THE DELICIOUSLY CHEESY HAPPINESS EQUATION

By
DUKE THAO

THE DELICIOUSLY CHEESY HAPPINESS EQUATION

Copyright © 2021 by Duke Thao

All rights reserved. Except as permitted by U.S. copyright law, no part of this work may be reproduced or distributed in any form by any means, or stored in a database or retrieval system, without permission in writing from the publisher.

When forms and sample documents appearing in this work are intended for reproduction, they will be marked as such. Reproduction of their use is authorized for educational use by educators, local school sites, and/or noncommercial or nonprofit entities that have purchased the book.

All third-party trademarks referenced or depicted herein are included solely for the purpose of illustration and are the property of their respective owners. Reference to these trademarks in no way indicate any relationship with, or endorsement by, the trademark owner.

Printed in the United States of America

For Shoua: My friend, mentor, hero, and mother.

CONTENTS

Introduction	1
Chapter One: The Happiness Equation	7
Understanding Happiness	8
The Happiness Equation	14
Deliciously Cheesy	20
Fun and Curiosity	20
Serious and Dangerous	39
Happiness Is a Balance	58
Summation of the Happiness Equation	63
Chapter Two: Clarity	67
The Suffering of Confusion and Happiness of Clarity	68
Better Questions, Better Clarity	74
What If	84
Shortcuts to Strength and Happiness	109
Nature's Teachings of Clarity	112
Raise the Inside	122
The Purposefulness of Our Being	130
Conductors of Information and Energy	143
A Pattern in Nature	148
Be an Awakening for Those to Come	157
Summation of Clarity	159

Chapter Three: The Heart — 165

- Hearts of Strength — 166
- Hearts of Destruction — 171
- Hearts That Transformed — 174
- A Test of Heart Strength — 178
- Happiness From Inside — 179
- Summation of the Heart — 183

Chapter Four: Wisdom — 189

- Balance of the Inside and Outside — 190
- The Forces of Living Beings — 196
  - *Desire* — 198
  - *Fear* — 200
  - *Ego* — 204
  - *Environmental Conditioning* — 213
  - *Clarity* — 217
- Awareness — 225
- Embedded Laws of the Heart — 230
  - *Inner Strength* — 236
  - *Love* — 242
  - *Wealth* — 244
- Summation of Wisdom — 249

Chapter Five: The Stars — 255

- Our Exciting and Amazing Journey to the Stars — 256
  - *To the Stars* — 258
  - *From the Stars* — 266
- Our Happiness Begins — 269
  - *Our Clarity Lights the Way* — 273
  - *Our Heart Powers Our Journey* — 288

Designing Our Information and Energy	291
The Magic of Doing	*296*
Putting It Inside	*306*
The Beautification of Our World	315
For the Coming Age of Freedom	*319*
Summation of The Stars	327
Acknowledgment	**333**
References	**335**
Index	**341**

INTRODUCTION

I once gave a speech titled *The Happiness Equation* at a Toastmaster event at work. It was my first Toastmaster speech, so the speech was mediocre at best. I didn't think much of it afterward. A couple of weeks later, a fellow team member, Matthew, publicly thanked me for the presentation's ideas. Matthew said that he had asked a girl out on a date, and she turned him down, but the ideas from *The Happiness Equation* helped him understand that he is in charge of his happiness, regardless of the external outcome. Despite being rejected, he used the ideas from the presentation and achieved happiness. Matthew's happiness became independent of the results outside.

Most of us simply exist in the winds of the elements outside. We live our lives to what will happen to us, and our happiness depends on the good things that will come our way. We are happy on sunny days and depressed during stormy days. We forget that the sun is always shining above the clouds. Our happiness is like the sun, always shining from inside. Through understanding and applying the Happiness Equation, we can release our happiness to let it shine through.

When I was twenty years old, I said something really silly without any thoughts or planning to predict my future happiness. I said, *"When I am 30, I would be happy if I am making $30,000.00 a year."* That was long ago, and the 30/30 sounds like a good round number and starting point to save, invest, and prepare for a better future. When I was 29 years old, I made one and a half million dollars, was happily married, and lived in a mini-mansion. Life couldn't be better, so I thought because *"I made it."* Little did I know that we never make it outside because

INTRODUCTION

our true journey is on the inside. The information and energy that empowers our happiness and strength live inside us.

Around that time, I remembered thinking that when I am 40 years old, I would be worth tens of millions of dollars and happily retire. It turns out I was very wrong because when I was 41, I was unemployed, divorced, and living in an apartment. A major national retailer offered me a job working in their receiving dock for $8.00 per hour. In my best month as a NASDAQ market maker, I made $330,000.00. At $8.00 per hour, it would take 240 months, or 19.83 years, to earn that amount—the outside volatility swings wildly against our expectations. A year later, short on funds, I moved in with my brother. I lived a life without clarity and inner strength, and that is how I arrived at being lost in the jungles of life.

I went past midlife, and I felt like someone lost in their late teens and not knowing what was ahead, and I didn't know what to do for a better journey ahead. There's a sense of embarrassment and shame in getting lost in life's jungle. I have questions that I need to find answers to because I did not have the answers then. Is my best life in the past? Where or how do I go forward from here to make it better and even more exciting? What do I need to learn from my past if I want a better life ahead? What do I need to learn from others? What is a better life?

Fortunately for me, after my divorce, I didn't take the path of trying to find a better life and happiness in bars and clubs or even meeting the next person. I felt that it was me that got me here, and if I did not correct it at the source, I would find another similar destination. I remember asking myself why beautiful beings like Siddhartha or Mother Theresa would work all their lives for others and have nothing for themselves. I want to know why because I want to experience their clarity, strength, and happiness. I needed to learn clarity, inner strength, and happiness from others who came before and attained inner peace, confidence, and strength against the changing outside elements. I want to define who I want to be on the inside, find out what it will take to find me, and begin my work towards a better me. My divorce became a blessing as it freed me to

THE DELICIOUSLY CHEESY HAPPINESS EQUATION

discover myself. I lived my life as a conditioned being in a changing world, and I received my results accordingly. Thus, I will need better information to guide and stronger energy for my drive.

I remember not knowing what to do but knowing what not to do. I wasn't going to use my time unwisely as I had done before. I unknowingly took my first step when I heard that one of my uncles offered to teach the nephews a traditional marriage liaison class, so I showed up to learn. On the non-traditional side, I bought audio CDs of a well-known motivational speaker and began listening and even taking notes. They are very small first steps in learning from others. In my traditional class, I realized inner strength is embedded in the traditional teachings of service as our minds and hearts strengthen to help others. We learn to understand and help resolve social issues. When we learn traditions, we also learn the embedded laws of the heart. Despite being new to me, the motivational material that I bought is a regurgitation of the information and energy of others repackaged to seem original. The speaker and his energy are original, but the material is not. The true source is more ancient. For example, great writers from ancient Greece, like Sophocles, learned to write tragedies 2500 years ago. Thus, great thinkers also learned the art of strength and happiness long ago. They share their understanding with us through time.

We often keep working with our conditioned self, but we hardly look for our better self. We keep looking at the world from a conditioned perspective instead of a clear perspective. For one thing, I did not know how to think for the benefit of others. We live our lives for others' happiness because it sows the seeds for further happiness for everyone around us. If we consider others' happiness, we make fewer mistakes. If we consider only our happiness, we make many mistakes as our desires and ego overwhelm our decisions. When we see the world for the happiness of others, we see a more beautiful world.

I also didn't know that I had to fall to rise to become better or that fear held me to my small comfort zone. Fear, failures, and suffering are at the edge of becoming better. My failure and

INTRODUCTION

embarrassment of further failure will help to sow the seeds to better me for others, including myself. When we face our fears, we expand and grow beyond our comfort zone into exciting adventures. There is no permanent destination for happiness outside, but we can arrive at lasting happiness inside our hearts' strength. As I began conducting better information and energy, I realized that I wanted to take it a step further. I decided to design my energy for how I want to feel in the external challenges. By designing my energy, I am designing how I will feel in the face of obstacles. I then put the information and energy I designed inside me. Many of us already put energy inside, but we do not design it with our clear minds. We normally design it in the spur of the moment with our desires and fears. I want to design my emotional energy while my mind is calm.

> *"No one saves us but ourselves. No one can, and no one may. We ourselves must walk the path."*
> — BUDDHA

Only we are responsible for the happiness of our life's journey. We determine the energy that drives everything we do. Thus, we need to understand our inner balance and the outside patterns and make sure they work well together. The outside elements will not adjust for us, but we have to live in balance with our changing world. Our understanding and inner energy should be clear, strong, and flexible to accommodate the fluctuating external challenges better.

Nothing from the outside can give us lasting happiness unless we give it to ourselves first. Most of the time, we simply keep looking for more of it from the outside, and we call it happiness when it is good and unhappiness when it is not so good. When we receive it, we are happy and unhappy when we do not receive it. Our happiness fluctuates with the changing elements outside. If our feelings fluctuate to the changing elements outside, our journey for lasting happiness must not be from the outside because that would make our happiness highly volatile.

THE DELICIOUSLY CHEESY HAPPINESS EQUATION

We feel happiness on the inside when there is a balance between our inner expectations and external reality. We must learn to attain our inner balance by choice and take charge of our happiness. First, we must clear up the information in our minds to focus the energy in our hearts. Once we have clear information and heart strength, we are free to determine our happiness. We will live in exciting and positive energy and share our happiness with others, and it becomes our life's meaningful purpose. We will live in clear information, strength, and happiness no matter what happens outside. Living is doing, giving, and sharing happiness every day. With better information and stronger energy inside, we will have the inner strength to begin our life's exciting journey. A daring and extraordinary life of great balance awaits.

> *"To live is the rarest thing in the world. Most people exist, that is all."*
> — OSCAR WILDE

CHAPTER ONE
The Happiness Equation

Happiness

"All human unhappiness comes from not facing reality squarely, exactly as it is."
— BUDDHA

THE HAPPINESS EQUATION

UNDERSTANDING HAPPINESS

> "When I was 5 years old, my mother always told me that happiness was the key to life. When I went to school, they asked me what I wanted to be when I grew up. I wrote down 'happy.' They told me I didn't understand the assignment, and I told them they didn't understand life."
>
> — JOHN LENNON

We live in the most beautiful place in the entire universe. For tens of trillions of miles in all directions, our Earth is the only place we know harboring all the beautiful life variations, and one of those variations is us, humans. Yet, many of us dwell in suffering and unhappiness in our beautiful world and then wish for an even better place afterward. Since our world is one of the most beautiful places in the universe, our peace and happiness should be here. Thus, the cause of our suffering must not be from the outside but from the inside. Therefore, we need a clear discovery of ourselves and our world to see and appreciate the most beautiful place in the universe. We have to clear up our perception from the inside to see the beauty outside.

In the many exciting adventures of our lives, we will experience both sunny days and stormy days. There will come moments in our lives when a storm overwhelms us, and we can't see where we are going. There is no hiding from the storm because the storm of confusion is inside our hearts. The cause of the storm is a large mismatch of our internal expectations against our current external reality. We are caught in an emotional storm because we thought our situation was a pleasant sunny day, but our reality is as dark as night. Our internal joy and happiness have now become pain and suffering. We find it difficult to bring happiness to our hearts. Our suffering heart is the internal source of our happiness, and now it is lost in confusion. In the unbearable storms of our lives, it would be great to find a

THE DELICIOUSLY CHEESY HAPPINESS EQUATION

shortcut to allow us to get out from under such storms and into the clear blue sky of happiness. We need a simple Happiness Equation to clarify our happiness level.

Instances of suffering in our lives are due to an internal difference between our heart's inner expectations and our external realities. When we run into an emotional storm that blinds our hearts' perceptions, there seems to be only one solution from the outside that will bring peace to our hearts. That desired solution is also the likely cause of our current suffering. By understanding the Happiness Equation, practicing it, and applying it, we will recover faster to bring peace to our hearts. The Happiness Equation will not solve our very powerful emotional imbalances immediately. But, it will allow our hearts to see with better emotional clarity. We can begin our journey to internal calm and happiness. We will better see when our Happiness Equation is disturbed and what we can do to bring it back into balance faster. We will see the simple variables that contribute to our suffering or happiness. Our understanding of the Happiness Equation will allow us to bring happiness to our hearts by acting on the variables within our control.

The Happiness Equation will help us manifest happiness inside, no matter what is going on the outside, and it will help us deal with difficult emotional situations. For easy situations, we will adjust automatically without help from the workings of the Happiness Equation.

Easy: Driving Bliss

My oldest daughter did not drive until she was eighteen years old. She is very spirited and generous with her time by volunteering and enjoying all sorts of activities in her young life. She volunteered at the children's museum, worked at a clothing retailer, and participated in many school activities. Because she didn't drive until she was eighteen, I had to drive her everywhere and pick her up. She did not like it whenever I was not on time. If I am thirty minutes late, I may get the silent treatment for that entire evening. Once I was three hours late, I got there, and she

THE HAPPINESS EQUATION

was happy and excited to go home and enjoy the evening. The difference is that when I was three hours late, I told her ahead of time that I had an event to attend. I asked her to find something fun to do downtown. She adjusted her expectations and, therefore, she was not disappointed when I came three hours late then. When I came thirty minutes late, I didn't tell her, so she didn't have time to adjust her expectations. Our clear communication helps to adjust the easy imbalances for happiness.

Our desires

> *"Live with cause and leave results to the great law of the universe. Pass each day in peaceful contemplation."*
> — ZENGETSU, A CHINESE ZEN MASTER OF THE TANG DYNASTY

Scholars and monks interpret the *desire* of Buddhism as dissatisfaction rather than a true desire to attain. They argue that enlightenment was once a desire, leading to a journey of clear understanding and peace. If we desire a certain outcome or a state of physical reality, we do not have it yet. Our desire creates another visionary realm in our hearts that is currently beyond our reach. We suffer because we want to be there, but we are not. If we could quantify it, the difference between our desired outcome and our current state is the value of our suffering. The greater the difference, the greater will be our level of suffering. Thus we have no suffering when we desire nothing beyond our current reality. There is no gap between our expectations and current reality when we desire nothing. When we no longer desire something, it has no power to pull at our hearts to create suffering inside.

Leo Tolstoy's short story *How Much Land Does a Man Require?* (1886) demonstrates the difference between our desire and how much we actually need or our expectations and reality. The difference in the amount is in the perception of what we think we need and our actual needs. Nothing in the world would satisfy our desires because such things will lead us to desire more. Our getting more will lead to an increase in expectations. An incredible amount of wealth in the world alone will not make us happy, but it can create fluctuations in our hearts' perceptions and social issues for unforeseen unhappiness. Unless we plan to share it with others for a purposeful cause, we need less than we think. We are social beings, and our happiness is in our balanced social relationships among colleagues, family members, and good friends.

If our happiness is not in the outside materials, it must be inside. Our clear internal understanding of the ways of our lives becomes our happiness. We achieve happiness by clearing up the confusion in our hearts. When we have a clear understanding of ourselves and our world, our misunderstood desires and dissatisfactions melt away in the clarity of our hearts' understanding. Without a clear, balanced internal understanding, our desires will continue to manufacture our unhappiness by wanting more regardless of how much we have.

A clash of expectations

We are not disappointed or happy simply because of our results, but we are unhappy or happy with our results versus our expectations. Thus, our inner expectations versus the outside reality determine our level of happiness. We also have expectations of each other which create happiness or unhappiness, depending on the outcomes. In many situations, the expectations are misguided to favor us, so we tend to have unhappiness. Thus, it is not our reality alone but the clash of our reality versus our expectations that create our happiness level.

> *"At a very basic simple level, we're unhappy when our expectations of reality exceed our experiences of reality."*
> — NAT WARE

The most difficult situations are not of the physical or even of the mind but of our hearts. The negative energies cloud our hearts and limit our mind's ability to think clearly. Therefore, we need to gain calm and clarity in our hearts as quickly as possible in difficult circumstances allowing us to use our minds effectively. We need our minds to solve the imbalance in our Happiness Equation. Only from a calm state of the heart can we think clearly to allow us better actions.

The Happiness Equation aims to help us navigate our lives' difficult events by bringing a clear understanding into our hearts. When we quantify our reality R and our expectations of reality $E(R)$ with simple mathematics, we will know exactly where we are regarding our hearts' inner balance. We will also know the cause of the imbalance and the solution to restoring internal happiness. Thus, the Happiness Equation will help us achieve quicker internal clarity of heart and mind. As a result, we will have become stronger at becoming happy.

Our anger

> "Anger stems when misplaced hope smashes into unforeseen reality. We don't shout every time something bad happens to us, only when it's bad and unexpected."
> — FROM STOIC PHILOSOPHY

Our anger is our emotional blindness and confusion created by an unexpectedly large difference between our reality R and expectations $E(R)$. We expected a certain result or outcome, and what we receive is much less than our expectations. When that happens, our anger will blind us to sound reasoning and an objective course of action to resolve the issue. Our anger will take us to the place of *Where the Wild Things Are* (1963), described by the author Maurice Sendak.

Our actions, driven by our anger, will do even more damage to the situation. Instead of applying our clear reason and logic for a better solution, our actions reflect our disappointment and hurt inside. As a result, the negative energy will cause further damage and harm.

THE DELICIOUSLY CHEESY HAPPINESS EQUATION

The unbearable negative energy of anger will sit inside and punish us, then conceive a retaliatory solution for its satisfaction at everyone's expense. Our anger overwhelms and clouds our perception of the outside, and we can't see clearly. Our anger will come from an imbalanced Happiness Equation due to our getting results much worse than expected. When we have a difficult emotional situation, we must learn to gain internal clarity in our hearts so that our minds can think of an objective and logical solution. The Happiness Equation allows us to see the depth of our unhappiness so we can begin to take better actions for balance.

Our suffering

> "At such a moment, it is not the physical pain which hurts the most; it is the mental agony caused by the injustice, the unreasonableness of it all."
> — VIKTOR FRANKL

Our greatest suffering is from the inside because our pain resides in the disappointment in our hearts. Our suffering comes from inside when we have a reality that does not match our expectations by a large amount. The difference between our reality R and our expectations of reality $E(R)$ becomes our suffering. Thus, we can alleviate our suffering by raising the reality R or adjusting our expectations $E(R)$ to match our R. The Happiness Equation helps us understand the balance of these two variables in our hearts.

Our happiness and contentment

> "Be content with what you have; rejoice in the way things are. When you realize there is nothing lacking, the whole world belongs to you."
> — LAO TZU

THE HAPPINESS EQUATION

When our expectations match our reality, our heart is at peace. There is nothing that is missing or out of balance in our lives. We don't want anything more than what we have because our current reality is what we desire. When we desire nothing beyond what we have, we find joy in our lives exactly the way they are. Everything is perfectly balanced, and we are happy.

We all have experienced a perfect day or moment, and we know why it is perfect. It is perfect because our expectations match our reality, and there is nothing else more we desire or want. Our happiness and inner peace come when we desire nothing more because everything is already perfect the way it is; this is because our reality and our expectations are the same. They are in balance with one another, and what we desire, we have. Thus, it is perfect.

THE HAPPINESS EQUATION

$$H = R - E(R)$$

Without a better understanding of happiness, we become lost in our senses' desires for pleasures and relaxation, and we call it happiness and unhappiness. We have a qualitative wish equation inside our minds, and we hope that we get all we desire and more to be happy. We get a blurry hope equation that hopes to receive our desires. Our happiness will fluctuate with the ups and downs of our lives.

The Happiness Equation uses simple mathematics to measure the differences between our reality R and our expectations $E(R)$, so we know exactly our happiness level. Our happiness level H depends on our reality R versus our expectations $E(R)$. By applying the Happiness Equation, we will understand the depth and cause of our state of happiness. With practice, even in a strong negative emotional state, we will be aware of the level of

THE DELICIOUSLY CHEESY HAPPINESS EQUATION

our unhappiness and the variables that are causing it. Then, we can begin to bring calm and balance to our hearts to find a solution to our happiness. The Happiness Equation will allow us to take charge of our lives' happiness, and our happiness becomes a choice.

The Happiness Equation is as follows:

> Happiness = Reality – Expectations of Reality.
>
> Let us use:
>
> H: Happiness
> R: Reality
> E (R): Expectation of Reality
>
> Our Happiness Equation is:
>
> $H = R - E(R)$

The Happiness Equation is a simple math formula. It will require numeric inputs.

Numeric Values Range:

> **Positive Values**
>
> 0 1 2 3 4 5 6 7 8 9 10
>
> 0 – Neutral
> 5 – Average Positive State
> 6 – Above average
> 8 – Strong positive state
> 10 – The best-case scenario

THE HAPPINESS EQUATION

> **Negative Values**
>
> 0 -1 -2 -3 -4 -5 -6 -7 -8 -9 -10
>
> 0 – Neutral
> -5 – Average Negative State
> -6 – Above average
> -8 – Strong negative state
> -10 – The worst-case scenario

Negative H, positive H, and H = 0

A negative H value in the Happiness Equation results in negative emotions, and a positive H results in positive and exciting emotions. When H = 0, we have happiness because everything is perfectly balanced. Our reality matches our expectations when H = 0, and we are in a happy and peaceful state.

We can balance our Happiness Equation by increasing the R by asking for more or by controlling our expectation E(R) from inside. The second method is always within our ability and clear internal understanding. The proper way to balance our Happiness Equation is to adjust our expectation E(R) to match our reality R. Changing our expectations occur on the inside through our clear understanding.

If we do not measure our happiness, we are not fully aware of the exact level and the variable responsible for our current happiness level. We will feel the negative impact of our imbalance, but we will not fully understand the depth, cause, and solution for our balance. If we can measure our happiness level H, we will know the exact level of our current state of happiness. We will also know the component that is responsible for our happiness. We can take action on how to go forward to achieving a balanced Happiness Equation. Once we measure our happiness, it will become real, and it will be simple to

THE DELICIOUSLY CHEESY HAPPINESS EQUATION

understand. The following diagram shows our happiness level through our changing reality.

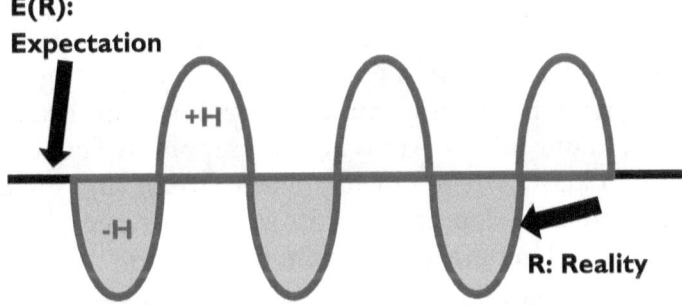

> *When we have a fixed expectation E(R), our happiness value H is negative or positive, depending on the value of our fluctuating reality R.*

Suffering and happiness

> "Forces beyond your control can take away everything you possess except one thing, your freedom to choose how you will respond to the situation."
> — VIKTOR FRANKL

When we have a large negative H, we experience extreme negative emotions like anger. For example, if we have an E(R) of 8 and our reality is −7, our happiness level is H = −7 − 8 = −15. Due to the large negative H, we will experience powerful negative emotions. We are in internal pain and suffering, and we become vulnerable. We may lose control of our thoughts and actions. The negative energy will take over and create havoc for ourselves and others. Our entire focus will be on immediately trying to return our reality R to the way it was to balance our Happiness Equation instead of searching for a logical solution to

THE HAPPINESS EQUATION

go forward. We may also retaliate in anger and become predictable and vulnerable to others.

If our happiness level H is -15, something we perceived to have an expectation E(R) of 8 now has a reality R of -7. Due to the large negative H, our hearts will be in pain and anguish. We will find it hard to accept the large negative H immediately. We will do anything hoping to get our reality R to be 8 again. The large negative H creates emotional pain in our hearts and confusion in our minds. Applying the Happiness Equation will allow us to know where our happiness level is and the cause. With our continued practice, we can balance our Happiness Equation at each moment faster from the inside.

When we have a large negative H, we must accept our reality R the way it is and adjust our perception. It is the one variable in our control. Once we accept our reality R, we can change our expectations E(R) to be -8. Our rebalanced Happiness Equation becomes $H = -8 - -8 = 0$, and we now begin to have calm and objectivity again. If we allow ourselves to stay in a negative emotional state for too long, our suffering and confusion cloud our perceptions. We must accept our new negative reality R as the cause of our negative H. Once we accept our negative reality, we can change our E(R) to match our new R. Our happiness level H is back in balance at $H = 0$. Our happiness begins on the inside.

When we are in pain and suffering, we will be vulnerable. We will be looking for a reality R to balance the large negative H. We will be open to others' manipulations. Soon, we will believe only their vision and understanding can cure our suffering. Their desires and visions will be our obedience and perceived happiness. We must internally balance our Happiness Equation, so we will no longer become vulnerable to others' manipulations.

An H value greater than +10 or less than -10

Volatility in our Happiness Equation creates addictions. We crave emotional volatility in our Happiness Equation because it presents opportunities to experience an exciting, positive H value greater than 10. When our emotions get rocked back and forth,

THE DELICIOUSLY CHEESY HAPPINESS EQUATION

there are opportunities to experience exciting, extreme positive swings. It is exciting to experience an H greater than 10, but exciting swings in H create addictions. A large negative H less than −10 creates strong negative emotions and confusion. A positive H greater than +10 is the emotional opposite. It creates excitement, but it does not mean that it is all good because the excitement also creates addiction and confusion. When we experience a large positive H, our expectations of reality going forward also change. Our expectation for the next event becomes higher. Sooner or later, it leads to a negative H.

$$\text{Large } +H$$
$$H = R - E(R)$$
$$H = 7 - 8 = 15$$

When our expectation $E(R)$ is -8, and suddenly the reality R becomes 7, we have an exciting positive H = 15. We expected a negative outcome due to the circumstance, but the result became positive. It is like a great movie where it seems our hero will lose. His expectation $E(R)$ is a -8. When his reality R suddenly becomes 7, our hero wins and gets the girl. The Happiness Equation is $H = 7 - -8 = 15$. In movies, a high positive H makes it exciting. In other events, the high positive H creates an addiction due to the excitement in our hearts. A large negative H level like −15 is the opposite, creating unbearable negative emotions.

To break away from the addiction of a large value of H, we have to take the average of our reality R over multiple periods. We will see our true happiness level H spread over time. We do many things in our lives over and over again. By taking the average R of multiple events over time, our measurement of reality becomes more accurate. If we plug our average R into the Happiness Equation, we will get a result that better reflects our true H level. A single happiness H event greater than +10 is meaningless if our average is negative over days, weeks, months, or years.

DELICIOUSLY CHEESY

FUN AND CURIOSITY

> *"Almost nothing material is needed for a happy life, for he who has understood existence."*
> — MARCUS AURELIUS

Ice cream and hot cocoa

Ice cream and hot cocoa are two of our most delicious creations. However, one is cold, and the other is hot. As delicious as they are, we enjoy the cold one on hot summer days and the hot one on cold winter days. The contrast between the two states brings out a higher positive H. The Happiness Equations of ice cream on a hot summer day and hot cocoa on a cold winter day are as follows:

<u>Ice cream in summer</u>
$H = R - E(R)$
$E(R)$ = outside temp and R = ice cream
$E(R) = -8$, hot
$R = 8$, cold
$H = 8 - 8 = +16$

<u>Hot cocoa in winter</u>
$H = R - E(R)$
$E(R)$ = outside temp and R = hot cocoa

THE DELICIOUSLY CHEESY HAPPINESS EQUATION

$$E(R) = -8, \text{ cold}$$
$$R = 8, \text{ hot}$$
$$H = 8 - -8 = +16$$

The hole in our heart

When we have a large negative H in our Happiness Equation due to our reality R being much less than our expectations E(R), we will have a large hole in the center of our heart. Our reality R clashes with our expectations E(R) to create a negative H. We become vulnerable to circumstances that are similar to what caused the hole. We will seek pleasures to numb our suffering or other external R to fill the hole inside. Our need to fill our hearts' holes makes us predictable and vulnerable to others' speeches and deceptions.

$$H = R - E(R)$$
$$H = -5 - 8 = -13$$
$$H = -13 \text{ creates a large hole in our hearts}$$

There is only one way to fill the hole in our hearts properly. We have to accept our new R and adjust our E(R) to match our current R. When our expectation E(R) matches our reality R, our Happiness Equation becomes balanced at H = 0. We no longer have a hole in our hearts when we accept our negative R and adjust our E(R) to match. We are no longer vulnerable to pleasures' enticement to numb our pain or others' speech and deception. There is no longer a hole inside to fill.

Depending on its creation and our intentions, the hole in our hearts can serve a purpose for us. For example, if our skill level is currently at five and we intend for our life's processes to run at a high skill level of nine, we will have a hole in our hearts. Therefore, we have to elevate our skill level to become nine to fill the hole in our hearts to ease our internal suffering. In this situation, the hole in our hearts can elevate our inner strength.

THE HAPPINESS EQUATION

However, if others or circumstances create a hole in our hearts, our emotional suffering will make us vulnerable and predictable. Thus, we may reach for external elements to fill the hole in our hearts to numb our suffering.

Why she had to go

> *"Why she had to go. I don't know why she wouldn't say."*
> — FROM THE BEATLES SONG "YESTERDAY" (1965)

When someone we love leaves our lives, there's usually only one reason why she had to go. She had to go because she wasn't happy. She wasn't happy for two reasons; her reality R is small or negative, or her expectations E(R) are large. Her Happiness Equation yielded a negative H. So, she had to go because she wasn't happy. She wouldn't say why because she's tired of telling us that she wants a better R. Sometimes, she is still trying to understand her Happiness Equation and her E(R). But, she had to go because her happiness level H was negative, and her Happiness Equations are as follows:

The first reason she had to go: Negative R
Average E(R) = 5
H = - 2 - 5 = - 7

The second reason she had to go: Large E(R)
Average R = 5
H = 5 - 9 = - 4

Sometimes, she had to go due to universal random factors. She wanted to stay, but she couldn't. When we want her to stay, and she wants to stay but she can't, both our Happiness Equations become:

H = 0 - 9 = - 9 or worse

THE DELICIOUSLY CHEESY HAPPINESS EQUATION

The happiness of surprises

We all love surprises because our H becomes positive due to the unexpectedness of the surprise. A positive H brings excitement to a normal expectation E(R). When we are surprised, we usually get a reality R greater than our expectation E(R). We love surprises because our H suddenly becomes positive, and a positive H always makes our events more exciting. We love a great deal because our R exceeds our E(R).

$$H = R - E(R)$$
$$E(R) = 5$$
$$\text{Surprise large } R = +9$$
$$H = 9 - 5 = +4$$

Some people never change

Some people keep working with the same inner expectations E(R), and they never change. They have a set fixed E(R) on the inside, and their happiness level H rises and falls depending on the reality R of their Happiness Equation. Their happiness is subject to an external reality R. They always look to the outside, hoping for a better R to give them a positive H. When they get more, they are happy, and when they get less, they are unhappy. They never change their inner expectations E(R) inside to take charge of their Happiness Equation.

$$H = R - E(R)$$
$$E(R) = \text{constant } 5$$
$$\text{If } R = 8, \text{ then } H = 8 - 5 = +3$$
They are happy

$$\text{If } R = 2, \text{ then } H = 2 - 5 = -3$$
They are unhappy

THE HAPPINESS EQUATION

Happiness is a choice

We have pain in our lives when our R is negative. Our pain will be unavoidable through the different changes. Our reality R is negative, causing the pain. When we have internal suffering in our lives, our happiness level H is negative. Whether our R is negative or not, our suffering is always optional. Our H level is our choice to make.

$$H = R - E(R)$$
$R = -7$, the pain of the negative R
$E(R) = 7$, we have positive expectations
Our Happiness Equation is
$$H = -7 - 7 = -14$$
We are suffering

We can change our expectations $E(R)$,
And our suffering becomes optional
When we change our expectations $E(R)$ from 7 to -7,
Our Happiness Equation becomes:
$$H = -7 - 7 = 0$$
We are still in pain due to $R = -7$,
But we are no longer suffering

The happiness of emotional maturity

When we have emotional maturity inside, we can control our emotions and focus on our joy and happiness, no matter what happens outside. We will have a balanced Happiness Equation because we can control our internal energy. Our mature emotional energy adjusts our expectations $E(R)$ in our Happiness Equation to the outside changes, our reality R. We can have a balanced Happiness Equation $H = R - E(R) = 0$ at any moment

THE DELICIOUSLY CHEESY HAPPINESS EQUATION

we choose. Our emotional maturity allows us to select our internal energy to balance our Happiness Equation.

The happiness of freedom

> "Our greatest freedom is the freedom to choose our attitude."
> — VIKTOR FRANKL

Our greatest freedom is the desire to be exactly at this place and time. If we require some relaxing and exotic destination to feel free, we are not free. Our freedom requires the exotic destination and the action of doing nothing. They are external realities of R. It is the same thing for the passage of time. We can be free of the passage of time by desiring to be in each moment. When we rejoice in this moment's happiness, our Happiness Equation is $H = R - E(R) = 0$ in both dimensions of space and time. We have exactly our hearts' space and time when we desire to be in the here and now. Our expectation $E(R)$ matches our reality R, and we are free in both space and time. So we become happy in the here and now.

The proof that money does not buy happiness

Money gives us the ability to buy things and provides us with more time for relaxation and pleasure. It can make our lives more comfortable, enjoyable, pleasurable, and exciting, but does money make us happy? Can money buy us happiness?

$$H = R - E(R)$$
Money will increase the R,
Thus, $H = R - E(R) = +H$
Happiness is $H = 0$, not $+H$

A Positive H level is exciting and pleasurable
Pleasure is a sensation

THE HAPPINESS EQUATION

Money buys excitement and pleasure, +H
But Happiness is H = 0

Money buys excitement, enjoyment, and pleasure,
but it does not buy happiness
Happiness happens on the inside
Happiness is when H = 0

Money can increase the number and amount of stimulants for our physical senses by raising our reality R. It can make our lives pleasurable and exciting due to raised external stimulants, but our happiness is in our hearts. We earned our happiness through a clear internal understanding of our minds and hearts to balance our Happiness Equation in our daily lives. Thus, money can buy pleasure and excitement, but it does not buy happiness. Our happiness happens through our internal ability to balance our Happiness Equation.

The suffering of desire

Our desire is the cause of our suffering because if we have a strong desire, we do not have the object of our desire yet. Therefore, our reality R is less than our expectation E(R). We will dwell on our object of desire, and it creates internal suffering. Our Happiness Equation and diagram with desire are as follow:

$$H = R - E(R).$$
Our desire creates an expectation E(R) = 8
Our current reality R = 4
Our Happiness Equation is: H = 4 - 8 = - 4.

THE DELICIOUSLY CHEESY HAPPINESS EQUATION

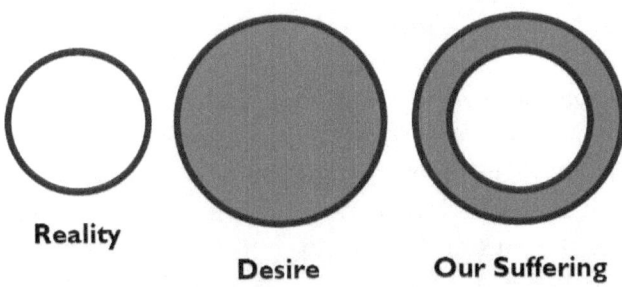

Our suffering does not come from the outside but from our desire's creation. Therefore, the difference between our desire and our reality is our suffering.

Our desire creates a suffering level of H = −4. If we do not neutralize the negative H by filling in the gap, our suffering leads to a hole in our hearts. When we have a hole in our hearts, we can raise our internal strength to achieve our objective or become vulnerable to enticements and traps. A person who can control their desires can control their happiness.

The happiness of forgiving others

> *"It's one of the greatest gifts you can give yourself, to forgive. Forgive everybody."*
> — MAYA ANGELOU

When someone takes our reality R into the red to make it negative, our happiness level becomes a large −H. Their action may be intentional, or maybe they cannot help themselves. Whether it is their intention or they cannot help themselves, we should move on from that level of commitment when someone makes our reality R negative. If they simply left it alone, our reality R would be at least zero or greater. To free ourselves from our past hopes, we have to forgive them. We have to forgive others before we can free ourselves to move on to better visions of our future.

THE HAPPINESS EQUATION

> *"Forgiveness removes the blockage that allows love to flow."*
> — MARIANNE WILLIAMSON

When we have no resentments, and no negative thoughts, what we have left are free-flowing constructive and positive thoughts. Our positive energy will create a positive future. When we forgive someone for hurting us, we can better balance our Happiness Equation. If we do not forgive, our Happiness Equation is $H = R - E(R) = -7 - 7 = -14$. We hold on to a past expectation $E(R)$ and reality R that do not match. When we forgive, we no longer require something from our past for our happiness. For this particular relationship, our reality $R = 0$ and our expectations $E(R) = 0$. Thus, our Happiness Equation becomes:

$$H = R - E(R) = 0$$
$$H = 0 - 0 = 0$$

When we no longer have an expectation $E(R)$ or a reality R for this relationship, our Happiness Equation is $H = 0 - 0 = 0$. When we forgive others, our happiness level is $H = 0$, allowing us to move forward. Thus, as a result of forgiveness, we have happiness inside.

Parting with no betrayals

Let's say we are in an intimate relationship because we deeply appreciate someone being in our lives; for us, their meaning or expectation is a 9. That is our $E(R)$ for the relationship. We then find out that they do not see the relationship in the same way. They see the relationship as a reality R of 5, casual and friendly only, and they would like to part ways regarding the intimate relationship. Our happiness equation becomes:

$$H = R - E(R) = 5 - 9 = -4$$

THE DELICIOUSLY CHEESY HAPPINESS EQUATION

There is still some pain as our overall Happiness Equation is negative, but the pain is more bearable. We are disappointed because they do not share the same feelings. Our reality R does not match our expectations E(R), but the other person did not take our reality R and make it negative through a betrayal. It is our high expectation E(R) that is creating an overall negative unhappiness level H. If we are to balance our Happiness Equation, we must accept our reality R and adjust our expectation E(R) to match. When there are no betrayals, the other person does not make the reality R negative. Even though our happiness level H is negative, the reality R is not. Therefore, the value of negative H is smaller, and our suffering is more bearable. We should still accept our reality R and adjust our expectation E(R) for a balanced happiness equation.

Change our E(R) to 5
Because R = 5
H = 5 - 5 = 0

A solution for Samantha

I used the Happiness Equation to solve a happiness problem for a friend. Samantha loved a man for years to the level of a 9, but he only saw the relationship as a 5, good friends to support each other for future happiness and success. Samantha initially ended the relationship because she went to look for better out there, but when better was not out there, she decided she wanted him back. For him, the intimate relationship ended permanently. However, he saved the friendship for a softer landing to remember better of each other.

Samantha is exceptionally driven, so she kept trying and hoping, for years, that she could change the situation and change his heart and mind. To help her achieve happiness, I wrote out the following solution below for Samantha. I hoped that seeing the simple solution, she would find it easier to accept the reality

THE HAPPINESS EQUATION

R and make an internal change in her expectation E(R) for her happiness.

Samantha's expectation $E(R) = 9$
Her reality $R = 5$
Samantha's Happiness Equation
$H = R - E(R), 5 - 9 = -4$
Her level of constant suffering is -4

For her happiness,
she needs to adjust her expectation $E(R)$ to 5
When her expectations $E(R) = 5$,
Her Happiness Equation becomes:
$H = 5 - 5 = 0$
Thus, she is happy

Whatever good things come into our lives, we desire more of them. When we can neutralize our desires, we can become truly happy. For Samantha's happiness, she needed to change her expectation E(R) to match her reality R. She may not get what she desires back in her life, but she will get happiness. When Samantha saw the clarity of the solution, she accepted her reality. She adjusted her expectation E(R) to match her reality R, and her Happiness Equation became balanced. After five and a half years, Samantha was able to move on. She didn't get what she wanted, but she got happiness because her Happiness Equation is now $H = 5 - 5 = 0$.

The unhappiness of untruth

When someone tells us an untruth, they have done something they should not, and the untruth is to cover up an action. If the truth comes out, it creates a large negative H in our Happiness Equation. When someone tells an untruth, and we find out, it hurts our ego because it makes us think that we are not worthy

THE DELICIOUSLY CHEESY HAPPINESS EQUATION

of their truth, and it breaks trust because an action of negative reality R is intentionally covered up. We are both betrayed and deceived.

For example, we are in a relationship with someone with an E(R) expectation of 7. When they tell us an untruth to cover up something hurtful they did, and when we find out later on, our reality R becomes -7. Our Happiness Equation becomes:

$$H = -7 - 7 = -14$$

Our Happiness Equation has a large negative H due to the impact of the untruth. However, if the person is courageous enough to tell us the truth immediately afterward, we can adjust our expectation E(R) to become -7, and our Happiness Equation remains balanced:

$$H = -7 - -7 = 0$$

The truth can set our hearts and minds free by allowing us to adjust our E(R) in the Happiness Equation for balance at H = 0. If they did something wrong and told us the truth, we would still have trust and friendship. However, finding out the truth through others will break our trust, and the relationship will end.

A pattern of telling untruths makes us become like Aesop's fable *The Boy Who Cried, Wolf.* If we have been telling untruths to others, then when we tell them the truth, they will not believe us. Thus, it is always best for us to tell others the truth to keep their Happiness Equation balanced regarding our integrity and our words. Then, they will believe us in the future when we need them to believe in our words.

The truth shall set us free

The truth will help set us free from our suffering in an emotionally painful situation. When our expectation E(R) is 8,

THE HAPPINESS EQUATION

and, due to an untruth, our reality R becomes -5, we have the following Happiness Equation:

$$\text{Our expectation} = 8$$
$$\text{Due to an untruth,}$$
$$\text{Our reality} = -5$$
$$H = -5 - 8 = -13$$

Because of the large negative H, we suffer from pain and confusion on the inside. We can become free of our internal suffering and confusion by accepting the truth. The truth will set us free from our internal suffering. When we accept our negative reality R, we free ourselves to change our expectations E(R) to match our reality R. Our suffering on the inside begins to ease. We become free of our emotional confusion and begin to become happy.

$$\text{Reality } R = -5$$
$$\text{Adjust our expectation } E(R) = -5$$
$$H = -5 - -5 = -5 + 5 = 0$$
$$\text{Our } H = 0$$
$$\text{The truth sets us free to be happy}$$

The happiness of honesty

When there is honesty, our expectations E(R) and our reality R are the same. They match each other. Because of honesty, our reality R equals our expectations E(R), and we have a balanced Happiness Equation with H = 0. Our words, which create expectations E(R) for others, match our actions, and R = E(R). Because of honesty, our Happiness Equations are balanced.

$$H = R - E(R) = 0$$

THE DELICIOUSLY CHEESY HAPPINESS EQUATION

The happiness of half-empty or half-full

> *"Comparison is the thief of joy."*
> — THEODORE ROOSEVELT

When we look at the world as half-full, we are in a positive emotional state because we are happy with what we have. But, on the other hand, when we view the world as half-empty, we are in a negative emotional state and desire more. The different states of emptiness are as follows:

$$\text{Empty} = 0, \text{Half} = 5, \text{ or Full} = 10$$

When we call it half-empty, we expect the glass to be full. If we are at half-empty at 5, we expect a full 10. Our half-empty Happiness Equation is:

$$\text{Half-empty: } H = R - E(R)$$
$$H = 5 - 10 = -5$$

We expect nothing when we call it half-full, and we are thankful for what is in front of us. If we are at half-full at 5, and we are expecting 0, our half-full Happiness Equation is:

$$\text{Half-full: } H = R - E(R)$$
$$H = 5 - 0 = 5$$

In calling our glass half-empty, we want more than what we have. When we desire more, we become unhappy. In calling our glass half-full, we are thankful for what we have. When we are thankful, we become happy. If we look at the world as half-full, it becomes easier for us to find happiness, as demonstrated by the two lists below.

THE HAPPINESS EQUATION

The list of unhappiness

- I am so poor as I have only $1,000 in the bank.
- I have a nine-to-five job that is not going anywhere, and we do the same thing repeatedly.
- I have only a simple house and a simple car.
- I wish that my life was fun and exciting.
- I have no one in my life to love me, and I am alone.

The list of happiness

- I have $1,000 in the bank, and I plan to save more. I am grateful to have a small cushion for unexpected emergencies.
- I have a secure job with great team members who help and support each other on exciting projects for our customers.
- My simple house and car fit perfectly with my current situation and purpose.
- I am free to enjoy all the city's exciting things, and if I want more, I can save and plan for anything I wish.
- I currently enjoy learning about myself, who I want to become, and preparing myself to receive new friends and companions.

> "He is a wise person who does not grieve for the things which he has not, but rejoices for those which he has."
> — EPICTETUS

Our list of unhappiness and happiness are the same—our perception of half-empty or half-full changes the energy to become positive or negative. When we criticize, it becomes half-empty and filled with unhappiness. We feel trapped in the negativity and smallness of our circumstances. When we are appreciative, it becomes half-full and overflowing with joy. We feel the freedom of having everything. Nothing is missing from

THE DELICIOUSLY CHEESY HAPPINESS EQUATION

our lives until we call it half-empty and deem it so. Our happiness does not depend on how much we have but on how much we criticize or appreciate it.

There is an African short story called *Farmer and a Wise Man* by an unknown author. A wise man met a farmer and introduced him to the value and wealth of diamonds. The wise man's words created a desire that led to suffering within the farmer. The farmer sold his land and went to look for diamonds to ease his suffering. He eventually went broke in a distant foreign land and took his own life. One day, the new owner found a shiny object in the small stream within the farmer's land. He took it to the same wise man, and sure enough, the land had diamonds. When we are content with what we have, our happiness blesses our lives with diamonds. When we are thankful and appreciative of what we currently have, our Happiness Equation level H becomes balanced. When we are thankful for those in our lives, they sparkle like diamonds.[2]

An easy task, a difficult task, and rising to a challenging task

Our tasks are neither difficult nor easy but relativity to our strength. When we bring an internal strength that matches the difficulty of the outside, our task becomes easy.

$$H = R(I) - E(R)$$
Our internal strength, $R(I) = 5$
The difficulty of the task, $E(R) = 5$
$$H = 5 - 5 = 0$$
We complete the task with ease

When we bring an internal strength that is less than the outside's difficulty level, our task becomes hard to do. The difficulty of the outside required task is still the same, but it becomes harder when we bring less internal strength.

$$H = R(I) - E(R)$$
$$R(I) = 2$$
$$E(R) = 5$$
$$H = 2 - 5 = -3$$

Our task becomes hard to do

When we desire amazing results, our challenging task has an expectation $E(R) = 9$. Thus, for our task to become easy to do, we have to raise our inner strength to match.

$$H = R(I) - E(R)$$
Our challenging task has $E(R) = 9$
We need an $R(I) = 9$
$$H = 9 - 9 = 0$$

**When we raise our inner strength $R(I)$ to 9,
Our challenging task becomes easy to do**

The happiness of being me

> *"Be happy for this moment. This moment is your life."*
> — OMAR KHAYYAM

The Mouse and the Wizard: a vague summary of a childhood short story by a forgotten author.

Once there lived a mouse that was unhappy being a mouse. The unhappy mouse went to see a wizard for a solution. The wizard had potions that could turn anyone into anything. Because the mouse was not happy being a mouse, he thought it

THE DELICIOUSLY CHEESY HAPPINESS EQUATION

would be interesting, or best, to become another living being or creature. However, the potions were expensive, and the mouse could not afford a potion that would transform him into something that he would like to be. The wizard happened to be doing house cleaning that day, and he found a bottle of potion without a label. Therefore he did not know what the mouse would turn into when he drank it. The wizard offered to sell the bottle to the mouse at a huge discount because it had no label. The mouse accepted it, paid for it, and then took the bottle back to his hole in the tree. He began pondering whether he should drink the potion to find happiness as another creature other than a mouse.

He thought about all the animals he could become, what would happen to him, and how he would feel. What if he became an elephant? He would be too big for his home. What if he became a whale? He would have to swim in the ocean and miss his friends here in the forest. What if he became a bird? He would still fit into his little hole in the tree, but he would have to eat worms. He thought about other possibilities and what if he became them. Finally, he concluded that he loved being a mouse because all the other animals had their unique unhappy state. He returned the potion to the wizard and lived happily being a mouse.

Using the Happiness Equation, we see how the mouse came to his decision. In the beginning, the mouse was unhappy. Thus, his Happiness Equation of being a mouse is $H = -4$. On the other hand, when he thinks about being an elephant, a whale, or a bird, the realities R in the Happiness Equation of these animals are negative due to the mouse changing his surroundings, habits, or friends to something he does not want. Therefore, the mouse's happiness level H is even worse for being these other animals.

$$\text{Mouse, } H = 2 - 6 = -4$$
$$\text{Elephant, } H = -4 - 6 = -10$$
$$\text{Whale, } H = -5 - 6 = -11$$
$$\text{Bird, } H = -3 - 6 = -9$$

THE HAPPINESS EQUATION

The mouse compares the happiness level of being a mouse to the average happiness level of becoming the other animals. Thus, the reality R is that of being a mouse, and his expectation E(R) is the average of the other animals. After realizing that the Happiness Equation for being the other animals results in a larger negative H value, the mouse appreciates being himself and finds happiness being a mouse.

The H for being a mouse = - 4

The Average H of taking potion:
(Elephant, whale, and bird)
= (-10 + -11 + - 9)/3 = - 10

Reality R = mouse
Expectations E(R) = other Animals
H = R (mouse) - E (other animals)
= - 4 - - 10 = + 6

By applying the Happiness Equation, we can see how the mouse concluded that there is no other better animal to be than being a mouse. The mouse is now happy to be a mouse. We can learn from the mouse's reflection and conclusion. The happiness of our being is in this form in the here and now. There are no other times, places, or creatures to become for our happiness, for this is our place, time, and life.

The good and bad of suffering

> "To live is to suffer, to survive is to find some meaning in the suffering."
> — FRIEDRICH NIETZSCHE

According to the First Noble Truth of Buddhism, life is suffering. However, there are many sides to suffering, and not all of our suffering is bad because it depends on how much we can see the suffering and, more importantly, what we choose to do with it. There is the helpless suffering of dwelling in a negative H because we feel sorry for ourselves. This suffering serves no purpose except to give ourselves an excuse to fail by blaming others for our situation. We reaffirm our negative emotional state as being right and doing nothing about it.

We then have the suffering created by our desires because we expected more than our current R. Our E(R) is greater than our R, and therefore we have a negative H in our Happiness Equation. We will raise our inner strength to raise our reality R and match our expectations E(R), thus alleviating our suffering. The suffering created by our desire will end up strengthening our inner self. Some forms of suffering lead to our strength as we elevate ourselves to overcome our suffering.

When someone manipulates our reality R and expectation E(R), the perception of a negative H creates suffering. This last form of suffering can be dangerous because once they create a negative H inside us, our hearts become lost and confused. Their words and wishes become our actions. We become manipulatable and predictable to the visions they create, which is mostly for their benefit. Therefore, to overcome suffering due to others' manipulation, we must raise our awareness and understanding to strengthen our inside.

SERIOUS AND DANGEROUS

The unhappiness of an insincere friend

> "An insincere friend is more to be feared than a wild beast; a wild beast will only wound your body, but an insincere friend will wound your heart and your mind."
>
> — BUDDHA

THE HAPPINESS EQUATION

An insincere friend:

In the Happiness Equation $H = R - E(R)$, we would expect our valued friendships to have an $E(R)$ of 7 or better because an acquaintance would have an $E(R)$ around 2 to 4 and a stranger 0. Because we have a positive expectation for our friendship, an insincere friend's betrayal makes our reality $R = -7$. Our Happiness Equation becomes:

$$H = -7 - 7 = -14$$

A wild beast:

We know a wild beast is capable of hurting us. A wild beast doesn't have to be a wild animal, but it could be a physically aggressive person. Because a wild beast can hurt us, our expectation $E(R)$ for the wild beast is -8. Therefore, an attack by a wild beast makes our Happiness Equation become:

$$H = -8 - -8 = 0$$

An insincere friend is more to be feared than a wild beast because a friend will have a large raised expectation $E(R)$ due to our friendship. When we are betrayed or hurt by an insincere friend, our negative R and positive $E(R)$ result in a large negative H of -14. Thus, our level of pain and suffering on the inside is -14. When a wild beast hurts us, the wound is outside only, and our happiness level is $H = 0$. A wild beast cannot hurt us inside because our expectation $E(R)$ is -8 for a wild beast. An insincere friend is more to be feared than a wild beast because an insincere friend deeply wounds our hearts. Therefore, we must also never become insincere friends to others by wounding their hearts.

The unhappiness of unkind speech

The unkind speech of others can create internal suffering. Their unkind speech has the potential to go to our internal source

THE DELICIOUSLY CHEESY HAPPINESS EQUATION

of strength and energy inside, to our hearts. When someone uses unkind speech to hurt us, they try to distort our reality R to be zero so that our Happiness Equations level H becomes negative.

Our balanced Happiness Equation
$H = 7 - 7 = 0$

With their unkind speech
Reality is distorted, $R = 0$
$H = 0 - 7 = -7$

They do so by creating a perception that our reality R is small. It is an opinion based on their need to feel important or, worse still, a closed mind intending to hurt others by attacking our inner strength.

Relationship betrayals

Sometimes we come across those close to us who would betray our friendship and trust for sudden reasons that do not make sense. Or, we might betray others' friendship and trust for the same reasons that do not make sense to them. Betrayals lead to pain and suffering in the hearts of those betrayed. The Happiness Equation will help us resolve the imbalance of our internal unhappiness of betrayals quicker. In our pain and suffering, the greatest desire at the time is for the pain to stop. The quickest way is to ask others to restore the reality R to what it was. That is asking someone else to change, and they have just created the large negative imbalanced H in our hearts. Their actions might be intentional, or maybe they cannot help themselves. If it is intentional, then it is designed to hurt us. If they cannot help themselves, it may happen many more times. Therefore, we should ease our suffering through our clear understanding and not rely on others' actions, for their hearts may be harder to change.

THE HAPPINESS EQUATION

We have an expectation E(R) of 7 or better for those close to us and that we trust. For the average person we meet on the street, we have an expectation E(R) = 0. We do not know them, and we have no expectations E(R) and no reality R. Our Happiness Equation for strangers we just met on the street is H = 0 − 0 = 0. When someone close to us breaks our trust, making our reality R = −7, our Happiness Equation becomes:

$$H = -7 - 7 = -14$$

When our Happiness Equation is a large negative H, we will have a hole in our hearts. Thus we will be in internal pain and suffering. Due to the large negative H inside, we will not have clarity of thinking and objectivity to resolve our imbalanced Happiness Equation. We can become predictable and vulnerable. When we accept our current situation and change it from the inside, we can adjust our expectation E(R) to become −7 for this particular friendship. We will no longer have an imbalanced Happiness Equation. The hole in our hearts will begin to disappear. When we adjust our expectation E(R) to match our reality R, our happiness equation becomes:

$$H = -7 - -7 = -7 + 7 = 0$$

In betrayals, we have the potential of having a large negative H that creates deep internal suffering. But once we accept our situation and our reality R, we can adjust our E(R) to match our R, and we will have a balance H to neutralize our deep internal suffering. For example, the Russian fable below illustrates the difference between others' words and actions.

The Scorpion and the Frog – a fable of Russian origin

> *A scorpion and a frog met on the bank of a stream. Wanting to get to the other side, the scorpion asks the frog to carry him across the river on his back. The frog, in turn, asks, "How do I know you won't sting me?" The*

THE DELICIOUSLY CHEESY HAPPINESS EQUATION

> *scorpion replies, "Because if I do, I will drown, and I will die too."*
>
> *The frog then asks, "What if when we get to the other side, you decide to sting me?" The scorpion replies, "When we get to the other side, I will be so grateful and happy that you have helped me. I would never sting you then."*
>
> *The frog is satisfied with the answers, and they set out. In midstream, the frog feels a sharp pain on his back, he turns around, and the scorpion is pulling its stinger out of his back. The frog feels the onset of paralysis and starts to sink. As they start to sink into the river, the frog turns to the scorpion and says, "You fool, why did you do that? Now we will both die."*
>
> *The scorpion replies, "I can't help it; it's my nature."*

The story of *The Scorpion and the Frog* shows that people's actions reflect their nature within. We can only validate others' intentions through their actions and not through their words. They may deceive us with their words, but they cannot help themselves with their actions.

Attacking our Happiness Equation

> "You will not be punished for your anger, you will be punished by your anger."
>
> — BUDDHA

Miyamoto Musashi (1584-1645) was a legendary samurai from sixteenth and seventeenth-century Japan. Musashi is considered one of Japan's greatest samurais. He wielded a first initial attack like no other samurai. Musashi used emotions as part of his first attack strategy. He attacked his opponents' internal energy long before his sword attacked them on the outside. He attacked his opponents' inside to create confusion and internal suffering in their hearts to destroy their source of strength for wielding their

THE HAPPINESS EQUATION

fighting skills and knowledge. His opponents became ineffective due to their internal suffering and confusion.

In 1604, Musashi challenged Yoshioka Seijuro, the master of the Yoshioka School, to a duel. Musashi intentionally arrived late, creating an imbalance in Seijuro's Happiness Equation. As a result, Seijuro became filled with rage and anger. With his rage, he attacked Musashi and was defeated. To avenge the honor of his brother, Yoshioka Denschichiro challenged Musashi to a duel. Musashi came late again, upsetting Denschichiro, and Musashi also defeated the younger brother. The Yoshioka brothers' rage and anger weakened their internal strength and decreased their ability to apply their skilled swordsmanship. The effectiveness of their skills and knowledge were only as good as their internal strength to wield it. Their ability to wield their skills came from the calm and stability of their hearts. Musashi knew that rage and anger would greatly reduce his opponents' inner strength and ability to wield their swordsmanship skills. Therefore, he first attacks his opponents' hearts to create rage and anger.

In 1612, Musashi fought his most famous duel against Sasaki Kojiro, the Demon of the Western Provinces. Only a tested legendary samurai would have the title *the Demon of the Western Provinces*. Musashi also came late in this duel — so late that they had to send someone from the island to go and get him. The fight was to take place on Ganryu Island. When Musashi did not show up at the scheduled time, they sent a messenger to get him. When the messenger arrived at where Musashi was staying, he was still sleeping. He got up and ate a nice breakfast before heading out to Ganryu Island for the duel with Kojiro. The following diagram shows Kojiro's strength when his heart is calm:

THE DELICIOUSLY CHEESY HAPPINESS EQUATION

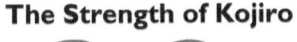

The Strength of Kojiro

Internal Strength   Skills and Knowledge

At peace and calm, the entire inner strength of Kojiro wielded his legendary skills and knowledge. He was at 100 percent on the inside and the outside.

When Musashi finally arrived, Kojiro was so upset that he stepped into the water to attack Musashi while Musashi was still on the boat. Unfortunately, Kojiro attacked Musashi with anger and rage instead of his legendary skills and knowledge. Musashi defeated Kojiro using only a bokken, a wooden sword. Musashi carved his bokken to be longer than Kojiro's long sword. By coming late, Musashi attacked Kojiro's inner strength without him being aware. Thus, Kojiro can no longer wield his entire lifelong samurai training and skills.

After the attack by Musashi

Kojiro

Clouded by Anger

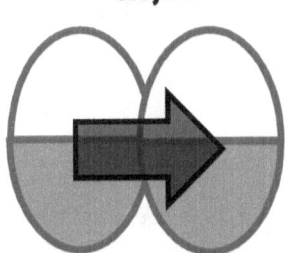

Internal Strength   Skills and Knowledge

By simply arriving very late, Musashi attacked Kojiro's inner strength. As a result, Kojiro became filled with rage,

THE HAPPINESS EQUATION

and without calm for inner strength, Kojiro could only wield part of his skills and knowledge.

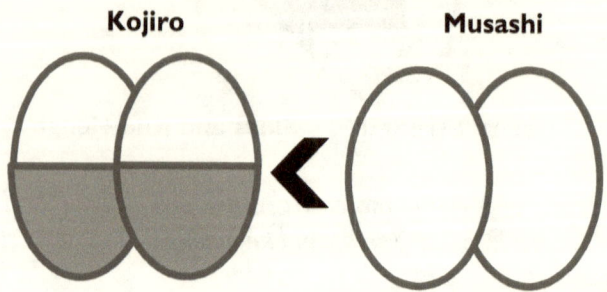

Kojiro's reduced skills and knowledge due to his internal rage were no match for Musashi's full-strength skills and knowledge wielded by his inner calm.

Kojiro is a legendary samurai warrior, and he would have found it honorable to accept a duel with Musashi or any worthy opponent. Therefore, his expectation $E(R)$ for the duel is an 8. However, when Musashi did not show up at the scheduled time but showed up very late, a proud legendary samurai felt disrespected, and his perceived reality R became -8. Thus, Kojiro's internal Happiness Equation becomes:

$$H = R - E(R)$$
$$H = -8 - 8 = -16$$

Kojiro's internal happiness level is a large negative H. Because his Happiness Equation is a large negative H, he is in internal emotional confusion due to rage and anger. He did not fight Musashi with complete access to his lifelong samurai skills and knowledge. Instead, he fought Musashi with skills and knowledge wielded by his elevated anger and rage. Against an equally skilled opponent who attacked him from multiple dimensions and time frames, Kojiro lost the duel.

THE DELICIOUSLY CHEESY HAPPINESS EQUATION

Musashi teaches us that someone will wreak havoc upon our hearts if we do not take charge of our inner strength. We will be in rage and anger, and we cannot wield our skills and knowledge. As a result of our internal rage and anger, we will fall to their external attacks. Understanding the Happiness Equation will make us more aware of attacks on our inner strength. Kojiro is one of the greatest samurais ever, and he lost to Musashi because Musashi used an initial attack, unlike anything Kojiro had ever seen before. Musashi attacks his opponents emotionally first so their imbalanced hearts can no longer effectively wield their skilled swordsmanship.

In Bruce Lee's book *Tao of Jeet Kune Do* (1975), he describes combination attacks as a series of set-up moves to open up the opponent for the final attack. Musashi's combination of attacks and set-up moves began well before the actual physical fight. His combination attacks begin with a designed attack on the heart to weaken his opponent's inner strength to set up for the final physical attack later.[1]

Attacking through deception

In William Shakespeare's tragedy *Othello* (1622), the Moroccan Venetian general Othello defeated himself by allowing Lago to counsel and mislead him and driving him mad with anger. Lago tells Othello that his wife Desdemona is unfaithful and manipulates circumstances to make it seem as if it were true. Without Othello being aware of it, Lago attacked Othello inside. As a result, Othello kills the woman he loves and loves him in an uncontrollable rage. After Othello realizes what he has done due to being deceived, he kills himself. The following Happiness Equation shows the large negative H of Othello's anger caused by deception:

$$\text{Othello loves Desdemona to an E(R) of 9}$$
$$\text{Lago manipulates Othello's R to appear to be } -9$$
$$H = -9 - 9 = -18$$

THE HAPPINESS EQUATION

Attacking with positive energy and deception

In the 1980s, a large refugee camp in Thailand housed many war refugees from Laos. There were approximately thirty-five to forty thousand refugees in the camp at its maximum capacity. The camp leader was himself a refugee, and he was safe from the dangers of his enemies in Laos. However, they sent an acquaintance and distant clan relative from Laos to visit him in the camp. The visitor from Laos promised the camp leader a leadership position if he and some people returned to Laos to help rebuild and heal. The camp leader was careful and went back by himself first to Laos to investigate and ask questions. He spoke with former enemies who welcomed him and toured him around the old country. Being satisfied that everything would be okay, he then took some people back with him by force to Laos, a country they had just taken great risks to flee. Once he returned with a group of his people, his former enemies asked him to be re-educated in the new system so that he would be able to serve the people better. He never made it out of the re-education camp and was never seen again. The following shows the manipulation of his Happiness Equation:

$$H = R - E(R)$$

His reality R of being in the refugee camp in Thailand is $R = 3$
His enemies created an expectation of returning to Laos of $E(R) = 9$
His Happiness Equations were:
$H = 3 - 9 = -6$ for staying in Thailand
$H = 9 - 9 = 0$ for returning to Laos

Their speech created a happiness level $H = -6$ in his Happiness Equation. The H of -6 created internal suffering that needed going back to Laos to ease the suffering. He moved back to Laos to try to raise his reality R to balance his Happiness Equation. Through positive deceptions, others can manipulate and create an imbalance in our Happiness Equation. We will be

THE DELICIOUSLY CHEESY HAPPINESS EQUATION

in their control and will act according to their design. Our actions to attain a balance H will be according to their design, guidance, and desires.

Maslow's hierarchy of needs

As human beings, we have internal needs that, if not met, create suffering inside. According to Abraham Maslow, the needs follow an order from basic physiological needs to advanced self-actualization needs. There are five categories in Maslow's hierarchy of needs built on top of each other like a pyramid. The ascension up Maslow's hierarchy of needs requires internal growth in understanding. According to Abraham Maslow, our hierarchy of needs is as follows:

- Physiological needs: health, food, water, shelter
- Safety needs: personal security, financial security, and emotional security
- Love/belonging needs: friends, family, and community
- Self-esteem needs: our self-worth and confidence
- Self-actualization needs: understanding and fulfilling our purpose beyond ourselves

Maslow's needs are so strong that others can use them to bait us to their design. It is not their words that trap us, but our lack of clear perceptions not to see the traps. The higher up we go in Maslow's pyramid, the harder it will be for others to attack us inside and trap our needs. We will have grown in awareness and internal strength to see the attacks and neutralize them by turning their attacks into opportunities for love and kindness, compassion, and inner strength.

The trapping of crabs

There is a fishing video on the trapping of Dungeness crabs using baited crab traps. Fishermen put bait in the trap and lower the trap to the seafloor. The crabs can taste the food in the water, and they come to investigate, making their way into the trap. The trap is designed to be easy to get in but impossible to get out of. The crabs' desire for sustenance and pleasure makes them become someone else's sustenance and pleasure. The crab is reaching for its basic need for sustenance. The desire for its basic needs blinds the crab to the trap.

If a crab could think beyond its basic needs, it would never climb into the trap. As humans, we can think, and we would not fall for such traps. For humans, it requires a stronger emotional trap for our hearts. It requires a trap for our desires of belonging and to be loved. Our desires, fears, and environmental conditioning sometimes prevent us from seeing the traps that others set for our hearts and minds. Once our hearts become trapped, we find it nearly impossible to get out. The traps for human hearts are more complicated because they are designed them to hook our desires and fears, higher up in Maslow's hierarchy of needs.

The trapping of crabs requires the use of Maslow's hierarchy of basic physiological needs. The trapping of human hearts uses Maslow's hierarchy of mid-level needs of love and belonging. We can see down the hierarchy into the crab traps, but we find it hard to see our own level's needs or above. If we go further up Maslow's hierarchy of needs into self-actualization, we will see all the traps below. To go up Maslow's hierarchy of needs, we will need to elevate our internal understanding of others and ourselves. Through our internal growth, we can see and neutralize the traps set by others for our hearts.

The trapping of me

I have had a Facebook account for a long time, but I was never active. There were times when I did not log on for years. Then, one day I logged onto Facebook, and I received a friend request from an attractive-looking woman who shares no mutual friends with me. Out of not wanting to be rude, I accepted the request. The next day, I received a *"Hi."* Again, not to be rude or secretly wishful, I replied, *"Hello, how are you doing?"* Before you know it,

THE DELICIOUSLY CHEESY HAPPINESS EQUATION

I started corresponding with someone who appeared genuine, available, successful, and intelligent. The person asked us to move to another Facebook downloaded application so we could communicate better. I remember thinking the words of Don Corleone from *The GodFather* (1972 Movie), *"What have I done to deserve this generosity?"*

One of my daughters looked at the profile and said that there's not enough history and friends, and thus, it has the potential to be a fake account. My other daughter was more direct and subtle. She simply texted me a picture of a cat and fish. I told them that the person appeared to be sophisticated and genuine in the conversation. I then watched Youtube videos of awkward moments from "90 Day Fiancé" and laughed. As we all think we are special, I thought, *"It cannot happen to me."* As it was my first time, I did not yet sense anything wrong. The person from the profile was attractive, kind, and appeared to have principles, and she was asking for nothing. A potential large expectation E(R) began to manifest in my Happiness Equation. Thus, my Happiness Equation could begin to look something like the below:

$$H = R - E(R)$$
$$H = 0 - 9 = -9$$

She said she was highly successful in her many businesses, and from time to time, she traded forex using tips from her godfather. I prefer the stock market as I have been developing a trading system for a long time. I didn't ask for proof, and I didn't care to trade currency, but she decided to show me her results from one trade. She made nearly $900,000.00, and she would donate 30 percent of it to charity for children and the poor — what a beautiful person, inside and out. She told me that she could show me how to trade forex. Again, I didn't really care to switch to trading something I did not understand. However, being a kind friend, I downloaded the brokerage firm app from the app

THE HAPPINESS EQUATION

store to my phone. I realized the predecessor name of the app, and it appeared to be a legitimate entity.

A couple of days later, she walked me through the mechanics of trading forex on the app using a simulation account. The next day, she walked me through the same thing, except that this time we entered the trade based on the tip of her godfather. The simulation account generated a 35 percent return in 10 minutes. The positive result did wow me. First, it was an attractive, available person; now, my expectation E(R) is being manipulated again by money. My Happiness Equation has two large E(R)s and now has the potential to look like the equations below:

$$H = R - E(R) - E(R)$$
$$H = 0 - 9 - 8 = -17$$

I took a walk and thought about further researching the idea of trading currency based on tips provided by my friend's godfather. If I were to do it, it would need to be legal, and I would still need to understand the contract sizes to design an exit plan when things go wrong. Insider trading is illegal, and I am unsure how it pertains to forex because it trades worldwide. She suggests that she could have her contact at the brokerage firm help me open the account as a favor. She returned twenty minutes later and asked if I had reached out to her contact yet. I told her that I would need to research the idea further, including opening the account. Most likely, I would open the account on my own. That is when her imbalanced Happiness Equation revealed her intention. After the demonstration, she had an expectation E(R) that needed an R for balance. My opening the account through her contact was her E(R). When I did not want to provide that realty R right away to match, her large expectation E(R) turned into a large negative H in her Happiness Equation and manifested negative emotional energy. Her negative energy revealed her intention. I felt that the trap was to steal my identity or funds when I opened the account.

THE DELICIOUSLY CHEESY HAPPINESS EQUATION

I got catfish, but I felt that I would have avoided the trap because I would never get into any situation for just me, but it had to benefit everyone, and it had to be legal. Better than a good first impression is a good last impression. Thus, I wasn't going to say anything or do anything unkind. Despite the temptation of love and money, my Happiness Equation H was never at -9 or -17, but more like -3 or -5 because I was not in it just for me. It had to make logical sense as well. If I had a large hole in my heart that needed to fill, my H level would be greater at -9 and -17. The Happiness Equation battle is as follows:

My Happiness Equation:
After the correspondence began, $H = 0 - 3 = -3$
With the forex simulation using the godfather's tip: $H = 0 - 3 - 2 = -5$

Her Happiness Equation:
After the demonstration, she had an $E(R) = -7$
When I did not open an account, $H = 0 - 7 = -7$

When I realized the deception,
I adjusted my R, and both my $E(R)$s $= 0$
$H = 0 - 0 - 0 = 0$

When I became thankful for the lesson,
$H = 5 - 0 = +5$

The deception and a smaller $-H$ made it easy to adjust my R and $E(R)$s. It may not even be a woman on the other side, or it could have transitioned to someone else to close the deal. Nevertheless, I am thankful for the lesson, so my Happiness Equation level H became positive.

THE HAPPINESS EQUATION

False prophets: the trapping of Maslow's hierarchy of needs

> *"Everyone is willing to give something for whatever it is they desire the most."*
> — HENRY OBERLANDER, SWINDLER, AND THIEF

The attacks on our inside can be subtle, straight-up belittling, deceiving, filled with kindness, or in the form of exciting promises from a false prophet. The purpose is always the same: create suffering and confusion in our hearts by distorting our reality R and expectations E(R). The attack from false prophets is most dangerous because we are unaware of an attack, and we commit to giving all of ourselves away for their designed purpose. They will play with our fears and desires until they can create an imbalanced Happiness Equation inside us. They will say something untruthfully kind to build trust, distract, and create confusion in our hearts. Sometimes, they can immediately detect a hole in our hearts and know we are vulnerable. A false prophet may entice others with a peaceful existence beyond. They will claim to have biblical powers and understanding from beyond, but their only power is knowing how to manipulate our hearts' desires and fears for their desires and self-importance. Our real test of inner strength is our ability to look into their hearts and see their intentions. If we are aware of attacks on our inside, we will be aware of verbal attacks by false prophets or someone who would try to create an imbalance in our Happiness Equation for their advantage. We will be able to see the attacks and emotional traps they set.

As described by Bruce Lee in his book *Tao of Jeet Kune Do*, regarding combination attacks, their initial kindness is part of a series of set-up moves to open us up for the final emotional attack later on. In a physical confrontation, the combination of attacks is normally all physical. However, sometimes, we will have an opponent, like Musashi, who leads with an emotional attack to create confusion and weaken his opponents' inner strength.

THE DELICIOUSLY CHEESY HAPPINESS EQUATION

In the world of false prophets, the combination attacks are led with emotional kindness to draw our hearts out. Once they have our hearts, a false prophet will then tell us that we are not worthy for all we have done and that our reality $R = 2$, and that we should be someone who needs to have an expectation $E(R)$ of 9. To imbalanced our Happiness Equation, they will create a desire and suffering where previously none existed. Then, they will exploit the suffering that they created. They will exploit Maslow's hierarchy of needs of love and belonging within us. Their power is the manipulation of our emotions. If we believe their words, we will have a Happiness Equation of:

$$H = R - E(R) = -2 - 9 = -7$$

When our happiness level H is -7 simply because of someone's speech, we have allowed others to manipulate our implied reality R and our Happiness Equation. We will take actions we hope will lead to a balance $H = 0$ again in the future if we give enough of ourselves to their cause. We are now in their emotional control. By understanding and practicing the Happiness Equation, we will be aware of their attacks and neutralize the internal attacks of false prophets. We will become free-flowing and flexible like water.

Be like water

> *"Be independent of the good and bad opinion of others."*
> — DOCTOR WAYNE DYER

When we wake up to a cold morning chill, there's a mist rising from the lake, and the water seems warm and comfortable to the touch. There's a mist because the heat from the lake is escaping into the cold air. The water feels warm and comfortable to the touch in the cold air. During the previous night, we did not want to touch the water then because, in the warm evening air, the water felt cold. The water temperature is not warmer than last

THE HAPPINESS EQUATION

night, but it is more stable than the fluctuating air temperatures. Our body was experiencing the warm air last night, making the water feel cold, and today we are experiencing the cold air making the water feel warm.

$$H = R - E(R)$$
$$\text{Sensation difference} = \text{Water(Temp.)} - \text{Air(Temp.)}$$

$$\text{Water is more stable} = 65$$

$$\text{Last night's air temperature} = 75$$
$$\text{Sensation difference} = 65 - 75 = -10$$

$$\text{This morning's air temperature} = 55$$
$$\text{Sensation difference} = 65 - 55 = +10$$

The air temperature fluctuation makes us think that the water temperature fluctuates between cold in the warm evening and warm in the cold morning. Our perceptions fluctuate due to our senses, and so we experience perceived fluctuations in sensations rather than true physical sensation volatility in the water temperature. Our mind's perception is moving and not the temperature of the water. The water's temperature doesn't change much, but the air temperature does, and we feel the difference between the two.

Our search for peace and happiness from external elements subjects our happiness to their volatility, like the changing air temperatures. When the air is hot, we will feel warm and happy. When the air is cold, we will feel cool and unhappy. The day-to-day temperature of the water in a lake hardly changes much due to the changing air temperatures. Our internal emotional understanding inside us is like the more constant temperature of the water in the lake. Our clarity in thinking and our understanding define our happiness. Our internal emotional self does not change much over time.

THE DELICIOUSLY CHEESY HAPPINESS EQUATION

When we raise our internal understanding, our happiness becomes independent of fluctuating external elements. We become independent of false prophets' words because we are free of others' good and bad opinions. Our internal happiness frees us from the inside. We will be happy no matter what is happening, as illustrated by the following Zen story of external volatility:

Is That So?

> The Zen master Hakuin was praised by his neighbors as one living a pure life.
>
> A beautiful Japanese girl whose parents owned a food store lived near him. Suddenly, without any warning, her parents discovered she was with child.
>
> This made her parents angry. She would not confess who the man was, but after much harassment, at last, she named Hakuin.
>
> In great anger, the parent went to the master. "Is that so?" was all he would say.
>
> After the child was born, it was brought to Hakuin. By this time, he had lost his reputation, which did not trouble him, but he took very good care of the child. He obtained milk from his neighbors and everything else he needed.
>
> A year later, the girl-mother could stand it no longer. She told her parents the truth — the real father of the child was a young man who worked in the fish market.
>
> The mother and father of the girl at once went to Hakuin to ask forgiveness, to apologize at length, and to get the child back.
>
> Hakuin was willing. In yielding the child, all he said was: "Is that so?"

HAPPINESS IS A BALANCE

The Happiness Equation of receiving and the Happiness Equation of giving

> *"You should never take more than you give, in the circle of life."*
> — ELTON JOHN

When we apply the Happiness Equation of receiving, we do less and hope to get more R against our expectation E(R) because it yields a positive H. However, our small contribution will lead to a small return in time. Thus, we will eventually get a negative H.

When we apply the Happiness Equation of giving, we raise the R we contribute to others' expectations E(R), and our larger R of giving yields a positive H into the world. Our extra efforts in contribution will also result in an equally large return.

- The Happiness Equation of receiving
    - We ask how we can get more for ourselves.
    - We hope to receive a positive H from the world.
- The Happiness Equation of giving
    - We ask how we can make it better for others.
    - We contribute a positive H to the world.

What we contribute to the world returns to us. What we give and what returns to us are always in balance. When we understand this balance, we will use the Happiness Equation of giving to contribute positive H to others. We will plant the seeds of a better future when we apply the Happiness Equation of giving.

THE DELICIOUSLY CHEESY HAPPINESS EQUATION

The balance of work and success

> *"The only place that success comes before work is in the dictionary."*
> — VINCE LOMBARDI

When our happiness level $H = 0$, our reality R and expectation $E(R)$ are equal in our Happiness Equation. Our balanced H is our happiness, and the required balance also applies to work and success. All the magical, exciting, happy, and wonderful things in our lives are a balance of our work and our reward. Even a clear internal understanding of happiness requires work to achieve. We must work for what we want, need, and desire. The wisdom of many great thinkers and achievers who came before teaches the required balance of work and receiving. It is written in "Galatians 6:7," in Zen stories, moral stories, songs, and poems. Our journey requires doing to balance our receiving. If we want to create a positive H, we must do more than others' expectations. Thus, it requires a large giving R in our effort.

We need to have a tested methodology as part of our plan for our success. Our edge for success only comes after hard work, making mistakes, and learning to do our tasks better for the next opportunities. If we do not have a process to achieve success, others will bait our desires with well-thought-out plans to win against us. The Wizard of Oz, who lives in the Emerald City, is not a real wizard, but he does have a well-thought-out plan. The Great and Powerful Oz is an elaborate illusion created to disguise a purpose: to attract those strong and desperate enough to come for the simple task of retrieving the broomstick of the Wicked Witch of the West. To do so would mean destroying the powerful Wicked Witch of the West. That is the real task in disguise. We must beware of great and powerful wizards, whose only power may be our mesmerization of their deception created by their desires. As times change, the new wizards broadcast their messages over Youtube or social media nowadays. However, their intention remains the same—they create imbalances in our

THE HAPPINESS EQUATION

Happiness Equation for their exploitations. Thus, we must learn and understand the balance of work and success for ourselves.

Aesop's *The Tortoise and the Hare* (620 BCE) tells the story of a hare racing a turtle. The turtle was behind when they started, but he eventually won. The hare was ahead and took a nap while the turtle persistently pushed forward and finished first. The animals represent talents, egos, and emotional intelligence at work. However, if we think literally in animal terms, we might not grasp the story's meaning because it does not make sense. We would see the comedy but not understand the moral lesson. It would make us laugh but not strengthen our hearts' understanding.

The hare represents a very talented individual who can achieve anything he wants, and he does, and then he stops to relax to enjoy life. The turtle represents someone who understands the way of life and knows that he must put forth persistent efforts every day. The hare achieves his goal and then stops to relax. However, one day, the hare realizes that the world has changed, and he is behind someone who was not as talented but persistently driven.

The hare is results-oriented, and when he got his results, he stopped. The tortoise is process-oriented, and he understands that he must persistently apply his process no matter what. *The Tortoise and the Hare is* a moral story of our human nature. If we dwell in relaxation and comfort, we will one day wake up and be outdated and outdone by someone who persistently keeps pushing forward. Thus the persistence of the heart is more important on our journey than the talent at the beginning because our heart's strength consistently balances work with the desired external result.

> *"Do not be deceived; God is not mocked: for whatever a man sows, that he will also reap."*
>
> — "GALATIANS 6:7"

THE DELICIOUSLY CHEESY HAPPINESS EQUATION

The expectation E(R) is the external result we expect to receive for our efforts. The reality R is the efforts we put into our work for the E(R). Because what we sow, we reap; there's no way to attain more than the effort we put into our work.

$$\text{Because } H = R - E(R) = 0$$
$$\text{Thus, } H = \text{reap} - \text{sow} = 0$$
$$\text{Reap} = \text{sow}$$

Because reap = sow,
If we to reap more, we must sow more

Many cultural traditions and moral stories teach the balance of work and reward. The following is a Zen story that demonstrates the balance of work and reward.

Washing Your Bowl

> *A monk told Joshu: "I have entered the monastery. Please teach me."*
> *Joshu asked, "Have you eaten."*
> *The monk replied, "Yes, I have eaten."*
> *Joshu said, "Then you had better wash your bowl."*
> *At that moment, the monk was enlightened*

The new monk became enlightened that we have to earn the sustenance of our lives every day by balancing it with the work it takes to receive that sustenance. The monk learned the balance that we reap whatever we sow. When we use one bowl, then we wash one bowl.

$$H = R(1 \text{ bowl}) - E(R(1 \text{ bowl})) = 0$$

The children's story *The Little Red Hen* tells of a little red hen who planted wheat, harvests it, and processes it into flour. She then uses the flour to bake bread. All the other animals did not

THE HAPPINESS EQUATION

want to help in the effort along the way, but when the little red hen finished baking the bread, they were willing to help eat it. The little red hen did not share the bread with the other animals because they were unwilling to help put in the work. She only shared it with her chicks. If we want sustenance, then we have to work for it.

The Happiness Equation for the Little Red Hen:
$$H = work - reward = 0$$
Balance

The Happiness Equation for the other animals:
$$H = 0 - reward = - reward$$
Negative H

Our challenging life

> "It is very difficult so that you have to find something which you are passionate about."
> — STEVE JOBS

> "There's no talent here, this is hard work. This is an obsession. Talent does not exist, we are all equal as human beings. You could be anyone if you put in the time. You will reach the top and that is that. I am not talented, I am obsessed."
> — CONOR MCGREGOR

Our lives must be difficult and challenging for these very accomplished individuals to deem it hard. Their advice is to find something we are passionate about and obsessed with, and the passion and obsession will drive our hearts. Our lives will still be challenging, but it will feel easy upon our hearts because we will

THE DELICIOUSLY CHEESY HAPPINESS EQUATION

love what we do. If we find passion and obsession, we will find success and happiness.

> *"Choose a job you love, and you will never have to work a day in your life."*
> — CONFUCIUS

In the fight to be first in flight in the late 1800s, the Wright brothers were up against the legendary Samuel Pierpont Langley, a highly educated, accomplished astronomer, physicist, and secretary of the Smithsonian Institute. The US government and the Smithsonian Institute had faith in Samuel Pierpont Langley and funded his quest for the first human flight. Samuel Pierpont Langley wanted to be first in flight because he wanted Thomas Edison and Alexander Graham Bell's fame and reputation. The Wright brothers were passionate about flight and approached the problem in many inventive and creative ways. On December 17th, 1903, the Wright brothers' love and passion for their work beat out Samuel Pierpont Langley's depth of funding, education, credentials, and need for admiration to achieve the first flight for humans. The heart of the tortoise beat out the talent of the hare. We must become a tortoise.

SUMMATION OF THE HAPPINESS EQUATION

> *"Occam's razor: the simplest explanation is likely the correct one."*
> — WILLIAM OF OCKHAM

Our happiness takes place inside us because inside our hearts is where we feel our joy and happiness. Because we feel our happiness inside, our source for happiness must be inside us, not

THE HAPPINESS EQUATION

outside. That is the simplest explanation. Thus, happiness happens through an internal understanding allowing us to adjust our expectations $E(R)$ to our changing realities $R(S)$ outside. Happiness happens on the inside, and, therefore, our key to happiness must be inside.

The simple Happiness Equation

> *"Peace comes from within, do not seek it without."*
> — BUDDHA

Without an equation to clearly show our current state of happiness, our mind will have a blurry qualitative hope and wish equation that solely depends on external elements for happiness. And, we will find lasting happiness elusive because our happiness level will fluctuate with the external changes.

The Happiness Equation is a simple equation with two variables that uses addition and subtraction to arrive at our happiness level H. The Happiness Equation $H = R - E(R)$ measures the difference between our inner expectation $E(R)$ and the external reality R. Its simplicity allows us to see the truth of our happiness level and the cause. We can adjust our expectation $E(R)$ to achieve internal balance and happiness at each moment.

The Happiness Equation allows us to better see into an emotionally difficult situation when strong negative emotions or even strong positive emotions create confusion in our hearts. So we will know our happiness level and the cause of our happiness. The expectation $E(R)$ is the most important and flexible component in The Happiness Equation. Our expectation $E(R)$ is independent of our reality R because it is within our control to change. Our expectation $E(R)$ is on the inside and based on our strength of understanding. When we experience pain and suffering due to a negative H, we normally try to change the external elements. We try to change our reality R to what it was to match our internal expectation $E(R)$. We may be asking someone who just created a large negative H in our Happiness

THE DELICIOUSLY CHEESY HAPPINESS EQUATION

Equation to change. Once we understand the workings of the Happiness Equation, our most direct change is internal. Accept our new reality R and change our expectation E(R) to match it.

The relativity of reality R and expectation E(R)

> "We suffer not from the events in our lives, but from our perceptions about them."
> — EPICTETUS

We cannot have peace and happiness in any state of our physical or financial reality R alone because the balance required is in our expectation E(R) relative to our R. A large E(R) leads to a large negative H. The greater our E(R) in our Happiness Equation, the greater is our internal suffering. It is not the absolute external level of R from the outside that matters. Our happiness depends on how well we understand ourselves to balance our inner expectation E(R) against our reality R.

In the Happiness Equation of giving, $H = R - E(R)$, we should raise our giving R because our contributions go into the world. The reality R we give to others is always within our control because it comes from inside our hearts' strength. Therefore, we can raise our giving R and contribute to each event or situation to improve it. When we raise our efforts for others, it will contribute a positive H to those around us, and it sows a better tomorrow for everyone.

A balanced and happy life

If we need or want something from this world, we must work for it. What we receive or desire E(R), we have to put in an equal effort of R. When we receive sustenance from the outside, we have to work for it. If we eat a meal, we have to wash the bowl. The Happiness Equation demonstrates the simple clarity of balance that we have to earn what we receive.

THE HAPPINESS EQUATION

Our search for happiness is our search for feelings, and our feelings are inside. Therefore, our real search is to understand ourselves and our world better. Then, we can adjust our expectations accordingly to take charge of our feelings through any external changes. A clear understanding will allow us to empower the energy that is our feelings. We can better define our expectation $E(R)$ against our reality R and, thus, balance our Happiness Equation from the inside.

> *"Watch your thoughts, they become your words; watch your words, they become your actions; watch your actions, they become your habits; watch your habits, they become your character; watch your character, it becomes your destiny."*
>
> — LAO TZU

What would complete our lives' journey for happiness is reaching a clear understanding. Therefore, we can balance our Happiness Equation in each changing moment of our lives. We will have $H = R - E(R) = 0$. When we are in charge of our expectations $E(R)$, we can find happiness in any reality R, and happiness in each moment becomes our choice.

CHAPTER TWO
Clarity

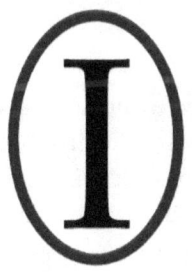

Information

"Becoming more awake involves seeing our confusion more clearly."
— RUMI

CLARITY

THE SUFFERING OF CONFUSION AND HAPPINESS OF CLARITY

The deception of the Buddha

> *"How many times must a man look up before he can see the sky?"*
> — BOB DYLAN

When the wife of King Suddhodana was expecting a child, she dreamt of a white elephant entering her body. The king went to seek wise men's counsel to help him interpret the meaning of her dream. After listening to the dream, the sages told the king that his wife would give birth to a son and that his son would be a great king or a great sage. For the child to take the path of being a king, he must not see these three things: a sick person, an old person, and a dead body. If he were to see these three things, the child would choose the life of a sage.

Shortly after Siddhartha was born to Queen Maya and King Suddhodana, the queen died from childbirth complications. King Suddhodana wanted to see his son follow in his footsteps, so he took extreme measures to prevent Siddhartha from seeing the three things foretold by the wise men. The king filled the young Siddhartha's life with all sorts of pleasures and comfort, tended to by beautiful young individuals. Siddhartha even got married and had a son. One day Siddhartha walked off the palace grounds and saw a sick person, an old person, and a dead body. When he asked the people with him about these odd and unusual events, they told him that being sick, old, or dying are ways of life. Sooner or later, we all will experience these undesirable states. Siddhartha realized that his life was a deception designed to mislead him to prevent him from knowing the truth. He saw a priest tending to a dead body with no fear or remorse but calm, caring kindness, and compassion. Siddhartha knew then that he

THE DELICIOUSLY CHEESY HAPPINESS EQUATION

wanted the life of a sage and to become peacefully calm like the priest in moments of hardships. So he left the comforts of his surroundings and went into the wilderness to seek the truth.[1]

When Siddhartha saw the three things foretold by the wise men, his expectations $E(R)$ and reality R no longer matched. His Happiness Equation, $H = R - E(R)$, suddenly had a large negative value that created deep suffering inside of him. Siddhartha's father designed his son's life for a reality R of 9, so the beauty and pleasure would anchor Siddhartha into that reality. Thus, Siddhartha had come to expect that life has an expectation $E(R)$ of 9. However, upon seeing the three things foretold by the wise men, he found out that life is a spectrum of reality with an average R closer to 5. Therefore, his different Happiness Equations are as follows:

His Happiness Equation was $H = 9 - 9 = 0$

With a new $R = 5$,
His new Happiness Equation is $H = 5 - 9 = -4$

Factoring life's unpleasant states:
Sickness, old age, and death
Sickness $= -2$, old age $= -5$, and death $= -10$
Factoring in these new states,
His average $R = ((5 - 2 - 5 - 10)/4) = (-12/4) = -3$

When Siddhartha factored in these unexpected additional negative R states, his Happiness Equation becomes:
$H = -3 - 9 = -12$

Because of the deception created by his father and upon finding out the truth, deep suffering emerged within Siddhartha's heart. This suffering drove him to seek the truth of a clear understanding of his life. He abandoned his title,

CLARITY

inheritance, family, and palace comfort to seek the truth of what life is. Due to the deep internal suffering in his heart, the comfort of the palace no longer mattered. To ease his suffering, he left to seek a clear understanding of the meaning of his life. He sought an expectation $E(R)$ that equals the reality R he witnessed. Siddartha was seeking clarity.

Clarity: the first of The Noble Eightfold Path is Right View

The First Noble Truth of Buddhism is that life is suffering. When Siddhartha Gautama came up with a way to alleviate suffering from life, he called his clear understanding *The Eightfold Path*, also known as *The Middle Way*. The extremes of life are pain and pleasure, but our existence is in the middle. The first of the *Eightfold Path* is *right understanding,* also known as *Right View*.

It is our clear perception that allows us to see the world better. We will no longer suffer inside when we can view the world with our clear perception. Our expectations will match our reality like a balanced Happiness Equation. Our better perception allows us to see clearly and take better actions that match our reality R.

Distorted View

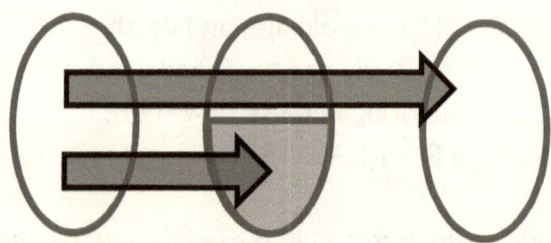

Our View   Our Distorted Filter   The World

Our internal distortions block our view of the world.

THE DELICIOUSLY CHEESY HAPPINESS EQUATION

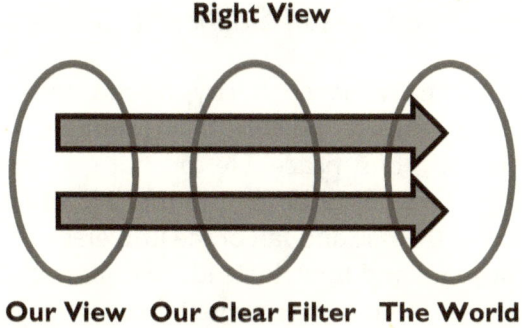

With Right View, we have a clear understanding to view the world.

When we have Right View, our expectation $E(R)$ equals our reality R, and our Happiness Equation is balanced at $H = R - E(R) = 0$. We have happiness inside our hearts; thus, our clear view helps ease our heart's suffering. The Happiness Equation is normally best applied to our lives' difficult events when our pain and suffering overwhelm our hearts, leaving us in confusion on the inside. The many variables and constant changes in our lives make it impossible to put it all into an equation for our complete clear analysis. However, the concept of the Happiness Equation still applies. We must match our expectations $E(R)$ to our reality R within our changing environments and our changing self throughout our life's journey. If we can see our world and our journey better, we can reflect on who we are and how or where we want to journey in our hearts and minds. Thus, we will match our inner expectations to our external realities.

When we clear up our hearts' confusion, we clear up our minds and find the right view. We will begin to know where we are going and have better expectations $E(R)$ regarding our world and its realities. Thus, the first of the Eightfold Path is to find a clear understanding to gain a clear perception. When we attain clarity of perception, our suffering ends, and happiness begins.

CLARITY

The clarity and happiness of Siddhartha Gautama

When Siddhartha achieved clarity, he did not reach beyond our world and gained powerful, mysterious, or mystical knowledge to bring him peace. He did not gain knowledge or understanding of the afterlife or pre-life. He did not gain an understanding of the rise and fall of the universe or the countless dimensions of space and time. Instead, he understood the heart's ways over desires, fears, environmental conditioning, and self-importance. He became free of the forces that clouded his perception. He became free of the ignorance of a distorted view when he understood the patterns of life. He gained a clear understanding of internal happiness, and he taught us how to free our hearts and minds for our happiness. His clarity allowed him to balance his Happiness Equation from the inside. He became free of fears and desires in his heart and his self-importance over others. He saw the connectedness of life in every living being. Siddhartha lived in happiness and clarity for all his days, applying his understanding to live in happiness and bring happiness to others. Siddhartha earned his wisdom through his journey of deception, suffering, and reflections. Siddhartha's enlightenment is his clear understanding of the internal forces.

Siddhartha gained a clear understanding that helped him overcome his father's deception. He found truth and beauty in accepting life's many different patterns of balance and changes. He found a balanced understanding of its joys as well as its sufferings. By reaching a clear view and seeing the beauty of life, he found an amazing and purposeful life. Once his internal confusion cleared, he lived a life he designed and brought others clarity, kindness, and happiness. Our clear understanding leads to an understanding of our purpose and inner strength.

How the Buddha met his mother

There's no doubt that a large part of Siddhartha's suffering came from not having been nurtured and loved by his biological mother. Along with his father's deception, Siddhartha's emptiness

THE DELICIOUSLY CHEESY HAPPINESS EQUATION

created internal suffering that drove him to seek salvation in a better understanding. When he awoke to reality and understood the processes and systems of life, he met his mother in nature's rest and growth cycles. She's a part of our universe's processes and systems, and so is he. They are both a part of the same universe's timeless processes and systems. The very short time they spent together is an unintentional random factor of the universe. Like many other factors, randomness is part of the impermanence of the cycles of rest and growth. Thus, we are to detach from our random factors to move forward to seek out a better understanding of our life's journey.

Siddhartha found his mother through his clear view. He understood the forces in his heart, the cycles of rest and growth, random factors, and detachments, thus, giving him peace for his life's journey.

The clarity and happiness of Helen Keller's enlightenment

> *Abbe Faria: In return for your help, I offer something priceless.*
> *Edmond: My freedom?*
> *Abbe Faria: No, freedom can be taken away, as you well know. I offer knowledge, everything I have learned. I will teach you, oh, economics, mathematics, philosophy, science.*
> — THE COUNT OF MONTE CRISTO (2002 MOVIE)

One of the most insightful people who ever lived saw the world only through her mind's awareness and imagination and the strength of her heart. She saw the world more clearly than many of us who have eyes to see and ears to hear. Because she was blind and deaf from a young age, Helen Keller received Anne Sullivan as her guide and personal teacher when she was seven years old. Since Helen Keller could not see or hear, Anne Sullivan taught Helen Keller language by spelling words into her hand. Helen Keller was given an object like a doll, and then Anne Sullivan would spell the letters of *doll* into her hand. At first, Helen did not understand that Anne Sullivan was trying to teach her words, thus, creating further frustrations. Approximately a month after their first meeting, Anne Sullivan ran water through Helen's hand, and then she spelled the word *water*. At that moment, Helen Keller finally understood that Anne Sullivan was trying to teach her words for communicating. According to the words of Helen Keller, *"That living word awakened my soul, gave it light, hope, joy, set it free."*

Helen's internal enlightenment on her education's importance led her to an exciting and amazing lifelong adventure in learning and growth. If she had not awakened to the importance of information, she would have been in darkness all her life. But instead, her sudden realization of the importance of information opened the door for her amazing life despite not hearing or seeing the world. Understanding the importance of information was crucial for Helen Keller's clarity, and it is true for us as well. We need clear information to understand better our life's journey toward a life of happiness. We can see life's patterns with our eyes and hear with our ears. But, we will also need to see them clearly with our minds and hearts.

BETTER QUESTIONS, BETTER CLARITY

"Doubt everything, be your own light."
— BUDDHA

Objectivity, independent thinking, and self-reliance

Marilyn vos Savant and Leonore Fleischer stated in their book *Brain Building in Just 12 Weeks* (1991) that the most crucial elements to our intellectual growth are developing objectivity and independent thinking. [2] When we have independent thinking, our thoughts remain ours without being constrained or influenced by other people's thoughts. In our having objectivity, we maintain calm in our hearts for our continued reason and logical thinking. The Happiness Equation quantifies our H level, giving us clarity and objectivity for internal happiness to be free to develop our independent thinking further.

In his essay "Self-Reliance" (1841), Ralph Waldo Emerson urges us to think independently outside social conditioning and social norms. We need to rely on our internal reason and logic or common sense instead of conforming to social environments or social norms. Thus, we will free our minds to think on their own. Thus, these accomplished thinkers urged us to think independently.

Albert Einstein's what if

> "Imagination is more important than knowledge. For knowledge is limited, whereas imagination embraces the entire world, stimulating progress, giving birth to evolution."
> — ALBERT EINSTEIN

In an educational school film from a long time ago, Albert Einstein imagined a beam of sunlight coming to Earth and then bouncing off into space. He imagined himself riding on that beam of light back into outer space. Then, he asked *what if* he is on that beam of light and travels very fast near the speed of light. From his questions, Albert Einstein deduced many of his theories. He theorized that space and time are part of the same field of the fabric of the universe. There is not a space field and a time field, but only a space-time field. Thus, according to the Theory of Special Relativity, time slows down when we approach light speed. He asks what-if questions regarding the nature of the universe, and when he set out to answer those questions, he worked out amazing insights into the universe's physical laws.

The incomplete questioning of the Oracle of Delphi

There's a story that before King Croesus of Lydia went to war against the powerful expanding Persian Empire of Cyrus the

CLARITY

Great, he went to the Oracle at Delphi to seek counsel. The Pythia is the high priestess of the Temple of Apollo, who is the Oracle at Delphi. Because its location was strategic to trade routes, Lydia, in ancient times, was a small but very wealthy kingdom in the Mediterranean. The expanding Persian Empire brought war to Lydia's borders. King Croesus went to the Oracle and asked what would happen if he went to war against the Persian Empire. The Oracle replied, *"You would destroy a mighty empire."* So in 547 BCE, King Croesus of Lydia attacked first and started the war with Persia. The Persian forces destroyed the Lydian army, and Croesus became the last king of Lydia. Eventually, Croesus made his way back to the Oracle at Delphi. He asked why the Oracle misled him into thinking that he would win against Persia. The Oracle replied, *"You didn't ask me which empire would be destroyed."*

Instead of objective questions, we tend to ask questions that will give us a favorable answer to receive more. We have to ask our questions objectively and not simply ask questions to receive a favorable answer. When we think of what's in it for us, it creates a blind spot in our hearts that blocks our mental clarity. The blockage in our minds hijacks our thinking and our questions. So, instead of asking an objective question, we will ask a question for a favorable answer. If our question is not objective because it reflects the blindness in our hearts and minds, then the answer we receive will also reflect our bias. A misleading and biased answer will lead to incorrect actions and unfavorable results.

The questions we ask eventually lead to actions toward our destiny. Because our questions create suffering within, our minds and hearts refocus on finding answers to them. Therefore, we have to ask better questions to get better answers for our actions to achieve a better destiny.

The first question

Our first question is our most important one because it leads to other questions for our lifelong journey. *"What do I want to do before I die?"* creates a list of exciting things to do in our lives. The bucket list is a list of things we want to do before we die, and it

THE DELICIOUSLY CHEESY HAPPINESS EQUATION

is often our first question. Once we complete our bucket list, it is generally associated with having done all the things we wanted to do to make our life feel complete so that we can die in peace. We have experienced all of life's pleasures and beauty. We didn't miss out on any exciting experiences, and therefore when we die, we can rest in peace. This question is typically the first question we ask ourselves so that our life will feel complete. But *what if* that first question with its bucket list of things to do is the wrong question? The question asks what is in it for us. By asking what is in it for us, we will have created our desire, suffering, and the need to fulfill that suffering. The answer leads us to reach for external elements to fulfill our inside needs to complete our journey.

What if that first question of asking what's in it for me so I can feel that I have lived creates an emotional blind spot in our hearts and minds? When we ask to receive, we ask questions from our emotional blind spots. Because the question lacks objectivity, the answer eventually leads to further suffering. It is never enough when we ask to receive, and it never ends. After our death, why would it matter how much pleasure or exciting experiences our physical human self has had. Instead of *"What do I want to do before I die?"* the better first question to ask should be *"What can I do so that I can live?"* We want to live a life filled with peace, purpose, and inner growth worthy of the energy and time we used for our life's journey. We want to live knowing that we are happy regardless of external circumstances. In our darkest moments, we want inner strength to shine the brightest. The first question, *"What do I want to do before I die?"* aims to receive pleasure, comfort, and relaxation for a meaningful life. The first question, "What do I need to do so that I can live?" aims to give and share happiness, leading to our inner strength and ability to create and share joy.

What do I want to do before I die?

The philosophical focus becomes; what do I want out of life? Thus, I want to travel and see the world, have an amazingly exciting and fun time, and relax in comfort and ease. When I die, I want to know that I have had a good, happy life to be at peace. I did not miss out on anything pleasurable, exciting, and fun that life offers. The question asks for external stimulants to complete our lives.

Our desires create an unhappy state that requires external stimulants for happiness. We want to experience an abundance of pleasure, and we want to experience less pain and suffering. Our enjoying life requires the experience of pleasure, comfort, relaxation, and exotic destinations. We are only excited because we will experience all the wonderful and fun things life offers. This first question appears to make sense because we experience all these exciting, wonderful, and relaxing pleasurable events. But if we live our life from the bucket list, then after experiencing all the pleasures of life and its curiosities, we would no longer have a reason to live.

> *"The literal meaning of life is whatever you're doing that prevents you from killing yourself."*
> — ALBERT CAMUS

When we ask, *"What do I want to do before I die?"* we become focused on finding external stimulants to go on living. We become self-focused and find patterns for meaning in our lives based on pleasure, comfort, and relaxation from the external. This first question requires favorable external circumstances for meaning and happiness in our lives. When the external sensory stimulants are no longer available, or our senses become saturated due to overstimulation, life becomes hard to live, and we want to check out, as Albert Camus described. The stimulants will be the same, we just had enough of them, and we no longer feel their excitement. If we live our lives according to "what's in it for me?", we will run into not having enough stimulants, which can lead to suffering, or we will have too much, and we become imbalanced, saturated, and bored, and suffer as well. Thus, the answer to happiness is not in the stimulants outside but in our understanding inside.

THE DELICIOUSLY CHEESY HAPPINESS EQUATION

The Best Donut Theory

> Mika: My father taught me this world was only a preparation for the next, that all we can ask is that we leave it having loved and being loved.
>
> Kai: I will search for you through 1,000 worlds and 10,000 lifetimes until I find you.
>
> Mika: I will wait for you in all of them.
>
> — THE 47 RONIN (2013 MOVIE)

Because they spent a very short time together, Mika and Kai's love and passion will carry into the next thousand worlds through ten thousand lifetimes. Similarly, the love and passion of Romeo and Juliet have remained fresh and intriguing for each new generation for four hundred years because their passionate love was for a very short time. Neither couple got a chance to dine at the super buffet of their love stories. They are not yet emotionally saturated with each other. They have not had their fill, and they remain hungry. We also did not get to dine at the buffet of their very short love story. Thus, we did not get our fill, and we are also hungry for more. The most memorable and best donut ever is the donut we had once as a child. It came in a positive surprise filled with a +H, and we also probably had to share it with someone. It leaves our hearts wanting more, which makes it so good and memorable. Some love stories in the world last only a couple of hours, and some in just a moment's smile, but they last an eternity in our hearts.

An amazingly memorable happy life does not require an overabundance of stimulants. We do not require an abundance of pleasure and experiences for our sustained intriguing happiness and excitement. We do not have to eat at the buffet for a fulfilling and satisfying life because life is more delicious when we are hungry. If we saturate ourselves with all the sensual and emotional flavors of life from a supreme buffet, our senses and emotions become dull. We will also become emotionally and physically out of balance. Our staying hungry is a requirement

CLARITY

for an exciting life. Our receiving fewer stimulants becomes more excitement and happiness as our hunger takes us on to other stimulating adventures of our creation. A great love story is not like a buffet but like the best donut. So, it leaves us hungry for more. Our best and most memorable life is through our love and kindness for others.

What do I need to do so that I can live?

The question of *"What do I need to do so that I can live?"* will lead us to ask other better questions for our journey. It will make us excited because we have so many wonderful ideas to make the world better and more beautiful for everyone. It leads to questions like, *"What do I want to give to life?"* We get to give our best selves. We will know that we have lived a good life when we die because we can see it in others' happiness. We are at peace because we have contributed to making it better for others. The answer to this first question will lead to our asking other better questions.

Our better first question asks, *"What do I have to offer and share with others?"* If we ask what we can give, we must improve and become better to give our best. The better first question will lead to our inner growth and strength, allowing us to better ourselves. It will also lead to happiness because we no longer ask what is in it for us from the outside. We will have a smaller expectation E(R) in our Happiness Equation, yielding a consistently better H. Our better first question leads to our strength and happiness. We will arrive at being thankful we can give. The more we give, the more we will have to give. When we are thankful, we live in happiness. The following Zen story demonstrates being thankful in giving:

> *The Giver Should Be Thankful*
>
> While Seisetsu was the master of Engaku in Kamakura he required larger quarters, since those in which he was teaching were overcrowded. Umezu Seibei, a merchant of Edo, decided to donate five hundred pieces of gold called

THE DELICIOUSLY CHEESY HAPPINESS EQUATION

ryo toward the construction of a more commodious school. This money he brought to the teacher.

Seisetsu said: "All right. I will take it."

Umezu gave Seisetsu the sack of gold, but he was dissatisfied with the attitude of the teacher. One might live a whole year on three ryo, and the merchant had not even been thanked for five hundred.

"In that sack are five hundred ryo," hinted Umezu.

"You told me that before," replied Seisetsu.

"Even if I am a wealthy merchant, five hundred ryo is a lot of money," said Umezu.

"Do you want me to thank you for it?" asked Seisetsu.

"You ought to," replied Uzemu.

Why should I?" inquired Seisetsu. "The giver should be thankful."

The Happiness Equations of the first questions

An incomplete question to the Oracle at Delphi led to a biased answer and disastrous result for King Croesus. Thus, our better questions lead to clear thinking, happiness, and strength for making our world better. When we have objectivity and independent thinking, we will ask better questions that lead to happiness. Now let's apply the Happiness Equation to our two first questions to understand their impact on our happiness. The Happiness Equations of the two first questions are below.

$$\text{What's in it for me?}$$
$$H = R - E(R)$$
$$R = 5$$
$$\text{We desire R from the world}$$
$$\text{We have a large } E(R) = 8$$
$$H = 5 - 8 = -3$$

CLARITY

> What can I do to make it better?
> $H = R - E(R)$
> $R = 5$
> We look to give R rather than receive
> Thus, we have reduced expectations
> We have a small $E(R) = 3$
> $H = 5 - 3 = +2$

When we ask a better first question, our hearts and minds are free to pursue a journey of clear thinking for a more purposeful and happy life. When we look for what's out there, we will not search for what is in here. We rather wait for something from the outside to be happy, and once we receive it, we may wait again for the next stimulant. Waiting for an R from the outside for happiness makes us try very hard to limit our efforts because we are waiting. The question, *"What do I want to do so that I can live?"* frees us from our desires and our waiting. When we are free of our desires, our Happiness Equation will generally be positive due to our lower expectation E(R) from external elements. When there is nothing in it for us, we get to become better. Our lives are an amazing journey in sharing joy and happiness with others, and with a better first question, we can happily serve our lives' purposeful journey.

Siddhartha and the swan

> *"Kindness is the sunshine in which virtue grows."*
> — ROBERT GREEN INGERSOLL

When Siddhartha was seven years old, he came across a wounded swan that his cousin Devadutta shot down. He took the swan and began to care for it when Devadutta showed up demanding the swan because he shot it down from the sky. Siddhartha argued that if the swan had been dead, then it would

THE DELICIOUSLY CHEESY HAPPINESS EQUATION

belong to Devadutta. But because the swan was still alive, it belonged to him, for he nurtures life. One asks, *"What's in for me?"* and the other asks, *"How can I make this situation better for others?"*

Instead of arguing, the two cousins agreed to take the matter to the wise men and elders. An elder pointed out that we do not want to suffer but would want to heal. If the swan could talk, it would want the same thing. Therefore, the swan belonged to someone who would want to heal it and make it better instead of someone who wanted it dead. The elders decided that the swan belonged to Siddhartha. The elder's compassionate wisdom sees the situation from others' perspectives and decides in favor of life and healing because we would also want the same thing.[3]

Siddhartha healed the swan, and afterward, it continued on its migratory pattern to nest in the Himalayas to continue its natural cycles of rest and growth. Our love and kindness will help others, so they may be able to fulfill their destiny. Those who come to take will injure and destroy life. They ask, *"What's in it for me?"* They would have taken the life of the swan. Those who come to give will heal and help others reach their destiny and purpose. They ask, *"How can I make this better for others?"*

> *"It's not what you look at that matters, it's what you see."*
> — HENRY DAVID THOREAU

Our perceptions define who we are, and our clear perceptions will better guide us in our life's journey. We can discover ourselves, our world, our universe, and our journey when we ask better questions of clarity to attain a better perception. What are our questions to the oracle? *What if* we ask more objective questions to achieve better perceptions?

WHAT IF

> "What if the computer was the most beautiful object, something you want to look at to have in your home? And what if instead of it being in the right hands, it was in everyone's hands?"
> — STEVE JOBS, *STEVE JOBS* (2015 MOVIE)

Our incomplete or biased questions lead to misleading answers that can misguide our lives. Our actions based on misleading answers lead to unfavorable results and further suffering. Our better and well-thought-out questions lead to better answers that open up our minds. Thus, our better questions lead to a better journey, happiness, and our destiny. *What if* we ask more objective and independent thinking questions?

My walk with Lily

> "Go wash in the Pool of Siloam."
> — "JOHN 9:7"

I enjoy taking walks with my kids. When we take walks among nature, we are in the company of our loved ones, immersed in the universe's timeless vibrations. One day we were walking around a lake, and we saw a squirrel living its best life because it was happily jumping from tree to tree and appeared to be having fun. One of my daughters is Lily. She's very compassionate, deep-thinking, and open-minded. Lily was next to me, so I said to Lily:

> "What if the conscious energy inside that drives that squirrel is the same energy that drives us? However, the internal energy stuck inside the squirrel's physical information has to make the best use of whatever evolutionary ability given to it by nature. Thus, it becomes a squirrel."

THE DELICIOUSLY CHEESY HAPPINESS EQUATION

Lily said, *"Maybe."* Maybe all life's consciousness comes from the same source because all the materials that make all living beings on our planet also come from the same source. They come from the earth and the stars. We all behave differently due to our genetic information and upbringing when nature combines with nurture. That is the process of the squirrel being and also us, human beings. The universe's laws are the same everywhere. For example, the force of gravity affects all things the same way. The laws of the universe do not differentiate between objects or different forms of living creatures.

The energy in a squirrel wields its vehicle body to the maximum of its ability or risks becoming extinct. The squirrel's mind and body constrain the perception of its internal energy to become a squirrel being. The squirrel's complete understanding of the universe is filtered through and limited by its biological evolution. The internal energy is limited to being a squirrel.

The squirrel needs to think it's a squirrel for its survival. As humans, our minds are free to be anything we want or desire, subject to the limitations of our biological design. Our level of freedom depends on how imaginative we are with our human mind's understanding. Our human-environmental conditioning, senses, and perceptions filter and influence everything we know about who we are. Like the squirrel being a squirrel, we have to be human.

The Squirrel

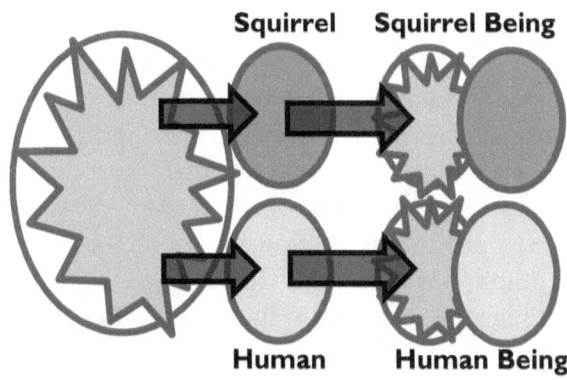

CLARITY

> *The conscious energy goes into the physical information that makes up the squirrel and learns to become a squirrel. The same conscious energy goes into the physical information that makes up a human being and learns to become a human.*

What if our human conditioning and our human mind do not constrain our perception? How would we see the universe? Who would we grow to become?

What if we could detach from our human perceptions and unleash our imagination to grow and expand further? Our compassion for others, our kindness, and our curiosity about the universe will be our only guides.

> *"In the sky, there is no distinction of east and west, we make our own distinctions and believe them to be true."*
> — BUDDHA

Our understanding of ourselves and all that we are is through the form of a human being. We learned East and West through conditioning. Our conscious energy currently resides in the physical form and understanding of a human being. Our connection to the universe is in the form of a human being.

All life is subject to the universe's fundamental laws. One day, our physical body will separate from our internal energy. It will deteriorate away, similar to the deterioration of the squirrel's physical body when it completes its life cycle. When we complete our life cycles, we give back the energy we borrow from the universe. Because our human energy resides in a more evolved species of this planet, we are more aware of other dimensions of existence beyond survival. Like the squirrel, our survival instincts and conditioning pull our actions. We are more aware of other laws or perceptions beyond our environmental conditioning as human beings. We have a more evolved conscious mind that is more self-aware than the squirrel.

THE DELICIOUSLY CHEESY HAPPINESS EQUATION

A wealthy squirrel

What if we were a person who had accumulated an abundant amount of wealth for our lifelong needs and comfort? What would that imply if we were a squirrel instead? We would be a squirrel that accumulated a large number of nuts. We would have enough nuts to last season after season for the rest of our squirrel life and our offspring's squirrel lives. Our offspring would not have to venture outside to gather nuts anymore. They are well-stocked, and those nuts are accumulating interest to grow into even more nuts. That would be nuts because there would be no challenges or excitement in their squirrel lives. They would simply live with abundance for the rest of their squirrel lives. Therefore, our intangible love is the best nuts to give our children to become internally strong, wise, and confident. They will be capable of gathering nuts season after season all their lives in any environment. Thus, the best nuts to give our children are an inner strength for gathering nuts and not plain old nuts from the trees. Therefore, they will be able to continue to dream better dreams and create better visions for tomorrow. Happiness is a clear understanding that empowers our inner strength and others.

A squirrel being a squirrel

What if the internal energy learns to be a squirrel, a sailfish, or a human? As humans, our energy learns to love and hate. As our energy learns to become its environment for survival, we forget that our energy is from a different source that is pure and simple.

The energy that is in the squirrel maximizes its ability to the evolved capability of its evolutionary vehicle-being. This world conditions us for maximum effectiveness for our survival. The conditioning serves us for a time in our life when we cannot think yet, but we act on our subconscious programming. As humans, we cannot live on our environmental conditioning alone throughout our lives. *What if* our environmental conditioning defines but limits who we are as a person? A squirrel can only be

CLARITY

a squirrel, but, as humans, we can be more than our original environmental programming. If we want to be more than our limitations, we would have to expand our minds and hearts beyond the original limitations that define our being.

The death of a squirrel

When a squirrel dies, the physical materials that make up its body get recycled back into nature, and the materials nurture or become other living things. *What if* the consciousness energy inside dissipates and gets recycled in a dimension beyond our senses and comprehension? In nature, patterns mimic each other from the very small to the very large and from one system to another. From a human perspective, my pattern is deemed more important than the squirrel due to our deeper emotional bond, more evolved awareness, or larger egotistical perception due to our human brain size. Gravity affects all the atoms in the universe in the same way. From nature's perspective, my pattern will be the same as the squirrel because the universe's laws apply equally to all living beings.

When my time ends, the consciousness and internal energy inside will dissipate to a dimension or a spectrum of understanding beyond our current human ability to perceive at this time. My body will dissipate and be recycled to become energy and materials for other beings. Where the squirrel's body goes, mine will go, and where the squirrel's spirit goes, mine will most likely also go. We may not even take our memories with us beyond this world because we do not remember the last set of memories. Our memories, which define us, could be only a tool for survival in our current form. *What if* my identity of *me* is a gift of the universe for survival in this space-time only? It does not exist in another realm. If we lived on Mars's surface, we would be a completely different species due to our adaptation to survive in that environment. Thus, our environment created our being for use only in this space and time.

Even if my consciousness awakens again, I will not have my memories or my emotional memories of this life because they

THE DELICIOUSLY CHEESY HAPPINESS EQUATION

will only link me to the good ole days of another life long ago. For every new awakening, I get new internal environmental conditioning for the challenges of that unique environment. My creation is for the space-time of my birth, and it does not exist in any other space-times or dimensions.

When I move on from this world like the squirrel, I get to take nothing with me, but it is the love that I leave behind for others that matters and lives on. This unique combination of information and energy that is *me* will never exist again in this or another dimension. Changes in space and time create different information and energy for new beings' environmental conditioning. My existence is a butterfly effect of countless conductions of this world's information and energy. Thus, it is made only for use in this particular unique space-time. Because this world's conditions created my being for use in this world, it will not exist in any other space-time. The uniqueness of the information and energy that is me is for one-time use only in this space-time. The expectation or hope of more me in this unique combination in another dimension is only a manifestation of our desires and imagination of our human form's need for survival in the internal and not necessarily a universal pattern of the external. Even Gilgamesh, the warrior king from one of the first human-written stories from ancient Sumeria, wanted to live forever.

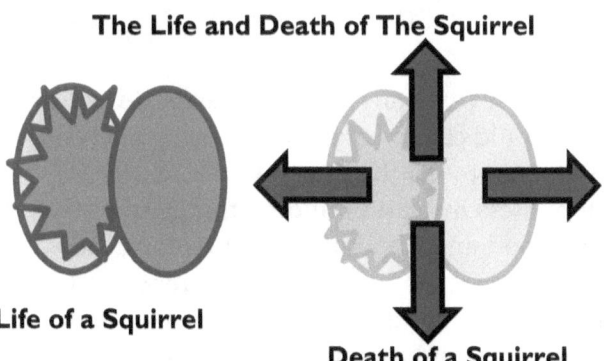

The Life and Death of The Squirrel

Life of a Squirrel

Death of a Squirrel

The law of conservation of energy states that the total energy of a system is always the same. The energy that makes up the

CLARITY

squirrel cannot be created or destroyed. The external energy gets recycled into becoming other beings. As patterns in nature mimic one another, *what if* the internal energy dissipates and gets recycled to become the consciousness energies of other living beings? *What if* the laws of physics apply to both states of energy? The energy of both the physical body and the squirrel's consciousness cannot be created or destroyed. *What if* they are both recycled to obey the law of conservation of energy?

What if everything about us is a multidimensional butterfly effect of information and energy across space and time? To think that we would exist again in another dimension is only our subconscious mind's wish for permanency. The conduction of information and energy of this space-time created us. This space-time created our understanding, pain, suffering, peace, happiness, and physical body for use in this environment. *What if* there is no other dimension for our unique combination, and our internal and external beings are impermanent? If that is true, then we have to solve our Happiness Equation in this space-time because there's no other existence. Our happiness of this form is only in this moment because we exist only in the here and now.

Reverse engineering happiness

> *"Start with the end in mind."*
> — DR. STEPHEN R COVEY

Happiness is everything that we ever desire or want to achieve. If we could change one thing about ourselves, we would change it to be happy all the time. Therefore, *What if* we reverse engineer happiness instead of finding things from the outside to make us feel good and hopefully bring us happiness? Thus, we start with our final objective of happiness and then work backward to figure out all the actions we need to take to reach our final destination of happiness. We will have a well-thought-out plan to achieve happiness by working backward toward our objective.

THE DELICIOUSLY CHEESY HAPPINESS EQUATION

- Our objective is a state of happiness. When we reach a state of happiness, we will have peace, purpose, and fulfillment.
- To have peace, purpose, and fulfillment will require clear thinking and a life lived for others.
- To have clear thinking and a life lived for others will require studying, thinking, and reflecting on our journey for our place and time.
- Studying, thinking, and reflecting on our journey for our place and time will require letting go of our environmental conditioning, desires, fears, and ego's need for importance.
- Letting go of our desires, fears, environmental conditioning, and ego's need for importance will require clarity in our minds and strength in our hearts.
- Raising the clarity of our minds and the strength of our hearts will require raising our awareness.
- To reach our state of happiness, we begin by raising our awareness of our processes and systems.

Everything is a process or system

> "Love is the bridge between you and everything."
> — RUMI

Our body is a biological system, and our physical world is an ecosystem. The plants and animals interact with each other in their system of symbiotic relationships. Our community and our world form our social system. Our sun and its planets make up our solar system. Therefore, systems embody what exists for interacting with each other.

What if everything is a process or a system? Processes and systems keep the universe and its components moving in constant balance through all the different changes. So everything is a part of a system run by processes from the very small to the very large.

- *Physicists postulate that superstrings vibrate to become quarks and other subatomic particles.*
- *The up quark and down quark become protons and neutrons.*
- *Electrons are fundamental particles.*
- *Protons, neutrons, and electrons become atoms.*
- *Atoms become molecules.*
- *Molecules become tissues.*
- *Tissues become organs.*
- *Organs become living beings.*
- *Living beings become families.*
- *Families become part of neighborhoods.*
- *Neighborhoods make up cities.*
- *Cities are in states or provinces.*
- *States or provinces make up countries.*
- *Countries make up our planet.*
- *Our planet is part of the solar system.*
- *Our solar system is part of the Milky Way galaxy.*
- *Our Milky Way galaxy is part of the local group of galaxies.*
- *The local group is part of the Virgo Supercluster.*
- *The Virgo Supercluster is part of the Pisces-Cetus Supercluster Complex, a galaxy filament.*
- *Galaxy filaments, galaxy walls, and large quasar groups make up the universe.*

To help explain dark energy responsible for our expanding universe, physicists postulate about the multiverse with an infinite number of big bangs and universes beyond our own. One day, we will gain the ability to see beyond our current limitations into an endless number of universes and dimensions. Still, at this time, galaxy filaments, galaxy walls, and large quasar groups are part of everything as far as we can see and understand for now. The largest known structure in the universe is the Hercules-Corona Borealis Great Wall discovered in 2013. It is ten billion light-years across.[14] Processes run all these systems every day, every hour, every minute, and every second, from the very small to the very large. If processes run all the systems, we must understand our world and our universe's processes and systems.

THE DELICIOUSLY CHEESY HAPPINESS EQUATION

Everything is a Process or a System

Everything is part of interconnecting systems, and processes run all the systems. Energy drives the processes.

Everyone and everything serves its purpose and performs its role to ensure that the system runs well through different cycles and changes. *What if* love is the energy that empowers the processes in many of these systems?

Everything is a perception

One of the greatest storages of wealth ever built by humans is the stock market, and its valuation is all perceptions. The stock market's valuation is the sum of all the participants' perceptions. It is the sum of all the fears and desires of every participant, big and small. If we put on a dark pair of sunglasses and look into the world, we would see a darker world. It is the same thing with a clear pair of glasses. Our view of the world changes depending on the color or strength of our glasses. *What if* we perceive the world through the clarity of the energy in our hearts? Our clarity of perception determines the actions we take. *What if* everything is perceptions?

We are born with a certain colored filter in our minds and hearts, and we look at the world with it throughout our entire lives. We are not even aware that we have a colored filter perception because that is all that we have ever known. Even though we live physically in the world, the world lives internally inside us through our colored perceptions. If we want to see the world with better clarity, we need to find better clarity in our minds and hearts to view the world. If we could remove our

CLARITY

colored perception, we would see all the beauty in the world of our space-time.

I am never wrong

> "But possibly the greatest barrier between anybody and a better intellect is the inability to admit mistakes."
> — MARILYN VOS SAVANT AND LEONORE FLEISCHER

What if I am never wrong? If I am never wrong, I will never have to change my ways. Changing requires accepting that I am wrong and then having to find a better way. If I am never wrong, I will never learn, and I will never grow to become better. Learning and growing are to accept that I am wrong and need to change by opening my mind to add new thoughts. The pain and suffering that I will experience will be someone else's fault because I am never wrong. Thus, I will blame others for my situation. If I am never wrong, I will never change. How can I change when I am not wrong? I do not have any problems because I am never wrong. The entire universe that has nurtured and supported life for billions of years must be wrong because I am never wrong. Therefore, the universe should adjust itself to me. I will never adjust to learn and grow but will always stay the same, from birth until death. I will never be able to see the beautiful world of *what if* I am wrong. When I am never wrong, I become wrong all the time.

What if I never fail?

> "Anyone who has never made a mistake has never tried anything new."
> — ALBERT EINSTEIN

If we never fail, we have never tested the boundaries of our limits. We have never tested the edge of our information and energy. At the boundary of our limits, we will fail at many tasks

THE DELICIOUSLY CHEESY HAPPINESS EQUATION

and succeed when we learn to do them better, and it is where our strength can rise and grow to become better, fantastic, or even amazing at times.

Our life is always exciting, fantastic, and amazing

What if our life is ever exciting, fantastic, and amazing? But we cannot see our exciting, fantastic, and amazing life because we haven't believed in its existence yet. We haven't believed it yet, because we haven't thought of it yet. We haven't thought of it yet, because we are stuck in what is missing from our life. We have not yet been able to make the best of what we have. *What if* we open up our minds and hearts to accept and realize that our life is exciting, fantastic, and amazing? Then we would feel the energy inside. When we feel the energy inside, it radiates outward into our world. *What if* today, we get to live our best life? We get to give our best from the inside and let that radiate into our world. Each day, we get to live our best life. Why is life so exciting and amazing every day? Because we get to connect to the universe and experience the happiness of our being. Why is the world ever so beautiful, giving, and kind?

Kindness is the fabric of social systems

> "Kindness in words creates confidence. Kindness in thinking creates profoundness. Kindness in giving in creates love."
> — LAO TZU

We communicate using energy as well as information. The energy from our hearts goes into others' hearts, and they will always remember how we made them feel. *What if* kindness and compassion allow us to see the beauty in the world? Our kindness and compassion strengthen the social fabric of our world. When Siddhartha Gautama left the palace to seek the truth regarding his place in the world, all the gurus he found could not help him ease his heart's suffering. When he reflected upon childhood memories and felt compassion for others less

CLARITY

fortunate than he, Siddhartha started seeing truth and beauty in the world. He saw the connectedness of everything, including his birth, his youth, and his family. His compassion for others allowed him to see and feel the love in social systems' processes across space and time. He saw his own life as a part of a process within systems, and he was able to see into the beauty of life. Our compassion and kindness for others allow us to see all the beauty in the world. Our hatred and anger make us see all the ugliness in the world. It is the same world viewed from different perceptions of the heart. Our perception determines the level of beauty in the world. The following Zen story demonstrates that the ultimate truth is kindness.

No Loving Kindness

There was an old woman in China who had supported a monk for over twenty years. She had built a little hut for him and fed him while he was meditating. Finally, she wondered just what progress he had made in all this time.

To find out, she obtained the help of a girl rich in desire. "Go and embrace him," she told her, "and then ask him suddenly: "What now?"

The girl called upon the monk and without much ado caressed him, asking him what he was going to do about it.

"An old tree grows on a cold rock in winter," replied the monk somewhat poetically. "Nowhere is there any warmth."

The girl returned and related what he had said.

"To think I fed that fellow for twenty years!" exclaimed the old woman in anger. "He showed no consideration for your needs, no disposition to explain your condition. He need not have responded to passion, but at least he should have evidenced some compassion."

THE DELICIOUSLY CHEESY HAPPINESS EQUATION

She at once went to the hut of the monk and burned it down.

Our discipline and our clear understanding of the ways are for our inner peace; they are for ourselves. Our compassion and kindness in our hearts are for others. Thus, our kindness is the best virtue because it strengthens the social fabric that connects us to others to create joy and happiness to share.

The 50-million-dollar solution

What if we achieve financial freedom to last for the duration of our life's journey? We can sit back and enjoy the abundance that life has to offer. In *The Saint* (1997 movie), Val Kilmer plays a thief who accumulates 50 million dollars, and he can retire in peace because he will have all the money he needs for the rest of his life.[4] *What if* we suddenly come across 50 million dollars, and we would be able to live comfortably for the rest of our life with no worries regarding food, shelter, and all the pleasures of life? We would be like the wealthy squirrel with all the nuts we could eat and all the trees for our shelter. The 50 million dollars would solve all our basic needs and desires, but then *what if*:

- The economic climate changed to affect our net worth.
- The 50 million dollars enlarges our self-importance. We isolate ourselves from loved ones and friends. We lose our social connection to love and to belong. We miss out on the happiness of people.
- We get bored because we have no challenges to motivate us.
- We develop certain comfortable and pleasurable habits that deteriorate away our inner strength.
- There is a crisis in the country or the world, many things change, and our money becomes worthless. So the 50 million dollars becomes meaningless.
- We gamble it all away in a couple of years.

CLARITY

We think the 50-million-dollar solution will solve all our problems and bring us lasting happiness. The reason and logic appear clear, simple, and straightforward. If we suddenly have 50 million dollars for the next 50 years, we will have a million dollars a year to spend on our comfort, needs, and desires. That is $83,333 a month. We will be okay for the rest of our lives. We can live comfortably in pleasure and just wait to die. *What if* we do not want to wait to die? *What if* we want to live in each moment?

Because we do not have it yet, we see the clear reason and logic of our satisfied needs and desires to make us happy. We do not see the many problems it will create if we suddenly have 50 million dollars. We act on our emotions when we are in a situation and not on our reason and logic when we view the situation from a distance. We cannot yet see many things like our enlarged self-importance when we have 50 million dollars and that our actions will reflect our enlarged ego. We do not see the changing force of desires in our close circle of friends, family members, acquaintances, or ourselves. Our future desires determine our actions, not our desires of today.

Reason and Logic vs. Actions

Reason and Logic of $50 million
Actions of $50 million

Once we have 50 million dollars, our actions will not match the reason and logic of the actions we thought we would take.

THE DELICIOUSLY CHEESY HAPPINESS EQUATION

The 50-million-dollar solution solves only our basic needs in Maslow's hierarchy of needs. It fulfills our basic needs and allows us to indulge in the pleasures of life. With 50 million dollars to make us all set so that we do not have to do anything, what would serve the purpose of our being? We would be like the wealthy squirrel with all the nuts we can eat, and we do not have to do anything. *What if* our journey in life is finding joy and happiness in the constant changes and challenges of uncertainty? Our basic needs' indulgences will have little meaning to us, and the 50 million dollar answer fulfills our basic needs, but it cannot meet our higher needs. The money will block our ascension to the higher needs of love and belonging or self-actualization. We are stuck in comfort, relaxation, and pleasures due to our basic needs already generously being met. The 50 million dollar solution will derail our ability to ascend Maslow's hierarchy of needs because our basic needs are satisfied. We will find it hard to grow in strength on the inside because we will have eliminated our need to become internally stronger. In *The Saint* (1997 movie), the hero's 50 million dollars wasn't enough to keep him happy. Shortly after hitting his target, he pursued a lady scientist's affection. Besides being beautiful, she had the potential to become the wealthiest person on the planet.

A king, an NFL owner, or a Fortune 500 CEO

> "To whom much is given, much will be required."
> — LUKE 12:46

What if we are a king, an NFL owner, or a Fortune 500 CEO? We see the riches, the estates, the palaces or mansions, the authority, the service, the respect, the pleasurable lifestyle, the confidence, and we desire it for ourselves. We do not see the strength of heart, the determination, the conditioning, sacrifices, stresses, and education that make a king, an NFL owner, or a Fortune 500 CEO. As emperors of their domain, their responsibilities and psychological stress of protecting the entire country or financial empire require extraordinary rewards. Their rewards appear to be a limitless abundance of lavish wealth, pleasure, and power. Their responsibilities are the care and well-being of all those in their domain against foreign and domestic enemies. They are rewarded for their discomfort so that others may relax and be comfortable. Suppose we want success so that we can experience a lavish lifestyle. In that case, we must develop the skills, knowledge, and inner strength to take on the responsibilities of others' happiness, comfort, and relaxation.

Unless we have the knowledge and strength of heart to run such a system, most of us will run it into decay and ruin very fast. If we want the benefits of a position of authority, we will have it when we have earned it through our development and growth to take on the challenges. Money is power, and receiving the benefits of power when we have not earned it will lead to abuse and destruction. The destination is not the money but our inner growth to become someone entrusted with the power to serve others.

In W.W. Jacobs's short story *The Monkey's Paw* (1902), wishing for money to solve our problems results in unforeseen drastic, dark, and undesirable consequences. Don't wish for material things and don't wish for free things, for there will be dark consequences that we cannot yet see. If we wish for money to fall from the sky to solve our problems, it comes with unexpected consequences that make our situation worse than before.

The Sword of Damocles story tells of a wealthy king named Dionysius, who ruled Syracuse long ago. His good friend was Damocles. King Dionysius was very rich and had many palaces and servants. His friend Damocles kept telling him how lucky he was and that he had everything a man could want. One day King Dionysius got tired of Damocles telling him how lucky he was and offered his riches to his friend for one day. When Damocles came to the palace the next day, he had access to all of King Dionysius's riches, comforts, and servants. Damocles was sitting at the dinner table when he suddenly saw a sword hanging above his head. It was only hanging from the ceiling by a single strand of horsehair. The sword was right above his head and looked like it might fall at any time to strike him down. He becomes filled

THE DELICIOUSLY CHEESY HAPPINESS EQUATION

with fear for his life, and the food and the wine become tasteless. He only wanted to get out of the palace. He asked his friend King Dionysius about the sword, and the king told him that he knew all about the sword.[5]

The sword represents the danger that others might come to take our lives so that they can take the wealth of the kingdom. It is the same thing for a CEO, an NFL owner, or a king. We need to raise our inner strength to earn the right to govern and serve such an entity to defend its people, wealth, treasures, processes, and systems. Thus, we need to have the inner strength to bring happiness to others. We cannot simply wish for something that we have not earned. Only those who have raised their inner strength can learn to live in balance with the danger of the sword because they have earned it.

Gifts of nature are just for our survival

> *"Pleasure is, and must remain, a side-effect or by-product, and is destroyed and spoiled to the degree to which it is made a goal in itself."*
> — VIKTOR FRANKL

What if our lives' pleasures are meant for our survival only because they make us want to live and earn more pleasure? They are gifts of nature, and by earning more, our lives become more bearable. Nature designed our pleasurable sense of taste to help nurture our bodies for survival. Nature designed our pleasurable sense of human physical intimacy to stimulate procreation for the survival of our species. Our pleasurable sense of relaxation makes us feel good while conserving energy by doing nothing. We developed the ability to walk upright to conserve energy long ago, becoming more efficient than the other primates. Our body conserves energy by giving us pleasurable sensations by not performing any tasks but being still. The pleasures of our lives are a means to an end. They serve a purpose for our existence, but they are not the purpose of our existence.

CLARITY

If we make comfort and relaxation our sole purpose, we will do less and consume more. The process of those actions will eventually lead to an imbalanced emotional and biological system. Our journey is for happiness, and our happiness is not the same as pleasure and comfort. We experience pleasure, and it is gone, but when we experience happiness, it stays in our hearts. Our happiness is for our hearts, and our pleasure is for our senses. We will never come to a time when robots serve us while we exist in pleasure, comfort, and relaxation for our entire life while we do nothing, unless, of course, the robots get more out of it than we do like in *The Matrix* (1999 movie).[7]

The emotional energy of happiness lives on in the conduction of information and energy. If we are pleasure-focused, when the pleasure is gone, so will the reason for our life to continue. We will look for other forms of pleasure to go on living or cease to exist. In addition, our comfort and relaxation are easy to do, and anyone can do comfort and relaxation. But, our discomfort takes great strength, understanding, and happiness to rise to the challenges and keep moving forward.

The happiness of suffering

> *"All the adversity I've had in my life, all my troubles and obstacles, have strengthened me... You may not realize it when it happens, but a kick in the teeth may be the best thing in the world for you."*
> — WALT DISNEY

We may think Walt Disney drew a mouse that captured our hearts and exploded into success. Instead, Walt Disney filed for bankruptcy seven times and failed at many ventures, including acting. His first successful cartoon character wasn't a mouse but a rabbit named Oswald The Lucky Rabbit. When Oswald The Lucky Rabbit became popular, Walt Disney lost the rights to his creation. Thus, his failure and suffering empowered his strength for the success of Disney.

THE DELICIOUSLY CHEESY HAPPINESS EQUATION

What if our strength only comes after suffering? *What if* the magical transformation for our internal strength lives at the edge of suffering? That is where the pressure turns coals into diamonds, hearts of confusion into clear focus, and failures into success. To journey to the edge requires our clear understanding and courage to accept discomfort and suffering. There are many kinds of suffering. We have physical suffering experienced by the senses, but our greatest suffering is the heart's internal suffering due to confusion.

We have internal suffering created by others to manipulate our actions. We have the internal suffering of feeling sorry for ourselves and refusing to take action for better balance. We suffer from internal confusion, and we do not know that we are suffering. Our internal confusion leads us to believe we are not suffering and deteriorating. Finally, we have the internal suffering we create inside to elevate ourselves to ease the suffering. A happiness level of negative H helps raise our inner strength by raising our giving R to balance our Happiness Equation. This last suffering is the happiness of suffering. Through its creation and our actions to ease the suffering, we will become stronger to achieve lasting happiness. When we do not get what we desire, we become internally stronger through our suffering. When we do not get what we want, we get raised internal strength.

Per Aspera ad Astra: Through suffering to the stars

> "The wound is where the light enters you."
> — RUMI

In an episode of PBS's *NOVA* from 2009 called *Becoming Human: First Steps*, scientists were trying to figure out why our human ancestors' brains suddenly grew tremendously around 250,000 years ago in east Africa. The fossil records indicated that our ancestors started developing more advanced tools due to our larger brains. They looked at the geological records and found that, around 250,000 years ago, there were thousand-year cycles of extreme wet and dry climate changes. Thus, our ancestors had to adapt constantly between abundance and starvation. The pressure and suffering of dealing with extremes made our human brains grow. Our ancestors grew from within to adapt to the external changing elements. The fluctuations between bountiful and lacking created an internal adjustment by increasing our brain size to adapt between the two extremes.[8] For example, even Siddartha's internal growth into awakening also comes only after wild swings of extreme pleasure and suffering. *What if* pressure and suffering raised our internal growth as a species? Our growth on the inside alleviates our suffering.

$$\text{The Happiness Equation:}$$
$$R(External) = R(E)$$
$$R(Internal) = R(I)$$
$$H = R(I) - R(E)$$

$$\text{We experience suffering when } R(I) < R(E)$$
$$H = R(I) - R(E) = -H$$

$$\text{By raising our } R(I) = R(E),$$
$$\text{We become stronger}$$
$$\text{Thus, } H = R(I) - R(E) = 0$$
$$\text{Our suffering goes away}$$

Our growth can only come through accepting and facing our challenges so that we can overcome them. Our pain and suffering strengthen the resolve within our hearts, and we become stronger. When we do not get what we want, we get inner strength instead. We cannot begin our work to discover ourselves and our world until we see the clarity of need and purpose. We cannot overcome something that we have not yet accepted that exists. We cannot grow stronger unless we have suffered. Therefore, we cannot find the strength to complete all our tasks

THE DELICIOUSLY CHEESY HAPPINESS EQUATION

for happiness until we have become stronger. According to the poem below by Aeschylus, wisdom comes with suffering:

> *God, whose law it is that he who learns must suffer.*
> *And even in our sleep, pain that cannot forget*
> *falls drop by drop upon the heart,*
> *and in our own despite, against our will,*
> *comes wisdom to us by the awful grace of God.*

In *Gone with the Wind* (1939 movie), Scarlett O'Hara starved and suffered, and finally, she decides that she will never be hungry again.[9] Our inner strength comes from the sum of Scarlett's famous line: *"As God is my witness, I'll never be hungry again."* Whenever we have moments that create great suffering, we create inner strength to ensure that the suffering does not happen again. The strength in our lives is a summation of our "I'll never be hungry again" moments. We commit to becoming stronger, so we don't suffer again.

> *"Everything that irritates us about others can lead us to an understanding of ourselves."*
> — CARL JUNG

Before we can become physically stronger, we have to carry heavier weights. Before we can become emotionally stronger, we have to carry heavier emotional weights. Those that irritate us will strengthen us because they will reveal the flaws we have left yet inside. Our greatest teachers are those who have come to test us the most with pain and suffering. They will make us stronger than anyone else can. We will know that we have become stronger on the inside when being tested, we can hold back negative thoughts and actions, and we can still focus on making logical decisions for everyone's happiness. We should bless those who came to challenge us to become better and stronger because they help raise our inner strength. In the beginning, it will hurt more, but through raising our tolerance and inner strength, we will feel little pain in the end. Those who love us bless our lives, and those who hurt us bless us with inner strength. Thus, everyone that we meet is a blessing.

Happiness through suffering

> "If you are irritated by every rub, how will you be polished?"
> — RUMI

In Margot Zemach's book *It Could Always Be Worse* (1976), a man wasn't happy with all the chaotic events going on in his little hut, so he went to see the Rabbi for help. He told the Rabbi about all the events that were driving him crazy. The Rabbi thought about it, and then he asked the man to bring the chickens, the rooster, and the goose into the house. The man's life became worse than before because the chickens were making all sorts of noises, the rooster was crowing in the morning hours, and the goose was honking.

After a while, the man and the Rabbi met again. The man tells the Rabbi how things have worsened in his little hut. The Rabbi thinks about it again and then asks the man to bring the goat into the house. The Rabbi asked the man to bring the cow into the house in their next meeting. With each animal's addition to the house, the man's situation became worse and worse, and he was at the point of breaking down. They met again, and the Rabbi instructed the man to release all the animals from the house. That night the man slept peacefully. The next day, they met again, and in joy, the man told the Rabbi, *"You made life sweet for me. With just my family in the hut, it's so quiet, so roomy, so peaceful...What a pleasure!"* [15] The man now had a higher tolerance for noise levels and distractions through his suffering. Our happiness depends on the strength of our tolerance for discomforts. Like the lake's water temperature, we do not sense the true discomfort level, but we sense the difference in our tolerance strength inside versus the discomfort level outside. Our happiness is the relativity of both factors. Through suffering, we raise our inner strength for happiness in most discomforts.

THE DELICIOUSLY CHEESY HAPPINESS EQUATION

Happiness = our tolerance - outside discomfort = 0

> "I had to live in the desert before I could understand the full value of grass in a green ditch."
> — ELLA MAILLART

We will make adjustments to our discomforts by raising our tolerance level. If we raise our tolerance level enough, what was once a distraction will no longer bother us. We have grown to tolerate it better. However, if we are irritated by someone, we have not yet raised our tolerance level to deal with it positively. Our peace does not come from getting rid of our distractions. Our peace of mind comes through raising our emotional tolerance for distractions. For example, a male lion's inner strength comes from being tested in the wild during his nomadic wandering years. We become stronger with every rejection, taunt, embarrassment, shortfall, or failure.

Comfort Zone

Limits	Expanded
Discomfort	Comfort Zone
Comfortable	

If we dwell in comfort without testing our limits, we live in a small area. By pushing beyond our comfort zone into our discomfort and beyond our limits, we will have raised our tolerance level to be comfortable in all areas.

CLARITY

The universe grants wishes

> "When you want something, all the universe conspires in helping you to achieve it."
> — PAULO COELHO

Powered flight evolved four times in all life variations; insects, pterosaurs, birds, and bats. *What if* a long time ago, someone from the dinosaur family saw a dragonfly and said, *"I wanted to fly just like that."* It saw the advantages of flight and wanted it with all of its heart. In time, the bird's ancestor developed feathers, wings, and the ability to fly in the air, and it became a bird.

What if we want the skills and the energy to accomplish all our tasks with joy? *What if* we want the strength of the heart to overcome our fears and our desires? *What if* we want the confidence to handle any challenging obstacles that come our way?

What if we do not get another life as we know it? As far as we can tell, there's only been one life that we have lived because we all do not remember any other lives. *What if a* peaceful afterlife is an invention of our hearts' and egos' desires? Nature designs us to want to survive and a peaceful existence tomorrow and beyond. Our consciousness may become aware again in another space and time, but it will not be a part of this life or a part of us any longer. The new consciousness will have its unique space-time, information to guide, and energy to drive.

The atoms that were once ours will belong to new beings of the new environment. Our consciousness's permanence could be like the permanence of atoms and molecules that live on through time. Thus we are reincarnated like atoms are recycled to become new beings. But, when we pass away, our atoms are recycled to become other living organisms, and the atoms are no longer ours. They belong to other living beings now. Without physical forms or memories to connect us to a prior conscious awakening, we have only this one life in the here and now. If we only have this one life, there's only one way to live: giving our best here and now.

What if the universe grants wishes? If the universe grants wishes, I wish for positive emotional energy every day for my being, drive, and sharing joy and happiness with others.

SHORTCUTS TO STRENGTH AND HAPPINESS

The wisdom of traditions

In many communities today, people still practice cultural traditions that originate before the Common Era. For example, in our own community's traditional wedding practices, two liaisons from each side of both families conduct the marriage proceedings. There are two from the groom's side and two from the bride's side. There is a lead, and there is an apprentice. It is similar to having lawyers from both sides present at a business negotiation to allow for structure, guidance, and objectivity. The wedding starts at the groom's house, goes to the bride's house, and finishes off back at the groom's house as the entire wedding party returns home.

The practice of sending off and conducting a traditional wedding ceremony requires an extensive understanding of cultural traditions, dialogues, and songs. The discussion, negotiation, and wedding ceremony have structure, poetic rhymes, and songs that teach and cultivate balance, competition, humility, friendship, family, and love. The benefits of learning and practicing traditional culture are gaining wisdom, humility, and kindness. Thus, we gain strength and confidence to create a balanced to serve others' happiness.

Traditions sometimes get a bad rap due to misunderstanding, misuse, and abuse, but most of the world's beautiful traditions have benefits that strengthen the heart for balance and happiness. The practice of the traditions helps to create confidence and build leaders to serve the community. As we learn traditions and help others in their time of need, it strengthens our confidence to solve complicated social issues. Therefore the purpose of traditions is love, kindness, humility, confidence, and leadership building. Because they make us better, our traditional cultural practices are shortcuts to our education for strength and happiness.

Our traditions carry thousands-of-years-old processes for cultivating and strengthening our hearts and minds for our life's journey. By cultivating our understanding of the laws of the heart, our traditions teach strength and confidence. The origins of many traditions date back to the beginning of time for humans. Unfortunately, some spiritual traditions have not adapted for change or have been hijacked for power by those in charge. The traditions' teachings should free others for happiness and balance instead of imposing our will over them.

Our traditions provide a guide from the beginning of life to the end and fill our thoughts and actions with kindness, confidence, peace, and purpose. They help us to develop courage and confidence to serve. Without traditions to guide us, we can become lost in the senses' desire for ease, comfort, and pleasures. Before we decide to give up being traditional, we need to find something stronger to guide our hearts. Otherwise, we will end up lost in the pleasures of the senses. We require the teachings of our traditions for our inner strength. When we invent a new gadget or process for ease and comfort, it does not make our tens of thousands-years-old traditions useless. If we abandon our traditions for an easy life, we will lack guidance for strengthening our hearts, and it will create confusion and hardship for our journey to come. Our traditions are hearts' education for our inner strength and happiness.

The importance of nature's traditions

What we believe inside will lead to our actions on the outside. Our traditions conduct timeless information and energy of

THE DELICIOUSLY CHEESY HAPPINESS EQUATION

wisdom to help strengthen our inside. Learning and understanding the ways of traditions help guide our beliefs for inner strength. Our planet's richest and deepest tradition is nature and all its balances of beautiful processes for all living organisms. Our nature on earth is the timeless and limitless universe at the local level. The many variables from space and time contributed to our planet's unique nature. Nature here on earth has adapted itself to the stars' movements and the universe's vibration. It has been in a constantly changing balance for billions of years. Thus our nature here on our planet is the adaptation of the universe at the local level. All that lives on earth are in balance with it or cease to exist. Nature is constantly changing, but each small change brings a new balance. All the creatures live in harmony with nature and depend on one another for survival. Like the bees and the flowers, the animals and the plants depend on each other. We cannot ignore nature's deep understanding of the universe's patterns. We cannot abandon our traditions learned from nature. We come from nature, are of nature, and will return to nature. If we are suffering, it is because we are out of balance with nature's deep traditions. Our nature is the universe at the local level, and our nature's patterns are the universe's regional traditions in motion.

The tradition of marriage

What if, a long time ago, our ancestors created the concept of marriage so that we would stop killing ourselves over mating rites? They realized that competition for procreation results in strong emotional demonstrations of male ego and strength. The male demonstrations of strength for mating rights can result in someone getting hurt or killed. The creation of marriage is a solution to neutralize our male ego's physical demonstrations. However, the wild animals in nature still display their male masculinity through physical demonstrations. The lions, elephants, hippos, and other animals still fight each other to the death, if need be, over mating rites. Their need for procreation unleashes actions of dominance and strength, which could result in injury or death. The energy of mating rights, not survival needs, results in extreme animal weaponry in the wild. In nature, extreme needs and desires result in extreme evolutionary weapons. Thus, one of the purposes of marriage is to tame the heart's uncontrollable energies so that we do not fight each other over procreation. The emotional force of social shame tames marriage's logical solution in human beings to make it work most of the time.

The evolution of traditions

The patterns in nature, filtered through our elder's understanding, become traditions for our social systems. Our traditions were created during a particular place and time to fulfill the needs and desires of that time. Our traditions are not absolute understanding because our understanding of nature is constantly growing and changing. Thus, our traditions serve as a shortcut to happiness for ourselves and others. As we understand more of nature and see new patterns to update our understanding, our traditions have to adapt to accommodate the changes, or they risk becoming outdated and eventually useless. A revelation from a thousand years ago may still be good for strengthening our hearts for our happiness. Still, it has to accommodate our growing understanding of the traditions in nature.

NATURE'S TEACHINGS OF CLARITY

"There is something of the marvelous in all things nature."
— ARISTOTLE

There are many perceptions, but there is only one reality, and nature has had billions of years to learn and adapt to it. We are just beginning to learn from nature's adaptation to discover the

THE DELICIOUSLY CHEESY HAPPINESS EQUATION

one reality. The Wright brothers were up against Samuel Pierpont Langley in the quest for the first flight human flight. Both teams took different approaches to flight. Samuel Pierpont Langley approached the idea of flight from power and propulsion. An arrow does not have any lift, but it flies in the air due to the power at launch. The Wright brothers modeled the *Wright Flyer* after observing the balance of birds in flight. They developed a three-axis control system that allows a pilot to steer and maintain balance. They based their work on patterns in nature. Samuel Pierpont Langley's Great Aerodrome flew straight into the Potomac River. Based on observations of nature's patterns, the Wright brothers' Wright Flyer flew into history. Nature's patterns and traditions stretch to the beginning of time and provide many answers to help guide our life's journey regarding our reality.

Fibonacci and fractal geometry

> "Nature uses only the longest threads to weave her patterns, so that each small piece of her fabric reveals the organization of the entire tapestry."
> — RICHARD FEYNMAN

Fibonacci and fractal geometry are mathematical patterns in nature, but the patterns are also found in human events because we are of nature in origin. Fibonacci is a pattern in nature, but we use it to track and time movements in the stock markets, a human social event. A Fibonacci number is the sum of the two prior numbers, $F(n) = F(n-1) + F(n-2)$. The following is an example of a Fibonacci sequence:

$$1, 1, 2, 3, 5, 8, 13, 21, 34, 55, 89, 144 \ldots$$

The Fibonacci sequence has its origin in Indian mathematics dating back to Acharya Pingala (200 BCE). It became the Fibonacci sequence after Leonardo Bonacci wrote *Liber Abaci*

CLARITY

(Book of Calculation) in 1202. Fibonacci is short for Filius Bonacci, meaning *"the son of Bonacci."* However, the name *Fibonacci* itself was only coined in 1838 by the Italian historian Guillaume Libri. Thus, Leonardo Bonacci never heard of the term Fibonacci, just like Confucius never heard of the name Confucius. His real name is *Kǒng Fūzǐ* (Master Kong) or more common *Kǒngzǐ*, and Confucius was coined in the late 16th century by Jesuit missionaries.

The Fibonacci sequence explains the growth rate in nature, from breeding animals to the growth of seashells. In human events, investors use Fibonacci patterns to understand and predict stock and commodity price movements. Likewise, we can use our tools to understand nature to forecast human social events and behaviors because we come from nature.

Fractal geometry, or fractal, is a branch of mathematics that shows repeating patterns in nature from the very small to the very large. One of the most famous fractal patterns is the *Mandelbrot set*, named after the mathematician Benoit Mandelbrot, which shows infinite repeating smaller and smaller geometric patterns when zooming into the geometric shape created by graphing the set. This concept was also illustrated by the Japanese artist Katsushika Hokusai's painting of *The Great Wave off Kanagawa* (1831). The painting demonstrates that the smaller and smaller wave patterns are the same as the larger wave. Thus, fractal geometry shows that the large patterns are the same as the small patterns in nature. Fractal is a pattern in nature, but it shows up in our human social events. For example, the stock and commodities chart patterns are the same for the small five-minute, hourly, daily, and larger weekly timeframes. Like Fibonacci and fractal geometry, nature's patterns appear in human social events and repeat themselves from the small to the large. Patterns in nature appear in our human events because we are of nature in origin.

THE DELICIOUSLY CHEESY HAPPINESS EQUATION

The cycle of rest and growth is a pattern in nature

> "Music is the space between the notes. It's not the notes you play; it's the notes you don't play."
> — MILES DAVIS

There are periods of rest in nature, and then there are periods of growth. There is the quiet resting of winter and the bountiful growth of summer. The peaceful quiet night follows the active and energetic day. One period is resting, and the other is the growth of energetic dances. The cycles follow each other and need each other. Our human perceptions limit our observation to our space-time of growth. We cannot see and understand the complete cycles of fractal geometric patterns in nature yet, including our complete cycle of rest and growth. At rest, our senses no longer connect to the physical universe. But according to Lao Tzu, what is not there makes what is there useful.

> "Thirty spokes share the hub of a wheel;
> yet it is its center that makes it useful.
> You can mold clay into a pot;
> yet, it is its emptiness that makes it useful.
> Cut doors and windows from the walls of a house;
> but the ultimate use of the house
> will depend on that part where nothing exists.
> Therefore, something is shaped into what is;
> but its usefulness comes from what is not."
> — LAO TZU

The beautiful monarch butterflies (scientific name: Danaus plexippus) complete a long cycle from Mexico through two stops in the US and southern Canada, and then they follow a long return trip to their starting point in Mexico. Each time they stop, they lay their eggs, and then they die. The next generation continues the journey to the next destination without any guidance from the previous generation. Thus, monarch butterflies do not get to see the entire cycle. Like monarch butterflies, we do not see the complete picture of our rest and growth cycles. We can only see what is filtered through our human senses while active in an energetic state of growth, not while we are at rest. Thus, we do not see the overall larger pattern of life's complete cycle. In nature, the patterns of life transcend one lifetime.

What do we want to be in the next life?

After my father passed away, my mother went through his belongings, and she found a letter he had written about what he wanted to be in the next life. He wanted to be an eagle flying high above. He wanted to be a large tiger in a forest away from the dangers of man. He wanted to be a military or public official, and with his status, he would marry three wives. His desire to be an eagle was to be safe from others. That would bring him peace. His desire to be a large tiger away from man was to be feared and safe at the same time. His desire to be a public official or military leader with three wives was his desire for self-importance and pleasure. *What if* we lived those lives in the next awakening of our consciousness? How would we know it is the gratification from a wish from a prior life? Once we are satisfied, what is next after that? *What if*, during those lives, we discovered we want a simple human life similar to the one we just lived? Do we even want to wait for the next life to find happiness in a hopeful imaginary creation, or do we want to find it in this one? *What if* the next life is simply a random factor of the universe, and we become a squirrel?

His desires show that his happiness in this life was unfulfilled, and thus, he is asking for it in the next life. Or he didn't achieve a clear understanding of happiness in this life. The requests he asked for in the next life for his happiness are manifestations of this life's environmental conditioning and desires. Our environmental conditioning in this life creates our being, desires, and suffering. The next life cannot fulfill our hearts' current desires and manifestations because the forces in this life created

THE DELICIOUSLY CHEESY HAPPINESS EQUATION

them. Each conscious awakening will have its own unique desires, manifestations, and heart sufferings. Thus, our happiness cannot be fulfilled in some hopeful imaginary dimensions or beings to come. This awakening created our dissatisfactions, and, thus, our answers are also here.

Are we going to wait for the next life to find happiness? Are we going to wait for the next life to decide that we will give it all to life? To prevent such desires in anticipation of our happiness in the next life, we should achieve clarity of understanding to find happiness in this one, so we are happy in the here and now. We can accept whatever comes next without hope for created expectations from our manifestations in this life. Our happiness comes from a clear inside to become our best for this moment and this life. It does not come from fulfilling the desires that manifest from our environmental conditioning in the form of a next life. In this life and all the other possible existences to come, our goal is to be happy. A happy life is a life of strength and giving our best. The full potential happiness of our being is in this form in the here and now. A better question to ask the Oracle is, *"Who do we want to become in this life for our happiness that would benefit others?"* Since we are stuck in human form and cannot become a tiger or an eagle, our transformation would have to occur inside. In this life, the next life, and every life, we will find peaceful happiness when we become someone who gives our best life for others' happiness. Happiness is a balance attainable here. Why wait for the next life for possible happiness when we can attain the happiness we desire in this life.

How long do we want to live?

> *"How many seas must the white dove sail before she sleeps in the sand?"*
> — BOB DYLAN

How long is too long of a life, and how short is too short of a life? If we lived to be ninety-plus years, some would consider that too long. If we live only for twenty years, some would consider that too short. How long is the perfect time to live, so it is not too long or not too short? *What if* we lived in the prime of our physical self at the age of twenty-five for exactly one hundred years? Would this make our length of time perfect? What if we lived for a thousand years in our physical prime and saw all our loved ones come and then go into ancient history? *What if* our perfect moment is one day only, but it lasts forever in our hearts? Is death better at ninety-five and suffering from old age than when we are at twenty, and we have most of our future ahead of us?

There is no amount of time we can live to say, "*Yes, I lived the perfect amount of time. That was perfect; now I can go in peace.*" There is no such thing. The answer is not in the length of time that we lived. Most of us do not get to decide the length of our lives. Our parents determine our beginning, and random factors determine our end. The answer is not how long we live but how we live and what purpose we serve during our time. Thus, how much are we willing to give of ourselves so that we can live and share happiness?

Our consciousness does not choose to come into this world and does not get to choose when to leave, but we can choose how to live our life. It is not how long we live that matters, but how we live and what kind of information and energy we conduct and share with others while alive because the quality of the moment lives on in our hearts. We want to live as long as we have a purpose for our life, and we can continue to give our best for our purpose of bringing happiness to share with others.

What we do not use, we will lose

I once visited a cave in Eureka Springs, Arkansas, with my family. The tour guide mentioned that they have trout in the cave's waters, but the fish are blind. The trout weren't born blind, but their being in the dark cave for a long time makes them blind. We were surprised to learn that the trout would lose nature's gift of vision in one lifetime. We felt sad that the trout had lost something that we consider very important to our normal daily

THE DELICIOUSLY CHEESY HAPPINESS EQUATION

lives; our sight allowing us to see the world. They became blind because, in the darkness, they hardly had use for their eyesight anymore. Maybe they wished it away for another more useful sense in their darkened environment. If we do not use our clarity of understanding, it might go away one day, and we will sit in the darkness of our minds and hearts.

Astronauts go into space, and when they return to Earth, they lose muscle mass, and they lose around 11 percent of bone mass after spending just six months in space. When we die, our consciousness disconnects and leaves our physical body. The physical body no longer serves a purpose and is no longer needed, and it begins decomposing immediately to return to the earth and universe. What we do not use, nature takes away.

When we use our body, mind, and inner energy to the best of our ability daily, it stays sharp and finely tuned. We can pressure our bodies, minds, and emotions, and the components grow to become stronger for our continued use. Nature designs our body and mind to be of use, or they will fade away. If we abuse our body, mind, or social relationships, we will also lose them.

Destroying a ten-thousand-year-old tradition forever

A forest is a tradition of ten thousand to a million years or even longer. When we destroy a forest, we destroy the traditions that have been there for tens of thousands of years. It will never return to what it was again. Even if we replant the trees, the forest's understandings, balances, and traditions are forever lost. The patriarchs and elders of that forest are forever gone. They are gone, and there is no one to teach the next generation about the forest's traditions. Nature is one of the greatest teachers in our search for understanding and meaning because it represents the wisdom of the constant balance and ongoing changes since the beginning of life on our planet.

CLARITY

The total disregard for traditions by the ducks at Lake Phalen

> *"Poverty is your treasure. Never exchange it for an easy life."*
> — ZENGETSU

Even the animals of our planet are in tune with the universe's vibrations and movements. When our planet's axis turns away from the sun and winter is in the northern hemisphere, those that could make the journey take off to the sky and head south for warmer weather. The turtles, frogs, and bears cannot migrate, and they hibernate or slow down their metabolism to rest for a long pause due to lower energy from the sun. It is a time of rest for the northern hemisphere. Then, when the northern axis turns toward the sun again, the animals journey north to take advantage of the bountiful dances of nature's growth after a long rest.

There is a posted sign at Lake Phalen in Saint Paul asking everyone not to feed the ducks. Lake Phalen got its name from Edward Phelan, one of the first settlers to Saint Paul, Minnesota. Edward Phelan emigrated from Derry, Ireland, in the late 1830s. Per the posted sign at Lake Phalen, the ducks will break their migratory patterns if we feed them. Instead of staying in tune with nature's traditions and flying south for the winter, they will stay around for winter because they are getting fed. In doing so, they cause unnecessary wear and tear to the lake's ecosystem. In addition, their attachment to ease and comfort will make them turn away from their ancestors' migratory traditions that have helped them stay strong for thousands of years. A duck that succumbs to ease of life abandons the ways and traditions of its ancestors. Thus, the desire for comfort and relaxation makes the ducks abandon their traditions for strength learned from nature.

If we were a duck born at Lake Phalen and our parents gave up our migratory traditions due to human feeding, we would lose that understanding required for our balance and strength. Instead of embracing the wisdom of our elders' traditions, we

THE DELICIOUSLY CHEESY HAPPINESS EQUATION

would now be living off the generosity of others. We gave up our ten-thousand-year-old tradition in one generation because we seek comfort and ease. Our life becomes challenging because we want easy. The migratory pattern is the elders' traditions and wisdom from their understanding of the patterns in nature. A duck that broke tradition for ease and comfort has abandoned a ten-thousand-year-old tradition designed to make it strong. The tradition of migration is lost forever. If we become ducks at Phalen, we will do less than required of our ancestors' traditions, leading to our suffering. We must not become ducks at Phalen but embrace our traditions' strength based on nature's wisdom.

> *"Look deep into nature, and then you will understand everything better."*
> — ALBERT EINSTEIN

Nature's patterns have been in a constant state of changing balance for billions of years. Our nature is the universe's tradition at the local level. Thus, Life's meaning blends into understanding nature's patterns, balances, processes, and systems. We lacked a simple understanding of our true origin in our human journey of over a million years. Our past understandings of our origin lack objectivity through observations. When we look to nature, we gain clarity regarding our ancestral journey of who we were to understand better who we are.

The pace and balance of nature

> *"Nature does not hurry, yet everything is accomplished."*
> — LAO TZU

Nature in the universe does not hurry but persistently moves along like a tortoise. There are no desires to pull or fears to push it to hurry. The laws of the universe create a constant state of balance with each new change without any struggle. There's no struggle because everything follows the law of nature to achieve balance. Our desire for more creates struggle and internal imbalance. Our human perception creates a difference between our reality R and expectations E(R), which sometimes generates unhappiness. In nature, there are no desires to create a difference between reality R and expectations E(R). Everything simply adjusts to each new change. The Happiness Equation of nature is balanced.

$$H = R - E(R)$$
$$\text{For nature, it is a constant } R = E(R)$$
$$H = R - E(R) = 0$$

Nature's pace runs at the pace of Aesop's turtle because it is very persistent. It is constantly in balance and rebalancing itself to accommodate for new changes. Nature's patterns are everywhere, and we are a part of nature. The patterns of nature are not limited to the forest, the lakes, the mountains, and the streams, but they are in our social events. Nature is our ancestry and our present. The materials borrowed from the universe become our bodies, and the universe's infinite understandings become our traditions and ways of life.

RAISE THE INSIDE

A tree falls in the forest

> *"Death is not the greatest loss in life. The greatest loss is what dies inside us while we live."*
> — NORMAN COUSINS

While walking in a park, I came upon a recently fallen tree due to a mild storm. It was a young tree still in midlife, and the storm was not that strong. I wondered why such a young tree would

THE DELICIOUSLY CHEESY HAPPINESS EQUATION

fall in a mild storm. I took a closer look at it, and I understood why the tree could not hold on in the storm and fell over. The young tree was rotten on the inside, and its core and inner strength were gone. The tree was rotten inside, and it didn't take a strong wind to knock it over. The tree lived in a system designed by and is a part of nature. Because its core was gone, it did not have the inner strength to hold on in a mild storm of nature. It could not weather nature's challenges.

Two Trees in a Storm

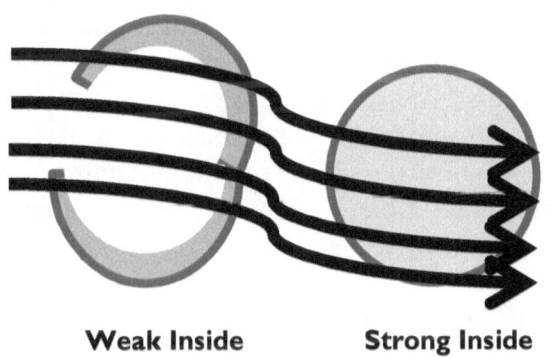

Weak Inside   **Strong Inside**

In the mild storm, the tree with the empty hollow inside falls. However, the tree with the strong inside remains standing.

Because we are part of nature, we can also be like that tree. When our inside is gone, we lack the internal strength to stand up to the storms of our lives. Without inner strength, it will not take much to knock us over. It is inner physical strength for a tree, but for us, our inner strength is our internal clarity and wisdom to rise to our challenges and storms. If we do not want to succumb to the same fate as that young tree, we should raise and strengthen the inside to withstand our lives' many storms. In nature's pattern, the strength is inside. Thus, we will need internal strength to withstand our lives' many storms.

CLARITY

> *"Life is a storm, my young friend. You will bask in the sunlight one moment, be shattered on the rocks the next. What makes you a man is what you do when that storm comes."*
> — ALEXANDRE DUMAS

When we raise our internal strength, we can handle any difficult matters with inner peace and calm. If we raise the inside for strength, our outside can weather any storms. Our lives' difficulties become more bearable because we will have the inner strength to face the many different challenges. If our fears, desires, self-importance, and environmental conditioning fill our inside, we will not have enough inner strength to withstand the natural and social storms that come into our lives. These forces create internal confusion to push and pull at our hearts. When we raise the inside, we raise our clarity of understanding, and clarity gives us the inner strength to weather any storm. When we raise the inside, we will raise the beauty and strength inside us.

The fountain of youth inside

> *"We all carry our own clock, and our clock ticks off at a rate compared to others that depend on the relative speed between us."*
> — BRIAN GREENE, THEORETICAL PHYSICIST

In 1513, Juan Ponce de Leon sought the fountain of youth in what is now Florida. He never found it because he was looking for it in the wrong place. He was looking for it in the outside world. Instead, the fountain of youth is inside.

Time slows down at near light speed or near large massive objects in the universe. When our heart is in high or low energy, the speed of time also changes. The duration of time stretches in our active and purposeful life, but the internal clock speeds up for each moment and appears shorter because life is exciting. We live longer, but our perception makes time flow appear faster. The passage of time in our lives runs on two clocks, our internal and our external, and both are subject to special relativity in

THE DELICIOUSLY CHEESY HAPPINESS EQUATION

nature and our hearts' relative energy inside. The passage of time is relative to energy out there in the universe and inside our hearts. Nature's patterns determine the pace of our external clock. Our internal understanding and emotional energy determine the pace of our internal clock. By raising the inside, we can slow down the passage of time for our external self. Our internal strength will drag and slow down the movement of our external clock as a life of purpose and strength will allow us to live longer to complete our journey's tasks. Our fountain of youth is in our minds and hearts.

The proof that raising the inside eliminates stress

> "When you choose to view your stress response as helpful, you create the biology of courage."
> — KAREN MCGONIGAL

Our desires create worries inside us because they create an expectation $E(R)$ greater than our reality R. We are stressed out when worrying about our high expectations $E(R)$. We are not stressed out simply because we are doing things. We are worried and stressed because of our inability to do things to the level of our expectation $E(R)$. In our Happiness Equation of giving, our effort R is less than the expectation $E(R)$ for stressful situations.

$$\text{Happiness Equation: Stress}$$
$$R \text{ is less than } E(R)$$
$$H = R - E(R) < 0 \text{ or } -H$$

We can increase our R to match the $E(R)$ by raising our inside and increasing our inner strength. When we raise the inside, we will find it easier to increase the R that we put forth into our tasks. Thus, our Happiness Equation becomes balanced. We raised our R to match our expectation $E(R)$ by raising our inside. Thus, we will have raised our inner strength to complete our tasks to our expectations $E(R)$, eliminating stress from our daily lives.

CLARITY

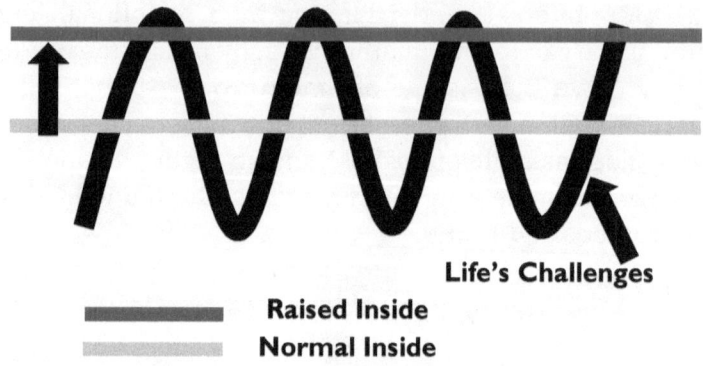

When we raise the inside, we can comfortably handle most of life's ups and downs.

How strong is our internal philosophy to apply ourselves? When we choose to raise the inside, we will accomplish all we need to do and want to do outside. If we neglect and destroy our inside, we will find easy tasks impossible to accomplish or even start. To raise the inside, we must change our emotional associations to the external patterns we want to change. We have to change the energy that drives us to serve our clear thinking rather than using our thinking to serve our useless or destructive emotional routines. Then, when we raise the inside, we can handle most challenges with less stress.

How far can you see?

> *"It's not the mountain we conquer but ourselves."*
> — EDMUND HILLARY

Imagine sitting on a beach by the ocean or on a large lake, and we are completely at peace. At the water's edge, we have an unobstructed view and can see into the distance. Our unobstructed clear view gives us peace. Now imagine we are in

THE DELICIOUSLY CHEESY HAPPINESS EQUATION

the dark, and we are not sure what lurks behind the darkness. We are not at peace because we cannot see visually with clarity. Therefore, we do not know what is in front of us or around us. Our thoughts and actions will reflect our level of clarity.

The peace we seek is clarity in our minds and hearts and not in our physical environment. Peace comes when we have a clear understanding of the balance in our world's processes and systems, and we can see into the distance of our life's journey. All life's creatures and components have learned and adapted to understand the balance of nature's processes and systems. If we seek the clarity of understanding in nature, we will find clarity of perception in physical darkness like Helen Keller. We will have clarity in our hearts and minds to see the world. Our actions will reflect our clarity.

Our obstruction preventing our clear view is a lack of clarity in our hearts and minds. When we climb the mountain inside to reach a clear internal understanding, our perceptions of the world will become clear. Our clear internal perception allows us to see into our lives' journeys, and we will have peace and happiness inside. With clarity, we will construct an expectation $E(R)$ that matches our reality R for a balance Happiness Equation of $H = R - E(R) = 0$. We can only travel to where we can see and not beyond that. Our journey will expand with our clear view, and so will our happiness in the journey.

The clarity of the fear of death

> "Death is not extinguishing the light; it is only putting out the lamp because the dawn has come."
> — RABINDRANATH TAGORE

Most of us fear death, but we hardly stop to ask what death is. *What if* death is only a human and earthly definition given to mark the completion of a cycle of our being? We currently do not have a complete understanding yet of the overall cycles of our lives. We are limited by what we can observe during our growth

CLARITY

cycle, and we do not know the complete cycle or cycle upon changing cycles. We define a small part of the completion of a cycle that we can see and label it death. Thus, it becomes a frightening, undesirable ending, but it may simply be a part of the cycles of rest and growth.

What if the fear of death is a gift for survival only? Without fear of death, we would check out at will when we no longer find our situation desirable. *What if* our fear of death is a fear of the unknown? Our fear of the unknown is fear due to lacking of clarity. We are afraid of the dark because we can't see, and our imagination creates worst-case *what-if* scenarios. To help alleviate our fear of death, the clarity we seek is not physical but rather our clarity in our hearts and minds for the cycles of nature. Thus, we will better understand and accept our journey through the different cycles of our rest and growth.

When we stand on a mountain top, we have peace because we have clarity of sight to see into the distant horizon with no obstruction. So likewise, when we ascend the mountain inside us, we will have peace because we can see our journey's distant horizon from our vantage point of view in our minds and hearts. Thus, the mountain we must ascend is inside.

What if our emotions become saturated in our life's journey? We become bored and need a new cycle to bring forth new energy. *What if* we need a better vantage point of understanding for clarity in our hearts and minds to conquer our fear of death? We are from nature, and we need to better see the patterns and cycles in nature. Our growth cycle connects our internal energy to our physical being here on earth, and our rest is when our internal energy no longer connects to our body. We connect with the physical universe in times of our growth, but we do not need to connect in times of our rest. It is not necessary. The egg sacks of insects do not need to be aware of winter's coldness because it is their time to rest.

THE DELICIOUSLY CHEESY HAPPINESS EQUATION

The growth on the inside

> "A jug fills drop by drop."
> — BUDDHA

The Chinese bamboo tree does not grow in the first, second, third, or fourth year of its life. In the fifth year, it then grows eighty feet in six weeks. The growth is on the inside all that time due to nature's watering, love, and caring. Our cultivating and raising the inside will also lead to explosive growth outside when the time is right. We will not get results right away, but we will get amazing results when the time is right.

The growth of the Chinese bamboo tree takes place on the inside, but it can be the other way around. Our unhealthy habits destroy our internal physical, mental, and emotional selves year after year. Yet, we continue and carry on as if the inside is still strong. We may still appear the same from the outside, but the inside is rotting away. Then, one day in a mild storm, we fall because our inner strength deteriorated from years of neglect and abuse.

We cannot change the outside and all its elements to make us comfortable or filled with joy and happiness. We can only strengthen our internal self to face the challenges of the elements outside by putting positive and exciting energy into our drive. Our clarity of information guides our journey, and our hearts' strength drives our efforts. When we raise the inside, we can rise to the challenging storms of our lives.

CLARITY

THE PURPOSEFULNESS OF OUR BEING

> *"He who has a why to live for can bear almost any how."*
> — FREDERICK NIETZSCHE

Our clear understanding of the patterns, processes, and systems across space and time becomes our guide to our life's journey toward happiness. We are not here simply to fulfill our desires because the information and energy from our space-time created those desires. The better we understand nature's processes and systems, the stronger our purpose and reason to live become. If we are born, live, experience pleasure or pain, and then die, what is the purpose of our existence? What is the why of it all? Why are we here? When we find an answer that makes sense, we alleviate our suffering. The purpose of life is not in our receiving but it is in our giving. What we consume is finished and gone from the world, and our consumption may also lead to a desire for more. However, what we give remains behind for others to enjoy. Our understanding of the why leads to our clear purpose for our existence. We are here to share our love and leave love behind for others. That is the pattern in our human journey of those that came before. That is also the pattern in nature.

The purposefulness of taking in energy

> *"Life is never made unbearable by circumstances, but only by lack of meaning and purpose."*
> — VIKTOR FRANKL

When Siddhartha Gautama left the palace to seek a clear understanding of life and alleviate his suffering, one of the many groups he studied with was the ascetics. For their spiritual journey, the ascetics would starve themselves to deprive their senses of pleasure. Siddhartha starved himself to the brink of

THE DELICIOUSLY CHEESY HAPPINESS EQUATION

death. One day, a village girl found him nearly dead along a riverbank and fed him some rice porridge. He then realized the why of eating: if he did not eat, his body, which houses his consciousness, would die. Thus, it would not serve any purpose when the body weakens and dies because the conscious mind dies along with the body's death. Understanding the need for balance led him to realize that our taking in pleasurable sustenance is only for a purpose; so that our body can live to serve. This understanding eventually led to the development of the balanced teaching known as *The Eightfold Path*, also known as *The Middle Way*.

The Middle Way is to live in balance with all the elements. For us to dwell in pleasure is incorrect, but to starve ourselves to the brink of death is also incorrect, for they both create an imbalanced physical body system. The way and why of eating is that it serves a purpose to nourish our body, which contains our mind and consciousness that serves life. With that kind of deep purposeful understanding, eating or consuming energy becomes balanced in serving a purpose for our journey. The pleasure of the senses is only a gift of nature, but the purpose is to nurture the body. The pleasurable taking in of energy is a means to a greater end for our life. Understanding the purpose overrides the desire for pleasurable sensations because we have wisdom and happiness to apply.

The deprivation of pleasurable sustenance brings pain and suffering to the senses. However, our understanding of the purpose of our actions brings happiness to our hearts. The strength of happiness outweighs and overrides the pain and suffering to the senses. Our eating is pleasurable for our senses so that we may take in energy. We have a purpose for taking in energy, and the happiness of our purposeful clarity within our hearts is stronger than our bodies' desire for pleasure. We will only take in exactly the energy we need for our purpose and balance.

CLARITY

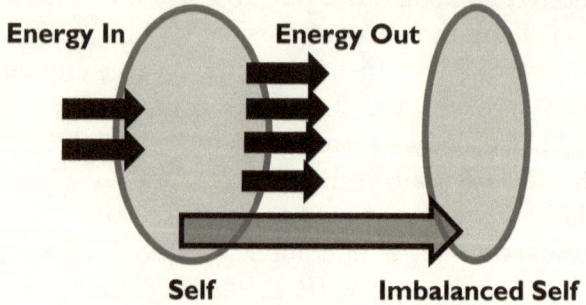

If we deprive ourselves of energy and use more than we take in, we weaken the physical body that houses the mind and consciousness.

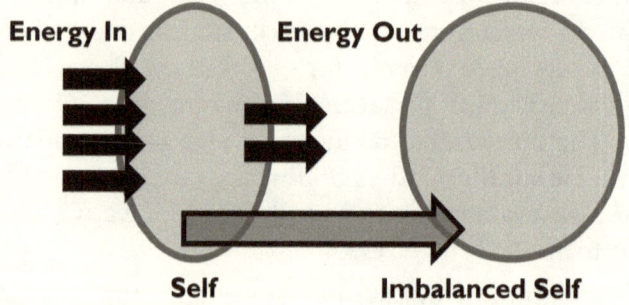

If our desire for pleasure takes in more energy than we use, nature stores our unused energy in the body.

Our ability to feel pain and our sense of pleasure guide us for survival. Neither of them is for us to dwell in or avoid. Just because it is pleasurable does not mean we should do it. Just because it is painful does not mean we should abstain from completing a task. We should do it because it makes sense for a purpose. Our pleasurable taking in of energy serves the purposeful why of our being. If we indulge in the senses' pleasures, it will imbalance our nature-designed physical body, mind, and heart. If we take in less energy than our body needs, it

THE DELICIOUSLY CHEESY HAPPINESS EQUATION

will weaken and cannot perform its tasks. Thus practices like asceticism serve only the purpose of discipline and are not a destination.

With purpose, we will take in exactly the energy we need. Our understanding of purpose maintains the balance of our biological and emotional systems. Pleasure is for the senses only, but it will consume us from the inside without a purpose to guide us. When we understand our purpose, it leads to our balance and happiness. Our physical body becomes balanced for a purposeful need of service. We do not need the complications and distractions of a dozen diet plans or workout routines for physical balance. The answer is a clear understanding within our minds and hearts to drive our actions for our physical balance.

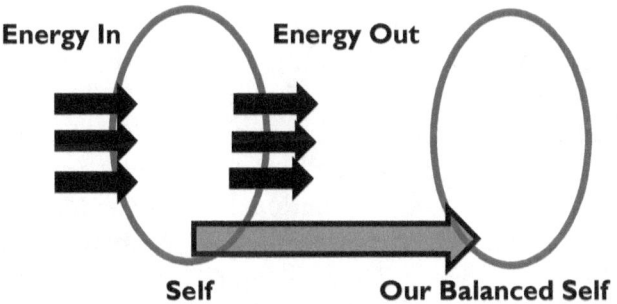

The way of balance is to take in only the amount of energy we use for our purpose. Thus, our physical body maintains its balance when we use what we take in.

The purposefulness of our being: shamanism, the Collector and his wife, and a baptism

> "A useless life is an early death."
> — JOHANN WOLFGANG VON GOETHE

CLARITY

Shamanism: Cessation of suffering in the service of healing

Some in our community still practice the traditional spiritual healing art of shamanism. A person does not seek to become a shaman, like a career, but the mystical healing service calls upon a person to become a shaman. The practice of shamanism dates back thousands of years in many different cultures worldwide. Some practices may date back as far as tens of thousands of years. Archeologists have found shaman burials dating to the Upper Paleolithic or Late Stone Age era of 50,000 - 12,000 years ago. A shaman is called into service in our cultural traditions because one does not decide whether to become a shaman. For many people who began the journey to become shamans, the calling is unexpected and often the farthest thing from their hearts and minds' intentions.

A shaman's journey begins with a physical pain that will not disappear. They will seek all kinds of remedies, including Western medicine. They will eventually seek the service of a shaman to help heal the pain. The shaman will perform a ceremony and then conclude that the pain is a sign of a calling to become a shaman. That is the cure to how their physical pain will go away. Once they accept their path, take on a mentor, and start learning and practicing becoming a shaman, their mysterious illness and pain disappear. They have found a purpose in living in others' healing, and they no longer have their original physical pain. My mother, a shaman, has been in the service of life and spiritual healing for over twenty years. In all that time, she has not had the devastating chest pain that called her to begin her journey as a shaman a long time ago.

The immortality of the Collector and the mortality of his wife

Taneleer Tivan, also known as *the Collector*, is a fictional character in the Marvel Universe comics. In the *Avengers: Infinity Wars* (2018 movie), Taneleer Tivan possessed the Reality Stone, one of the six Infinity Stones. The Collector is an immortal or has the power of immortality. He had a wife a long time ago, but she gave up her immortality and passed on due to lacking purpose in her life. *Matani Tivan* passed on from our universe because she no longer had a reason to live. Taneleer reflected on his own life, and he found a purpose to go on living. He became a collector of rare and unique items of the universe. He maintained his immortal status by finding a purpose to live in the service of the universe. Things in the universe do not necessarily die due to age but due to lacking a purpose to serve others. Thus, Taneleer Tivan's purposeful service to the universe keeps him immortal.[6]

A Baptism: Cultivation of purpose

We had a fantastic opportunity to attend my nephew's baptism, and I walked away from it very impressed with the whole process of creating purpose in a young life. There was great support from the congregation elders, friends, church members, and family. I also walked away with an understanding and greater appreciation of the spiritual teaching and the process of cultivating love, kindness, strength, and confidence in the up-and-coming members. Through being baptized, the kingdom of heaven welcomes my nephew. He is welcomed into the kingdom of heaven because he will be at peace, knowing his purpose now and into the future. He will gladly fulfill that destiny with encouragement, love, and confidence. Being in the kingdom of heaven, he will find the reasons, energy, courage, and strength for a long, pleasant, challenging, and yet purposeful and happy life in the service of others.

All things, living things, organisms, processes, and systems serve a purpose beyond themselves. If not, they will become useless, obsolete, and deteriorate away. When we become useless, changes come along to make room for those who are more of use. In staying purposely useful for others, we will find focus, balance, peace, health, and long life because others need our service in this world. We will be of service and have a reason and purpose to live. With our purposeful life, we will also have happiness inside. In the great laws of life beyond our desires and pleasures, our strength and lasting happiness are in our service to others.

Finding heaven

> *"The Tao that can be told is not the eternal Tao."*
> — LAO TZU

As a child, my cousin and I once talked about death and what happens afterward. My cousin said that right after the moment of death, we open our eyes again, and then our spirit would see the stairway to heaven. When I was nine years old, I saw the stairway to heaven over the Pacific Ocean on our flight to the USA. I remember telling myself that I could see the stairway to heaven because we were up in the clouds, but I couldn't understand why I saw it and others did not. Sometime in my mid-twenties, I finally realized that the stairway to heaven I saw over the Pacific Ocean was the slanted wing of our aircraft. My childhood understanding and my angle of perception created my view of the stairway to heaven.

After his enlightenment, someone came to ask the Buddha about heaven and the afterlife. The Buddha replied,

> *"I cannot tell you about heaven or the afterlife. I can only tell you about finding happiness in this life, in the here and now. But, the fact that you asked me about heaven implies that you are suffering and wanted to find happiness in a peaceful existence in the afterlife."*

Our world is one of the most beautiful places in the entire cosmos. There is nothing like it light-years in all directions. The beautiful balance of our world has supported life for over a billion years. The person asked about heaven because he desired another place, time, or dimension beyond our world's beauty to be happy. For happiness, he desired more than one of the most beautiful places in the universe. The desire for another mystical

THE DELICIOUSLY CHEESY HAPPINESS EQUATION

place or time is also the cause of the suffering preventing him from finding heaven here and now.

Finding Heaven in Another Realm

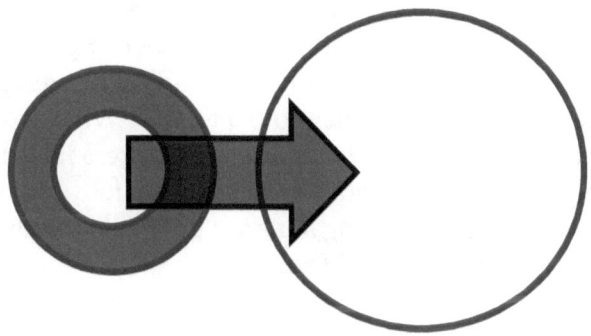

To find heaven in another realm, we want to escape from the confines of our suffering and transcend into some other clear, peaceful space of existence, detached from our world.

In my traditional cultural practices, the funeral process guides the deceased to awaiting grandparents in the afterlife. The spirits of our deceased loved ones are guided to the memories of simpler times from childhood, with grandparents eagerly waiting for their arrival. In our desire for the simpler times of our past, we create an imaginary realm for our future. *What if* the assumption such a journey is like King Croesus asking the Oracle at Delphi is an incomplete question? *What if* our desire for the simpler times of our pasts leads us to ask incorrect questions regarding nature's patterns? We want simpler, peaceful times from our past, and our desires cause us to ask incomplete or biased questions regarding heaven or the afterlife. The answer and pattern in nature will be different from our desires' creation.

We cannot reasonably construct an afterlife where we will meet our loving family and caring friends again. We did not know our family and friends before we got here, and we will not know them afterward. Like the idea of time travel, it will create endless unanswerable questions, dilemmas, and paradoxes. What age will they be? They will want to be in the prime of their lives as we do as well. If so, they will not seem like elder family members. *What if* they did not like their physical appearances while here? How will they look? *What if* we started as a family but branched into multiple families upon families due to divorce and remarrying others? *What if* we passed away very young and never knew our family? *What if* we never met our parents? Who would we meet in the afterlife, or how would we recognize them? *What if* we do not want to meet our parents? What would our name be? *What if* the squirrel could talk to express its desires for a peaceful existence? It would want heaven too. The squirrel would want youthful, relaxing summer days filled with endless acorn trees among family and friends.

> *"No hell below us. Above us only sky."*
> — JOHN LENNON, SONG "IMAGINE" (1971)

We let our happiness be confined and defined by our emotional understanding of a human being. We wish to create for a future place and time a lasting peaceful existence of our past that we want more of, and we want to do nothing while receiving our happiness. Our internal emotional expectations will most likely differ from the universe's timeless patterns. Our reality R in the universe will differ from our expectation E(R) regarding the afterlife. Our expectations were created here by our desires, and most likely, they do not reflect the timeless processes and patterns in the universe. When we find heaven, we will have a deep sense of peace and understanding that everything makes sense now and forever in whatever we do. When we find heaven, we will find the meaning of happiness and, most likely, our purpose as well. Our hearts will let us know because we will feel it inside. Our contentment, love, kindness, and purpose will drive our actions to service life. From serving life, we will gain inner strength for a balanced journey. As we are already in heaven, we will desire nothing, and there is nothing else to desire. *What if* our desiring nothing alleviates our suffering and helps us move closer to finding heaven? When we find our life's

THE DELICIOUSLY CHEESY HAPPINESS EQUATION

purpose for lasting peace and happiness, will we also find heaven?

> *"Heaven is a place on Earth."*
> — BELINDA CARLISLE

Finding Heaven Here

Through finding a clear understanding and purpose, we expand into finding lasting peaceful happiness in this world.

Is there a blissful, stress-free place in the great beyond called the afterlife, where we get everything we want that we did not get here while doing nothing to earn it, including an eternity with our family and friends? The answer is most likely *"No,"* Whatever happens after will be according to the laws of the universe and not according to our desires. Thus, finding heaven is a choice for now and in this life. Our peace and freedom are not in our consciousness's awakening in a peaceful afterlife or another dimension among loved ones. That is a creation reflecting our desire for carefree simpler times from long ago. The information and energy in this life created the idea of a peaceful heavenly existence after death; thus, heaven cannot exist in the afterlife because this life's desires created it. Heavenly peace exists only in this life when we have enough clarity to see it. *What if* heaven is here, but we have not yet had the breakthrough in clear spiritual understanding to see and feel it yet? Thus, we need to make an internal adjustment to understand and feel heavenly peace and happiness.

When we clear our perception and find heaven, we will wonder no more. Our desires, fears, self-importance, and environmental conditioning will no longer drive our being. We will have a clear understanding of purpose in our minds and hearts. We will be free from the forces that push and pull to create suffering in our hearts. Finding heaven here and now makes our destination a journey because it is inside. Our understanding stays with us through all our life's changes for lasting peace and happiness. If we can't find heaven yet, it is because the internal confusions still cloud our hearts' perceptions. The following Zen story illustrates that we have to undo the many programs in our minds and hearts to reach a state of lasting happiness.

Joshua's Zen

> *Joshu began the study of Zen when he was sixty years old and continued until he was eighty,*
> *when he realized Zen.*
> *He taught from the age of eighty until he was one hundred and twenty.*
> *A student once asked him: "If I haven't anything in my mind, what shall I do?"*
> *Joshu replied: "Throw it out."*
> *"But if I haven't anything, how can I throw it out?" continued the questioner.*
> *"Well," said Joshu, "then carry it out."*

The one thing we desire most

More than anything, we desire an end to our suffering. We desire peace more than anything, so many of our tombstones at our final resting place state, *"Rest in peace."* We desire a reality R that matches our expectation E(R) because that would give us peace. Unfortunately, our E(R) is misguided by misinformation and desires, so we suffer. Our suffering sometimes creates a strong need for an exciting and amazing life of pleasure. In Buddhism, breaking free of samsara is breaking free of the cycles of death and rebirth. When we no longer suffer in this world because we have a clear understanding, we are free. If we were to take samsara literally, why would we want to break free from the circles of life and death and live in another peaceful realm beyond and do nothing for eternity? What purpose would it serve? What would we do there, and how would we transcend to the next level beyond samsara? At this time, we do not know anything outside the boundaries of birth and death. No one has gone outside of samsara and returned to tell us how peaceful it is there. Thus, the desire for freedom in the physical universe by going into another realm is only in our imagination's creation. Our freedom from samsara takes place in this life only through our clear understanding of our life's journey.

Once we understand the clarity of our life's journey, we can find meaning through a purposeful existence. Our clarity of understanding and our purposeful life free us from our suffering. Our freedom from samsara is internal and not in another realm of existence. We no longer suffer when we can balance our Happiness Equation by changing our expectation $E(R)$ to match our reality R instead of reaching for more R to match our misinformed $E(R)$. When we are free, we no longer ask what's in it for us, but we can ask how we can better serve. We will have the one thing we desire most, an end to our suffering for lasting inner peace while still alive in human form. We will have peace at last.

After our life's journey

If our life's journey consists of being born, experiencing pleasure or pain, being healthy, getting sick, growing old, and then dying, what is in it for us? What is the purpose of our existence or the why of it all? When we look to nature's pattern for answers, there's nothing really in it for us individually. Nature recycles everything for a new beginning. There's nothing for our ego's self-importance or reward of a peaceful afterlife.

CLARITY

The pleasures of the senses are for our survival and childhood desires. Our ego's need for self-importance across space and time creates a desire for something for ourselves. So as far as we know it, heaven in the afterlife is a mere creation of our deep desire to want something eternally better when it ends here. What exists beyond will be completely different from the answers given by our desires' wishful incomplete questions to the oracle. Our human desires and imagination may only exist in this form. Beyond this existence is an alien world beyond our current comprehension, but the alien information and energy will become us, just like our human life here.

We will not get our desires from this life in the afterlife. The thing we want most in the afterlife is a manifestation of this life's desires. Our internal self and external self are a part of the impermanence of the universe. Our desires' bias will ask incomplete questions of our internal oracle. When we reflect on life from nature's patterns, we cannot take anything with us, not the money or even the memories. It is the love we leave behind for others that matters. Our love and kindness live on through the next generation for their information and energy. Everything serves a purpose, and our purpose is that we are a conductor of information and energy for a more beautiful world for others. Every person that has ever lived has left behind information and energy for others and those still to come.

CONDUCTORS OF INFORMATION AND ENERGY

> "When the singer's gone. Let the song go on."
> — ART GARFUNKEL

Information

Our life's journey is about how we can make it better for others. Life is not about us because it has been here for billions of years before we existed and will be here for billions more after we are gone. Our love and contributions stay in the world for the benefit of others. Our information and energy live on to serve others' journeys.

> "When an old man dies, a library burns to the ground."
> — AN AFRICAN PROVERB

In many traditional cultures today, the understanding and ways are kept and passed on through teachings given orally by an elder. This practice is becoming less true as books, computers, and websites store traditional and cultural information. Our cultures and traditions become less restricted to an elder's oral communication from one generation to another. However, it may remain true in many traditional cultures worldwide for a long time yet. But, even if we do not conduct information, we still conduct emotional energy from one generation to another. More than just a library of information burns to the ground when an elder passes away. The community's energy and strength are also lost, and we have to light the energy within for the next generation. We conduct information and energy from one generation to the next.

CLARITY

We receive energies that once belonged to plants and animals. They received that energy from another source and so on to the true source of the sun. Our body contains genetic information for building a living being, passed on for millions of years while constantly changing and evolving. One day our body will nourish others, and the information in our genetic material will pass on to others. We are conductors of information and energy in the natural world when we take in energy and pass on our genes. We are also conductors of information and energy in the social world when we pass information, energy, and traditions to the next generation for survival and strength. Thus, perhaps we are only conductors of information and energy and nothing more.

Energy

> "Carve your names on hearts, not tombstones. A legacy is etched into the minds of others and the stories they share about you."
> — SHANNON L. ADLER

The Dishwashing Machine Hypothesis:

When we reflect on what we do all our lives, we conduct information and energy from one life to another. Sometimes it is so subtle that we do not realize its depth. For example, one of my siblings has a software engineering degree and works in a lead capacity for a software company. He has a dishwasher at home, but it is never used to wash dishes. Instead, he washes his dishes in the sink, and he uses the dishwasher to store and dry the hand-washed dishes. One of my other siblings and her husband do their dishes in the sink, and they also use the dishwasher to store and dry their dishes. She has a four-year college degree in business and is well aware of the dishwashing machine's labor-saving property.

There's a reason why they both wash their dishes in the sink and then use the dishwasher to store and dry their dishes. When our parents bought our first house a long time ago, it came with

THE DELICIOUSLY CHEESY HAPPINESS EQUATION

a dishwasher. We did not know how to operate the dishwasher properly because we'd never had one before. My parents cautioned and discouraged us not to use the dishwasher because "it could start a fire and burn the house down." They conditioned into us the energy of fear that went deep into our hearts if we used the dishwasher and created a habit around it. We did all our dishes in the sink, and we used the dishwasher racks to store and dry our dishes. That is what my brother and my sister do with their dishwashers today. They use it to dry their dishes as was done a long time ago.

We do things according to our conditioned behaviors and not our superior reason and logic. The subtle energy conducted by the Dishwashing Machine Hypothesis overwhelms our reason and logic of what makes sense. It keeps us from using a dishwashing machine designed for labor efficiency. But, what else is inside keeping us from freeing ourselves to other better possibilities that would streamline our emotional energy for better efficiency? How do we proactively free our heart's energy to accept new processes or systems that would make our efforts more efficient and then apply them? How do we free ourselves of energies that have been there for thousands of years? How do we undo and remove the outdated and useless energies of the Dishwashing Machine Hypothesis of other areas inside us?

Information guides and energy drives

> *"Knowing is not enough; we must apply. Willing is not enough; we must do."*
> — JOHANN WOLFGANG VON GOETHE

Og Mandino's book The Greatest Salesman in the World (1968) states that the most valuable items passed on from mentor to apprentice are not the abundant wealth earned. Instead, the ten scrolls that contained information and wisdom to empower an apprentice's mind and heart for lifelong success and happiness are the most treasured items. The information and energy of the scrolls are the real treasures, not the accumulated

CLARITY

wealth. The scrolls provide information to guide and energy to drive.[11]

Our energy is even more important than information because it creates actions to apply our information. Without our energy, the information, skills, and knowledge would sit there, collect dust, and eventually fade with time. Our energy is our driving force to apply our information. We can change the strength of the information and energy to make it better and stronger going forward, and we will get everything done. We conduct information and energy from one generation to the next.

Conductors of Information and Energy

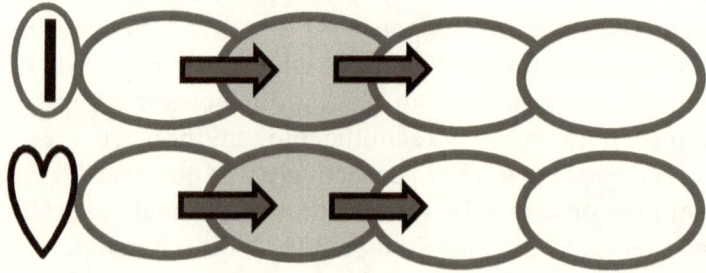

We are a link in the infinite chain of information and energy conduction.

The empowering energy of love, kindness, and compassion

> *"Even after all this time, the sun never says to the earth, 'You owe me.' Look what happens with a love like that. It lights the whole sky."*
> — HAFIZ

The strength of love is why our human family grew from families into villages, towns, cities, and countries. Because we grew and flourished into today, it shows that love is stronger than hatred and fear. If hatred and fear were stronger, we would have annihilated each other long ago. Love and kindness lead to life and growth. Hatred and fear lead to deterioration and death.

THE DELICIOUSLY CHEESY HAPPINESS EQUATION

Today, we are here because love's positive energy is much stronger than the negative energy of hatred and fear.

When we say something, we communicate both information and energy. Strong negative energy clouds our message, while positive energy allows others to receive our message.

> "Raise your words, not your voices, for it is rain that grows flowers, not thunder."
>
> — RUMI

Dark Energy and Clear Information

When we yell at someone, dark negative energy fills our message, and they cannot hear the clear message we are conveying.

Clear Energy and Clear Information

When we communicate with clear positive energy, they will hear our clear message because the energy does not cloud our communication.

CLARITY

We are conductors of information and energy. Our conducting of clear information and strong energy lead to strength and happiness, while clouded information and dark energy lead to pain and suffering. Information guides and energy drives. Our clear information shows us what to do, and our strong energy makes doing it possible. Thus, we are conductors of information and energy across space and time for others' benefit.

A PATTERN IN NATURE

> *"Wherever you stand, be the soul of that place."*
> — RUMI

Make the Next Generation Stronger

In nature, the life-giving soft rain makes things grow, not the thunder. Our kind speech and empowering words are like the life-giving and nurturing rain for the empowering of souls. Our loud and sharp criticisms of others do nothing to nurture and empower anyone, but it only destroys confidence in their hearts and breeds anger. We conduct information and energy from generation to generation. If we pass on better information and more empowering energy, the next generation will become stronger. It is a pattern in nature that our love strengthens the next generation. Our future generation is up against the strong competitive forces of nature embedded in our human lives. They require the best information and energy from us to make them stronger to rise to the challenges of *natural selection* or *survival of the fittest*.

THE DELICIOUSLY CHEESY HAPPINESS EQUATION

The survival of the fittest

Herbert Spence first used the phrase *survival of the fittest* after reading Charles Darwin's *On the Origin of Species* (1859). Charles Darwin called it *natural selection,* and Herbert Spencer called it *survival of the fittest.* Both terms stuck with us but in different circles. However, "*the survival of the fittest*" became more mainstream, and *natural selection* stayed in academics. The phrase "*the survival of the fittest*" brings to mind Charles Darwin and the bountiful variations of life's adaptations in the Galapagos Islands. In the Galapagos Islands, he became aware of the pattern of natural selection in nature and then shared his discovery with us. From Charles Darwin's natural selection came the theory of evolution, which reshaped our thinking regarding how we became human beings. For the first time in our history, we can understand and see how we became humans. His insight came from observations of nature's patterns, but it brought clarity to our human journey because we are a part of nature.

The survival of the fittest is a balance in nature where the wild of life lives. The balance is the constant growth needed to survive as all the other species adjust to the constant changes. If one side gains too much advantage, the other will cease to exist, thus dooming both. Where life exists, balance is required. Both species need each other to survive, grow, and move forward. The lions need the zebras to survive, and the zebras need the lions to stay strong for their survival. The adversaries need each other to live and to grow to become stronger.

Evolution is the genetic learning and growth of a species

The elephants, lions, zebras, gazelles, and other wild animals live on the edge of survival of the fittest. We also live in this world with its laws of nature. Our ancestry and our basic conditioning are still animal emotions in origin. The survival of the fittest is not just for the animals but in our everyday social events, interactions, and challenges as patterns in nature make their way into our social customs and daily lives. Our business competitions in the human world are very much survival of the fittest, with life and death on the line for businesses and corporations no longer strong enough to compete.

The wild animals continue to live at the forefront of nature's law of survival of the fittest every day. They are conditioned for survival in nature or risk becoming extinct. The tame and zoo animals are no match for the ferocity of the law of natural selection. Tame animals have the protection of human love and kindness. A lion of the same size is three times stronger than a German shepherd because nature's survival breeds strength and endurance. The fight for survival lives at the edge of the survival of the fittest.

The man in black

In *The Princess Bride* (1987 movie), a Sicilian, a giant, and a Spaniard kidnapped Princess Buttercup to start a war with Guilder, the sworn enemy of the kingdom of Florin. After almost getting away, the three kidnappers realized a mysterious man in black was in hot pursuit of them. Vizzini is the Sicilian mastermind, and he instructs the Spaniard to kill the man in black while he and the giant escape with the princess. Inigo Montoya, the Spaniard, wanting to avenge his father's death, studied fencing for twenty years. Confident he would defeat the man in black, Inigo asked his boss Vizzini to let him fight left-handed, or else it would be too easy. The man in black is Buttercup's love Westley, who was rumored to be dead but has been on a pirate ship for the last five years. The man in black outthought outfought and outclassed Inigo to defeat him in the fencing duel, and then he continued after his love, Buttercup.[12]

How can someone who had been missing for only five years be able to defeat someone who has been studying fencing for twenty years for a purpose? Westley triumphed over Inigo because Westley uses his fencing skills for survival every day onboard a pirate ship. Westley needed his fencing skills for the survival of the fittest, while Inigo simply studied fencing. Inigo Montoya was very knowledgeable in fencing, but he was no match for someone living in the wild and who had been using it for survival every day. Life lives at the edge of survival of the fittest, and it does not live in the classroom or practice. The beings that live on the edge of survival of the fittest have extraordinary strengths and senses that developed over time for their particular survival niche. Nature tested them through the evolution of countless life forms over countless lifetimes.

A simple purpose: Empower their inside

The world runs at the persistent pace of *The Tortoise and the Hare* fable and Herbert Spencer's *survival of the fittest*. Each new generation makes adjustments to becoming stronger or risks extinction. When we conduct better information and stronger energy, it helps to make the next generation stronger. They have better information to guide and stronger energy to drive. Our future generation's cultivation brings great excitement and expectation because it can make their reality $R2 > R1$ for their future Happiness Equation $H2 = R2 - E(R2)$. The greatest and most fulfilling adventure of our life is as a parent and a guide to the fantastic beings who will inherit our world. We have a simple purpose: make the next generation stronger. Our purpose is to give them the inner strength to better adapt to the forces of nature in our society. Thus, they will succeed in making their world better.

Our nature is the information that makes up our body's characteristics, and our nurture is the element responsible for the energy that drives all of us. Our nature is a random factor of the universe. Our nurture is our choice in love, encouragement, and guidance for our loved ones. So it is not nature versus nurture, but nature combined with nurture, which makes up our being.

CLARITY

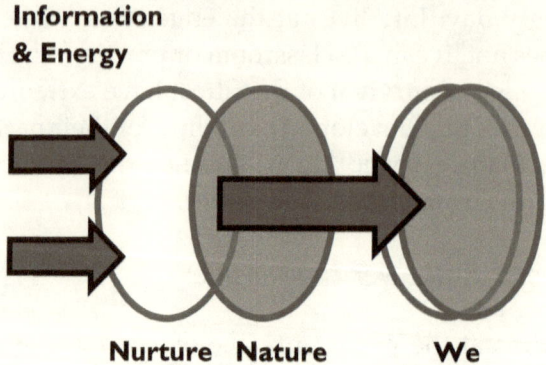

Our nurture applies information and energy to the physical information of our nature to become us.

We are conductors of information and energy, and we can make the next generation stronger through our nurturing of their strength. The force of the survival of the fittest and *The Tortoise and the Hare* keep everything changing and growing. So each generation must grow and become stronger to stay with the challenging pace and balance. They will need inner strength to keep running just to stay in the same place. Their raised inner strength will come from our ability to nurture their nature. So we must pay it forward to the next generation through our nurturing of their heart's strength.

A father's blessing

In "Genesis 27:5-7", Isaac was old and wanted to bless his eldest son Esau. At first, Esau was not interested. Esau enjoyed hunting and was always gone. However, their mother, Rebekah, wanted their younger son Jacob to receive Isaac's blessing instead. Isaac is old and nearly blind, so he cannot see well. Through Rebekah's deception, Isaac gives his blessing to Jacob. Thus, when Esau finally came around to ask for his birthright, Isaac realized that he had already given it to Jacob.

THE DELICIOUSLY CHEESY HAPPINESS EQUATION

Our blessings for our kids become a self-fulfilling prophecy for their lives, whether the blessing is good or bad. With good blessings, their hearts strengthened for confidence to face the challenges of their life's journeys. Our sharp criticisms and curses rip into hearts and weaken their inner strength for their lifelong journey. A father's blessing doesn't have to be limited to one child or the other, like Isaac's story from the Bible. We can bless all our children, no matter how many we have, and it will strengthen their hearts. The message from the beginning of time is that our children need our blessings for their inner strength to take on their future challenges.

In the music video "Runaway Train" by the band Soul Asylum, in the beginning, it says, *"There are over one million youth lost on the streets of America."*[10] Over one million kids are lost on America's streets because they did not receive our blessings for their inner strength. Our kids are emotionally lost on the inside first, becoming lost on the streets outside.

A mother's love

> *"I have a son, who is my heart. A wonderful young man, daring and loving and strong and kind."*
> — MAYA ANGELOU

I once watched a television program on a study of two mothers who yielded different offspring outcomes. One of them always produces healthy offspring, and the other always produces unhealthy offspring. The offspring of the first mother is genetically healthy and strong into adulthood. The second mother produces offspring that become obese, develop heart conditions, or become diabetic. The researchers thought that one mother might have good genes while the other might carry poor genes. So the researchers switched the kittens at birth, and the offspring still turned out the same for the two mothers.

The mother who raised genetically healthy offspring did just that again, even though she received the other mother's

CLARITY

genetically inferior kittens. The mother who raised poor genetic offspring did the same as before despite receiving genetically superior kittens from the other mother. One mother raised her babies with love and care, while the other mother neglected her babies.

The first mother would lick and clean her babies while the other mother left her babies alone. The love and care of a parent have the potential to reach into their offspring's genes and alter them in one generation. A mother's love has the power to strengthen our hearts at the subconscious level to empower us all our lives. Due to her love, their genes will strengthen, or due to her neglect and criticism, their genes will weaken. Love strengthens our future generation, while neglect and criticism weaken them subconsciously. The nurturing of their nature is a requirement for their internal strength. Love is a pattern required in nature for strength, and we are part of nature.

> *"But baby can't be broken 'cause you see she had the finest teacher — that was me."*
> — MELISSA MANCHESTER

I had an opportunity to attend my youngest daughter's parent-teacher conference in grade school. The teachers made the students present what they learned throughout the year. It was really special to see my daughter demonstrate her presentation and communication skills. She was so excited throughout the entire presentation. However, I noticed that her positive energy waned at the end when it came time to reveal her grades. She received two Bs, three Cs, and two Ds. I thought she was doing better myself. I asked the teachers if they knew that she falls on the spectrum and is in a special education class with the school's linguistic teacher. They said they did not know that. I told them that she works really hard, but sometimes, it is challenging for her to grasp a new idea. Thus, she will keep working in the wrong direction.

THE DELICIOUSLY CHEESY HAPPINESS EQUATION

On the drive home, she said that she was sorry for her bad grades and that I must be disappointed in her. I told her not to be sorry, that I am very proud of her because she has the heart of a lion, she works really hard, and that the teachers did not understand how to teach her. I told her that she would do great in the future, and if she did not understand anything, she should let me know from now on so we could work together to make sure she understood each topic. She's in high school now, and she still gets the occasional B, but the rest are all As.

Empowering the Next Generation

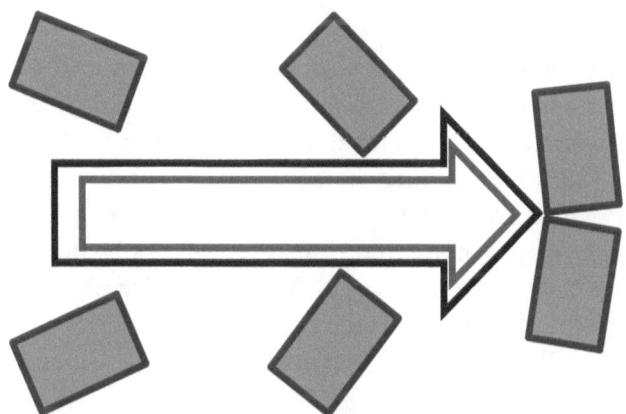

We must empower the next generation's internal information and energy to break through any obstacles. They already have better information than us; we need to put great energy and strength into their hearts.

> *"All that I am or ever hope to be, I owe to my angel mother."*
> — ABRAHAM LINCOLN

There's a special story of how a mother's love and encouragement made a difference in a young man's life. One day Thomas Edison came home and gave a paper to his mother. He told her, *"My teacher gave this paper to me and told me to only give it to my mother."* His mother's eyes were tearful as she read the letter aloud to her child: *"Your son is a genius. This school is too small for him and doesn't have enough good teachers for training him. Please teach him yourself."*

Thomas Edison eventually became one of the greatest inventors of the century. Many years after his mother died, he was looking through old family possessions, and suddenly, he saw a folded paper in the corner of a drawer of a desk. Thomas Edison took it and opened it up. On the paper was written: *"Your son is addled (mentally ill). We won't let him come to school anymore."* Thomas Edison cried for hours, and then he wrote in his diary: *"Thomas Alva Edison was an addled child that, by a hero mother, became the genius of the century."*[13]

The most precious and greatest garden that we plant for the abundance of tomorrow is our children. They are our most precious treasures, and our endeavor for their strength and happiness is one of the greatest and most exciting adventures of our lives. Our greatest purpose is the next generation's love, care, and empowerment. Time flows in their direction, and they will inherit tomorrow's space and time. We will not be here for them any longer. They will face obstacles and challenges unlike anything we have seen before. They will need their strength of heart to face the challenges that come their way. Thus, we must raise their inside.

BE AN AWAKENING FOR THOSE TO COME

> "As far as we can discern, the sole purpose of human existence is to kindle a light in the darkness of mere being."
> — CARL JUNG

We are most likely only a conductor of information and energy across space and time for others' benefit. Thus, our life's journey is for others. We live our best life when we contribute clear information and strong energy that empowers those in other places and times. Those that came before and lived great purposeful lives have empowered others.

Rice, Ruth, and Yang

In 2014, I had a wonderful opportunity to hear Condoleezza Rice speak at the Northrop Auditorium at the University of Minnesota. Unfortunately, I did not know much about her political views or personal history before her speaking engagement. I only knew that she was the US Secretary of State under former President George W. Bush. Condoleezza Rice shared with the audience that her grandfather set his mind to cultivating and promoting education in their family by taking out a loan to buy encyclopedias for the family. As a result of his awakening to education's importance, he made sacrifices for his family's future. Thus, his family's heart focused on the importance of education, and his lineage strengthened through conducting better information. Condoleezza Rice credits her grandfather's awakening to education's importance for their family's inner strength.

In the "Book of Ruth" from the Bible, Ruth is a Moabite who married Mahlon, the son of Naomi and Elimelech. Due to a famine in Bethlehem, Naomi and her husband Elimelech moved to the land of Moab. When Naomi and Elimelech's son Mahlon

CLARITY

came of age, he married Ruth, a Moabite. After Mahlon died, Ruth left her people and followed her mother-in-law back to Bethlehem. Naomi asked Ruth to go back to her people, but she told her mother-in-law, *"Where you go, I will go. Where you die, I will die and be buried there too."* Naomi knew that she could not convince Ruth to return to her people, so both women went back together to live in Bethlehem. In Bethlehem, Ruth eventually married Boaz and gave birth to a son named Obed. Obed became the father of Jesse, who then became the father of David, King David. They say behind every good man is a good woman. *What if* that good woman is your great-grandmother whose love and devotion strengthened the heart of your entire lineage?

A grandfather of a family in the Yang clan provided a similar awakening for his family. The Yang grandfather was the middle child and a son of a family whose father passed away when he was fourteen. When a tragedy like that happens, the family struggles without their patriarch. There's no one to lead them in performing the family's many challenging tasks. The mother can only watch the children and farm a little plot of land to feed the family. A father figure is needed to farm a larger plot of land and balance clan relationships in a traditional way of life.

Growing up poor, the Yang grandfather vowed that the community would need his services one day, and he would be there for his community. Through his suffering, he strengthened the energy in his heart, and he worked hard in the field and saved all that he could. He took it upon himself to give his best effort to learn traditions and cultural practices whenever an opportunity came. He welcomed traveling Buddhist monks to stay at his home and talked with them. He provided food and shelter to them in exchange for their teachings and wisdom. He learned to give love and kindness to others while empowering his information and energy. The Yang grandfather rose through his clan's ranks and became its leader; he became a spiritual healer, a clan leader, a loving husband, a strong father, a wise grandfather, and a town official. He spread his love, strength, and guidance throughout the community for most of his life. To this day, his descendants are capable and accomplished in the community. They are kind, generous, and strong in their hearts. They point to their grandfather's awakening for their inner strength. The Yang grandfather also made his destiny and self-prophecy come true. He became needed in the service of the community for most of his adult life.

SUMMATION OF CLARITY

Happiness inside

We all have the potential to discover and share happiness. However, some of us are waiting for happiness to come from the outside. Some are waiting for suffering to strengthen our hearts. Yet, we all have the gift of unlimited happiness should we decide to empower it from within when we seek a better understanding and strengthen our hearts for a life of balanced happiness.

In Bob Dylan's song "Blowin' in the Wind" (1963), there is a line that goes, *"Yes, and how many years can some people exist before they're allowed to be free? The answer is blowin' in the wind."* If we do not ask better questions, our freedom and happiness will be subject to external elements, and the answer to our happiness will be *"blowin' in the wind."* It will rise and fall with the changing external elements. When we ask better questions and receive better answers, we will find clarity in our hearts and minds. We will achieve happiness on the inside and become free. Therefore, our task is to find a clear understanding of ourselves, our world, and our journey. Our happiness will no longer be subject to external elements, but it will be inside, and our happiness will be our choice.

The smallness of our beginning

We are born into and live in a small region of space and time, and its social-cultural information and energy imprint upon our

CLARITY

minds and hearts. Others' joy, suffering, and purpose become ours, and we think it is our joy, suffering, and purpose. Yet, we just arrived not too long ago. To better understand our world, we will need to expand our minds and hearts to accept other thoughts and patterns different from our beginning. At the same time, we may want to discard the outdated information and negative energies from our environmental conditioning. Our lives can influence and reach other space-times, and information and energy from different space-times can influence ours. Therefore, we must expand our information, heart's strength, and imagination to include other knowledge, traditions, and energies from other space-times beyond our own.

To find who we are and our purpose, we need to seek the clarity of our journey first. We need clarity in our minds and hearts to see our world and journey. If not, we may be living someone else's life, pain, and suffering, without ever achieving or becoming what Ralph Waldo Emerson calls *self-reliant*. We must accept better information and energy to become self-reliant to determine our happiness and freedom. Once we gain clarity into our life's patterns and processes, we will understand the why of our being. We will have internal happiness to see the beauty of our world better. To reach clarity of understanding, we need to begin by asking better questions.

A better question

The journey to a happy and purposeful life starts with a better first question. A better first question asks, *"What do I want to do so that I can live?"* A better first question frees us to give to others because, through giving, we share happiness, and we grow internally to become stronger so that we can give even more. Sometimes, we ask the incorrect first question, *"What do I want to do before I die?"* It is a question that asks, *"What is in it for me?"* We will find happiness elusive because the constant expectation and hope of receiving more will create suffering within our hearts. Instead of becoming better, we will halt our growth because we will wait to receive happiness from the outside. When we can see

THE DELICIOUSLY CHEESY HAPPINESS EQUATION

past our desires, we stop asking what is in it for us, and we start asking better questions. If we do not see past our desires, we will ask biased questions to fulfill our dissatisfaction. Biased, incomplete questions lead to biased answers, leading to unfavorable results and suffering.

The correct first question will lead to many other insightful questions of *what if,* further leading to our minds' clarity and hearts' strength. We will find timeless patterns that have worked for other living beings since time began. Everything is a system run by processes. When we ask a better first question, we will receive a better answer to gain clear insight into our world's processes and systems. Thus, we can become purposely better to service the systems for everyone's benefit. Such is the way of our traditions, learned from nature.

The wisdom of traditions came from patterns in nature

We will discover that all our lasting traditions have their roots in nature's patterns, and the tradition's development served a unique purpose. Our traditions are shortcuts to our education for our hearts to achieve success, strength, happiness, and inner peace. We cannot abandon our traditions unless we have found something better and stronger to replace them. If we simply abandon our traditions out of a desire for ease and comfort, we will become lost on the inside like the ducks at Lake Phalen.

The plants and animals have their processes for their systems that evolved to accommodate changes. Our traditions are shortcuts to the processes that run our social systems. Like everything else, traditions change and evolve due to our growing understanding of patterns in nature. Unfortunately, traditions sometimes get hijacked for ego and power and, thus, receive a bad rap. All living beings live in balance with and learn from nature. Nature has all the answers because it has the deepest tradition going back to the beginning of life on our planet. The ducks do not have it marked in the sky that it is time to fly south because a certain date has come. Their balance with nature gives them that clear understanding.

CLARITY

A worthy life based on nature's balance is not a life of comfort, ease, and relaxation because our life's challenges live on the edge of the survival of the fittest. A challenging life will lead to our becoming stronger. What we do not use will go away, and what we use every day will strengthen. If we dwell in comfort and pleasure, our body, mind, and spirit will deteriorate. If we do not use it or abuse it, we will lose it. For nature gives and strengthens what we need, and what we no longer need, it takes it away. For the survival of the fittest, nature requires that we stay strong. Those who do not have a strong inside may fall in a mild storm. It is a nature's pattern that we must raise the strength inside for strength outside.

A conductor of information and energy

Our life is a mere link in an endless chain of conductors of information and energy. The pattern from the beginning of time is that our life is in the service of others. We conductor information and energy going forward. When we take more for our desire and importance, it will leave less for others. As a result, the system will suffer stress and challenging periods in the future.

We always solve our challenges to the level of our minds' clarity and hearts' strength. Thus, we take actions that maximize our internal understanding. The physical and sensual pleasures in our life are a gift of nature. However, indulging in pleasure leads to imbalances in our body, mind, emotions, and spirit. Happiness takes place in the clarity of our minds and the strength of our hearts. When we raise the inside for internal strength, we can resolve issues with love and kindness for everyone, thereby creating a better today and tomorrow. A clear mind and a strong heart will lead to lasting joy and happiness because we have the inner strength to face our challenges and share happiness with others.

We are conductors of information and energy. Our purpose is to empower the information and energy in the link that is our life. Soon enough, we will become a distant memory in time like those

THE DELICIOUSLY CHEESY HAPPINESS EQUATION

who came before. We can best serve our purpose by sharing love and leaving love behind for others. Our life here is for the benefit of others and those to come. For example, once Siddhartha Gautama achieved enlightenment and found a way to ease suffering, he set out to teach happiness to others all his life. For the next forty-five years, he became a conductor of information and energy in the service of life. The strength and clarity of his information and energy live on through being conducted by others.

> *"Your work is to discover your world and then with all your heart give yourself to it."*
> — BUDDHA

CLARITY

CHAPTER THREE
The Heart

Energy

"Educating the mind without educating the heart is no education at all."
— ARISTOTLE

THE HEART

HEARTS OF STRENGTH

> *"The way is not in the sky. The way is in the heart."*
> — BUDDHA

Superman: a heart strengthened by love

The most well-known and most loved superhero of all time is Superman. There are other much stronger superheroes, but only Superman is willing to give it all to save us. The overall strength of Superman is part information and part energy. The information is his Kryptonian DNA that becomes his physical strength. The energy is his Kansas upbringing filled with love, compassion, kindness, and humility that make up his inner strength. Superman's internal energy is the strength of his heart. It is the source of his true power because it drives his superior Kryptonian DNA.

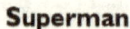

Superman is the combination of the inner strength of his Kansas upbringing and his alien Kryptonian DNA.

When we think of Superman's amazing powers, we think of his advanced alien Kryptonian genes that give him superhuman strength and the ability to fly. We see the strength of his Kryptonian DNA, but we miss the beauty and strength of his

THE DELICIOUSLY CHEESY HAPPINESS EQUATION

heart. We hardly think of his humble Kansas upbringing, filled with love and humility. We see the sky, but we miss the power of the heart. Jonathan and Martha Kent never had a child, and being simple farmers, raised Clark Kent in simple ways but filled with love, principles, kindness, and humility. The love and nurturing of Jonathan and Martha Kent are the secret to Superman's power. Superman has faced foes as powerful or even more powerful than him, but his love for others made him triumphant. For example, Superman fought the three Kryptonians that escaped from the Phantom Zone. They have similar powers, but he defeated them through his heart's strength.[1]

In another DC Comics Universe storyline, *Justice League: The Flashpoint Paradox* (2013 Movie), Flash is the main character. The Kryptonian baby Kal-El was never raised in Kansas by Jonathan and Martha Kent to become Superman. Flash wants to save his mother from death, so he turns back time to save his mother. In doing so, he unknowingly changed many other timelines, including eliminating his existence as the Flash. Instead of being found by Jonathan and Martha Kent in Kansas, the baby Kal-El's capsule fell into the US government's possession. They found the Kryptonian baby and imprisoned him underground in red light into adulthood. Kal-El was an emotionally frail superbeing as an adult with Kryptonian genes but without his Kansas upbringing. Although he has the physical powers of Superman, he could not fully utilize his superpowers.[2] Without his heart's inner strength to drive his Kryptonian DNA, he was a minor character, not the superhero we know as Superman. The secret of Superman's power is his heart's strength.

THE HEART

Superhero

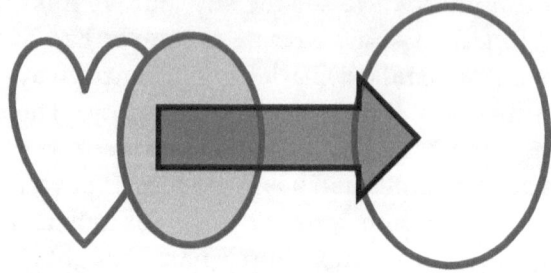

The beauty inside amplifies the superpower to become a superhero.

Our clarity of information guides us, but our energy drives our actions and determines our happiness level. We can focus and strengthen our energy to become more effective and happy. To do so, we need to learn from other sources or learn through experiences. Learning from experiences will take longer because it may be a long time before we experience an event that would strengthen our energy.

Lessons for strengthening our hearts do not necessarily need to come from a great classic novel, inspirational religious stories, or scriptures. It only needs to come from an exciting story that makes emotional sense. It can be real or fictional, but it needs to be exciting to capture our interest and, at the same time, make emotional sense to our hearts. What makes sense to our hearts, we will appreciate its beautiful lessons for our inner strength and happiness.

The tested heart of a great king

The wise ruler known as Genghis Khan was born as Temujin around 1162 in northern Mongolia. The name Genghis Khan means universal ruler. At the age of thirteen, Temujin's father, the leader of their tribe, died, and his tribe abandoned his family to the wild. He realized then that he could not trust in clan hierarchy and lineage but only rely on the strength of a person's

THE DELICIOUSLY CHEESY HAPPINESS EQUATION

heart. Temujin's insight into human nature at that young age implies an incredible discipline in thought and elevated awareness regarding human nature. By learning from a bad situation, he made the best out of being abandoned by his tribe. He understood that he needed to trust only in the strength of those with strong hearts. From his suffering and clarity, his inner strength grew.

Temujin had a childhood friend named Jamukha, who became his blood brother early on and later became his adversary. The Merkits, a Mongolian tribe of Turkic origin, abducted Temujin's wife, Borte. With Jamukha and his father's ally, Toghrul, Temujin defeated the Merkits and rescued his wife. However, as Jamukha and Temujin grew in strength, they drifted apart, becoming rivals. Each believed in a different system of leadership. Jamukha believed in aristocracy, promoting through class and lineage. But, due to his childhood experience, Temujin believed in relying on a person's inner strength and character. Therefore, Temujin believed in the meritocratic method of promoting through character strength. Temujin's leadership philosophy attracted more and more followers because those willing to work hard could rise in Temujin's government system.

In 1187, Jamukha launched a surprise attack with around thirty thousand soldiers against Temujin and decisively beat him. Temujin tried to defend with his remaining force, but it wasn't enough to prevent defeat. In defeat, Temujin accepted the responsibility for his failure, and he became a better commander for those who counted on his leadership. He began training his army to learn new skills and strategies in all warfare capacities, and he also trained them to fight together as one army. Temujin even designed the next fight at a location of choice where it would allow him to ambush Jamukha's men by provoking them to pursue a fleeing unit into a trap. Finally, in the year 1204, their two armies fought each other again. Temujin destroyed Jamukha's army this time, and Jamukha fled the battlefield.

A year later, Jamukha's two generals betrayed him and turned him over to Temujin. The two generals thought Temujin would reward them for turning in his enemy. However, the man that would become Genghis Khan believed in an individual heart's strength, and he had no use for those with corrupted hearts that would turn against their own khan. Temujin executed the two generals immediately for being traitors to their khan. Temujin forgave his onetime blood brother and offered Jamukha a high position in his government. However, Jamukha declined, saying that there is only one sun underneath the sky, and underneath Mongolia, there should only be one khan. He asked for and was granted an honorable death without spilling any blood.[3]

When Temujin lost to Jamukha in their first battle, he accepted the responsibility for his defeat. His actions show clear thinking, love, and kindness for his people by focusing on the positives in a bad situation. By accepting responsibility for his defeat, he matched his perception of his army's capability to its current reality. He realized that his army was not good enough to win against a strong opponent. Therefore, he balanced his Happiness Equation regarding expectations $E(R)$ and reality R of his army's strength. Then, Temujin raised the strength R of his army to the expectation $E(R)$ he desired. If Temujin had dwelled in anguish and vengeance, he might have rushed to seek revenge, and he would have had similar results as when he had lost to Jamukha in their first battle.

Once Temujin accepted the reality R that Jamukha beat him because Jamukha outwitted, outmaneuvered, and outclassed him in skills, numbers, and strategies, he realized that his army needed to improve. As their commander, he needed to improve. So Temujin set out to train his army to make it better, and they became the best in the world for their time. From the suffering of his defeat by Jamukha, Temujin rose in strength to become stronger. The Mongolian army was unstoppable wherever they went, from Asia to Persia and Eastern Europe. His love for his people gave him the strength to make his army stronger so that his soldiers would never be humiliated on the battlefield again. One of our greatest endeavors is to raise the inner strength of others. Genghis Khan became the wise ruler through his mind's clarity, heart's strength, and love for his people. He raised the inner strength of his people. The strength of his heart came about through being tested by his pain and suffering in the wild.

HEARTS OF DESTRUCTION

> *"The measure of a man is what he does with power."*
> — PLATO

The tormented heart of a superior being

One of Superman's greatest adversaries is a being called Doomsday. A prehistoric Kryptonian scientist aimed to create the ultimate warrior, creating Doomsday by accelerating his genetic evolution. Doomsday is physically superior to Superman and cannot die. To create a living superweapon that cannot die, the scientist exposed Doomsday's genetic material to countless suffering and death until his genes learned to overcome all obstacles, including death. Doomsday turned on his creator and killed him, and then he escaped into other worlds. After another alien race temporarily defeated Doomsday, they put him into a casket and shot him into space. The capsule landed on Earth, and the impact burrowed Doomsday deep underground.[4]

The sum of the suffering strengthened his genes and became the energy in his heart. All he knew through his countless exposures to suffering and death was pain, rage, and destruction of life. Thus, Doomsday is a genetically superior being powered by the energy of his tormented heart.

THE HEART

Supervillain

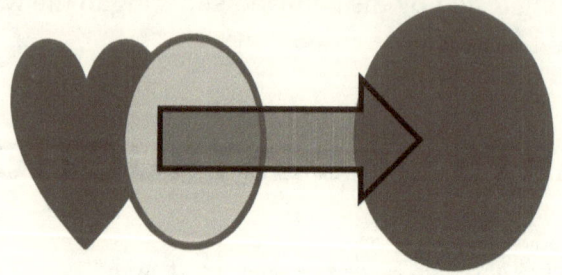

The darkness inside drives the superpower to become a supervillain.

A twisted heart with the power of our entire universe

One of Marvel Universe comics' greatest powers is the *Infinity Gauntlet*, with all the six Infinity Stones working together in unison. The Infinity Stones are the soul, time, space, mind, reality, and power gem. When the stones work together as one, the wielder's wish regarding everything in the universe becomes a reality. In the comic book series *The Infinity Gauntlet (1991)*, Thanos, an Eternal of Titan, united the six stones and wielded the ultimate power in our universe. Even all-powerful Eternity, the embodiment of all there ever is and ever was in our universe, is no match for the power of the Infinity Gauntlet wielded by Thanos. The coming together of the six Infinity Stones served a purpose for Thanos. Death appeared to Thanos in the form of a woman, and he fell in love with Mistress Death. He sought the power of the Infinity Stones to impress and win the heart of Mistress Death. As a gift for her, Thanos destroyed half the living beings in the universe.[5]

If we have the greatest force of power in the universe, we would probably wish for something simple, childish, and silly as death to our enemies or all the riches in the universe. Thanos wasn't happy, so he pursued the ultimate power in the universe. Even after getting it, he still wasn't happy. The greatest power in

THE DELICIOUSLY CHEESY HAPPINESS EQUATION

the universe wielded by a twisted heart can only destroy and bring pain and suffering to others. It cannot create and bring happiness to the bearer. The external power can only amplify what is in the heart of its bearer.

A confused heart from beyond

In the Marvel Universe comics series *Marvel Super Heroes Secret Wars (1984)*, a being called the *Beyonder* came to our universe seeking to learn the nature of desire. The Beyonder was the only living entity in his entire universe, a universe much larger than our own. Because he was all there ever was and all that there is, he needed nothing else and desired nothing. He has no desire or even a concept of desire. Desire is of the heart, and never having known desire, his heart became confused when he glimpsed into our universe and saw it for the first time. Being all the energies of an entire supermassive universe much larger than our own, the Beyonder is more powerful than any being in our universe.

A doorway briefly opened into another universe called the Beyond-Realm during a laboratory accident at a nuclear power plant on Earth. Some of the energies from that universe escaped and turned Owen Reece into the *Molecule Man*. The rest of the energy gained consciousness and became the Beyonder. During that brief moment of the accident, the Beyonder caught a glimpse of our universe, and he saw desire and didn't know what it was. He was intrigued and became curious about desire. So he came into our universe to investigate and learn the nature of desire. Far from our Milky Way Galaxy, the Beyonder destroyed an entire galaxy and created Battleworld. He transported teams of superheroes and supervillains there to fight each other for desire. The winner would be rewarded and given whatever they desire by the Beyonder.[6]

In the series *Secret Wars II (1985)*, the Beyonder came to Earth, and, among many other disastrous misadventures, he became fascinated with the idea of intimate love. He pursued a romantic relationship with a girl from Earth. He tried to win her heart by

THE HEART

using his powers to take her to exotic places, give her gifts, and even control her, but his actions only upset her. The Beyonder was trying to win her heart by showing off his powers. Unfortunately, doing so did not impress her at all. Even with all his powers, he could not win a woman's heart because he did not understand desire, which is of the heart. The Beyonder was confused because of his lack of understanding of the ways of the heart. His powers, which contained energies much greater than our universe, were useless in bringing happiness to himself and others. The Beyonder's great powers wielded by his confused heart did not bring him happiness, but they amplified the confusion in his heart and wreaked havoc and destruction upon our universe.

The Beyonder decided to build a large incubation chamber and put all his energy into it. He wanted to be born, grow up, and learn to understand and grasp the concept of desire. However, the Beyonder finally gets his wish in another universe in the end.[7]

HEARTS THAT TRANSFORMED

The becoming of Doctor Strange, Sorcerer Supreme

> "Get up! Pick up your mat and go on home."
> — "MARK 2:1-12"

Doctor Stephen Vincent Strange was a highly successful surgeon whose only focus was on making money. Then, an automobile accident shattered his hands, and he could no longer perform surgery. He soon became broke because he spent all his money trying to restore his hands to what they were. Being broke, homeless, and hoping the mystical powers could heal his hand,

THE DELICIOUSLY CHEESY HAPPINESS EQUATION

Doctor Strange journeyed to the Himalayas to study under a sorcerer. In his development and education for both heart and mind, he eventually realized that he created the internal obstacles preventing him from freeing himself from his past.

An obstacle that created a mental and emotional blockage for Doctor Strange was his desire to be a medical doctor to save lives because he could not save his sister. However, once he let go of his past and accepted that he could not have saved his sister, it freed him for a new calling elsewhere. He freed himself to refocus his heart and mind to become a sorcerer for the next chapter of his purposeful being, and he became the new Sorcerer Supreme known as Doctor Strange.

In his journey to becoming Sorcerer Supreme, it was not about healing his hands but something more important on the inside. His journey was about clearing his mind and heart to find a better understanding, for a stronger new belief to service life in other ways. He eventually saw reality differently and transformed his inner strength to serve the new vision. He found a new clear understanding to service life, not as Doctor Stephen Vincent Strange, the brilliant surgeon, but as Doctor Strange, Sorcerer Supreme.[8]

The temptations of the heart of Macbeth

In William Shakespeare's tragedy *Macbeth* (1606), after achieving victory over their enemies, Norway and Ireland, the Scottish general and nobleman Macbeth won favor and praise from King Duncan. That wasn't enough for Macbeth, and he desired more. Soon after, three witches came, and they gave Macbeth a prophecy foretelling him that he would be king. They even made him invincible by saying that no man born of a woman could kill him. His temptation and imagination made him take King Duncan's life, and Macbeth became king of Scotland. The witches' words are the temptations of our misguided hearts' desires. Their words created a negative H in Macbeth's Happiness Equation, and the hole in his heart took over his actions

THE HEART

$$H = R - E(R) = 0$$
The witches' words raised Macbeth's expectation E(R)
$$H = R - 2E(R) = -H$$

The three witches of Macbeth are the embodiment and personification of our imagination's temptations and desires. Macbeth's tragedy came about because his inner strength was not strong enough to neutralize his misguided imagination. His ego's desire for self-importance led him to take actions that did not agree with the principles of love, kindness, and humility. Macbeth thought he was invincible because the witches told him that no man born of a woman could kill him. In the end, Macduff defeated Macbeth. Macduff was born from his mother's womb through a C-section. The prophecy presuming invincibility had an untold loophole.

The heart of beauty and the beast within

> *"It is only from the heart that one can see rightly; what is essential is invisible to the eye."*
> — ANTOINE DE SAINT- EXUPÉRY

In the mirror, we cannot see the depth and color of our hearts that radiate emotional energy onto others' hearts. If we want to know our hearts' clarity, depth, and color, we must look at the world around us. The level of beauty in our world reflects the level of our inner beauty.

Gabrielle-Suzanne Barbot de Villeneuve wrote *Beauty and the Beast* (1740) and entertained us with a love story of contrast, but she also wrote the story to inspire us to be better from within. When we change our internal energy, our external world changes. In *Beauty and the Beast*, the prince was a selfish and ugly person inside his heart who denied an old woman shelter from a storm. She wasn't just an old woman but an enchantress who came to test the beauty of his heart. She transformed the prince's outside to reflect what was inside of him. Due to being an ugly

THE DELICIOUSLY CHEESY HAPPINESS EQUATION

beast inside, the prince became an ugly beast on the outside. As a result, the world around him, his entire kingdom, went into darkness. When we are capable of, and we turn away from, helping those in need, the darkness in our hearts reveals itself, and its energies amplify outward into our world.

> *"You must be the change you wish to see in the world."*
> — MAHATMA GANDHI

With the help of his staff, the Beast gradually transformed and raised his inside to become beautiful. He made tough decisions of sacrifices in favor of others by allowing Belle to go and save her father, knowing that if she did not come back, they would no longer be able to return to become people again. He raised the inside for beauty and strength. He made decisions out of love and compassion for others rather than for himself. His new internal beauty allowed him to consider others before his own needs. He made difficult decisions for others that required sacrifice. His outside eventually transformed to reflect his inner beauty. His entire kingdom and those around him transformed to become beautiful again. The prince is both Beauty and the Beast. If we wish for our world to be more beautiful, we need to raise our inside. When we raise our inside's beauty, we have the strength to make difficult decisions in favor of others over our needs. The beauty in the world is only a reflection of the beauty inside us. For a beautiful world, we have to raise our inner beauty.

THE HEART

A TEST OF HEART STRENGTH

Waiting for two marshmallows

Albert Einstein is famous for having an exceptionally high 200 IQ. Maybe they shouldn't have emphasized Albert Einstein's 200 IQ so much but instead focused on his emotional energy and heart's intelligence, the true source of his strength that drives his 200 IQ. There is a test of inner strength called the Marshmallow Test. It is a strength test with a much higher correlation for future success than a standard intelligence quotient (IQ) test. An IQ test measures a person's intelligence, such as short-term memory, analytical thinking, mathematical skill, or other recognition ability. The marshmallow test only measures one's ability to delay gratification with the aid of reason and logic by making a sacrifice today for more abundance tomorrow. The marshmallow test measures our ability to use our IQ properly; it does not measure our IQ value. Thus, it measures the strength of our hearts' drive.

The marshmallow test puts a child into a room. An adult comes in and offers the child one marshmallow now but then tells the child that if he or she waits until the adult returns, the child will receive two marshmallows instead of one. The child willing to wait for two marshmallows has a higher probability of future success than someone who scores well on a standard IQ test. To score well on an IQ test shows the ability to learn, the gift of our genes. It is like Superman's Kryptonian DNA, except for the mind. The Persian poet Rumi describes the results of an IQ test as the first intelligence.

The intelligence of the mind without heart strength makes one a mad scientist. Re-engineered Kryptonian DNA with a tortured heart turns one into a monster. To pass the marshmallow test requires the inner strength of a strong heart. It takes someone willing to make a sacrifice now to have greater abundance later on. The strength on the inside is Superman's Kansas upbringing of a strong heart. Rumi describes our heart's strength as our second intelligence. Someone who passes the marshmallow test can reason and think in the face of desires and temptations and can still make the correct decision not to consume now, allowing it to grow to double later on. A child is not aware of being tested and will act with the pure intention of the heart. Therefore, the child's level of heart strength decides in the marshmallow test.

Our impulsive actions result in a lesser tomorrow because we consume the seeds that would yield more tomorrow. The marshmallow test shows our heart's strength to control our impulses at the subconscious level. A strong heart makes a difficult choice now for more abundance later on. Passing the marshmallow test demonstrates self-control in favor of reason and logic for better things to come. The marshmallow test is a test of discipline and inner strength. Those with the heart's strength to pass the marshmallow test show a great ability to control their emotions and energy. To make better decisions for our future happiness, we will need to pass this simple test of inner strength.

HAPPINESS FROM INSIDE

"No man is free who is not master of himself."
— EPICTETUS

Siddhartha battled a demon called Mara the Tempter on the night of his enlightenment. Mara attacked Siddhartha with arrows, but Siddhartha turned them into flowers. He turned Mara's hate and anger into opportunities for love and kindness. Mara is not a real demon but a manifestation of our hearts' imaginations, desires, fears, and temptations. Mara, the Tempter, is the same as the three witches that visited Macbeth. They are the manifestations

THE HEART

of our confusion and unhappiness. Their further cultivation will lead to more unhappiness and suffering.

When we have clarity of our thoughts to take charge of our emotions, we will have conquered our desires and temptations. We will have conquered ourselves. Our joy, happiness, and what makes sense for everyone will drive our actions instead of our desires and fears. When we can remove our desires and our fears, we are free to make better decisions with clear thinking that makes sense. We are happy and at peace from the inside because we have cleared up our internal confusion and conquered ourselves inside.

Better than winning a thousand battles

> "It is better to conquer yourself than to win a thousand battles. Then it cannot be taken away from you by angels, demons, heaven, or hell."
> — BUDDHA

When we conquer ourselves, we will have happiness inside no matter what is happening on the outside. Thus, our happiness lives inside us, and it cannot be taken away by anyone or anything.

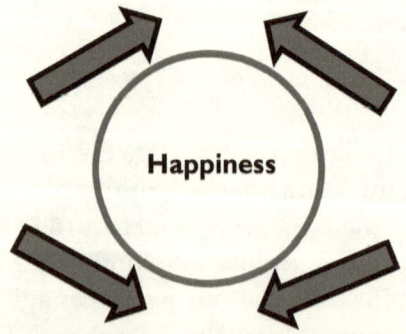

Better than winning a Thousand Battles

Our happiness cannot be taken away by external factors such as an angel's temptations, a mean person, the desire

THE DELICIOUSLY CHEESY HAPPINESS EQUATION

for comfort and relaxation, or the suffering of an undesirable place.

We can deflect and neutralize external attacks to our inside by turning them into opportunities for positive changes. Our internal happiness is better than winning a thousand battles. Through conquering ourselves, we free ourselves to be happy. Better than all the wealth and pleasures of the world is our happiness. Our happiness comes from a clear understanding that we are in charge of the internal energy that drives our being. We can choose happiness in all the outside elements because the external elements are not factors for our happiness. The most admirable person is a conquered self who can bring calm, positive energy, and common sense to improve any situation.

A heart at peace

Zen in a Beggar's Life

Tosui was a well-known Zen teacher of his time. He had lived in several temples and taught in various provinces. The last temple he visited accumulated so many adherents that Tosui told them he was going to quit the lecture business entirely. He advised them to disperse and to go wherever they desired. After that, no one could find any trace of him.

Three years later, one of his disciples discovered him living with some beggars under a bridge in Kyoto. He at once implored Tosui to teach him.

"If you can do as I do for even a couple of days, I might," Tosui replied.

So, the former disciple dressed as a beggar and spent a day with Tosui. The following day one of the beggars died. Tosui and his pupil carried the body off at midnight and buried it on a mountainside. After that, they returned to their shelter under the bridge.

THE HEART

> *Tosui slept soundly the remainder of the night, but the disciple could not sleep. When morning came, Tosui said: "We do not have to beg for food today. Our dead friend has left some over there." But the disciple was unable to eat a single bite of it.*
>
> *"I have said you could not do as I," concluded Tosui. "Get out of here and do not bother me again."*

Because he is a beggar, Tosui does not have many material possessions. However, what he has matches his expectations. His small reality R matches his small expectation E(R). Tosui's Happiness Equation is balanced, and he is happy. Tosui has little material possession, and his Happiness Equation is:

$$H = R - E(R)$$
$$R = 1$$
$$E(R) = 1$$
$$H = 1 - 1 = 0$$

The happiness and balance of Tosui may appear simple, but it is practiced diligently on the inside by a disciplined mind. It takes great internal strength to live in peace and happiness despite any external environment. To conquer ourselves, we have to work to raise the clarity and strength of our inside. Thus, we can live in balance with all the different elements outside.

SUMMATION OF THE HEART

> "We are slowed down sound and light waves, a walking bundle of frequencies tuned into the cosmos. We are souls dressed up in sacred biochemical garments, and our bodies are the instruments through which our souls play their music."
> — ALBERT EINSTEIN

The energy of the inside

The choices we make become our future. Our actions are dependent on our clarity of information and our strength of heart. We are a combination of our internal energy and our external information. Our heart's internal energy drives the external information of the body and mind to become our external physical manifestation in the world. Others will call that manifestation by our given name. The energy of our heart, amplified by our physical being, radiates outward to become actions. To others, the physical manifestation of the outside will become the definition of who we are. However, the true source is from inside of our hearts. The strength of our heart is greater than the strength of the reason and logic of it all. The energy from our hearts powers our bodies and our minds. Thus, we must start by raising our heart's strength to apply the reason and logic of our understanding. To do so, we must conquer our hearts from the inside. Information guides, but energy drives.

The heart's strength is not only defined by its ability to endure suffering and persist, but a strong heart is also love, kindness, and compassion for others. A strong heart is tough and durable but also gentle and kind. It is calm in a difficult emotional storm allowing us to use our reason and logic. A strong heart is kind and compassionate to others because our lives are in balance with theirs. Our clarity of understanding and our love for others strengthen our hearts. When we love others, we will give the best

THE HEART

of ourselves to them. Our heart is an exponent in enhancing the effectiveness of our minds and our physical bodies. We can increase the exponential factor over our minds and physical strength by raising our hearts' strength. Our overall strength equation is as follows:

$$\text{Strength} = (\text{mind} * (\text{physical strength or superpower}))^{\text{heart}}$$
$$\text{Thus, Strength: } S = (M*PS)^H$$

The different energies of the heart

Our hearts' energies have carried our species for a million years or longer. Our hearts lie at the center of our emotions, which is the energy that drives our physical bodies. Many of the species of our planet have the capability and drive of the heart. Our emotions come from an older part of the brain. Our human frontal lobe's development and growth came more recently to adapt to wild climate swings. Our hearts' strength will continue to carry us for thousands and millions of years more to come because our energy drives our mental and physical being.

Strong energy

Our strong energy inside will allow us to endure difficult circumstances and make decisions of love and kindness for others. The strength of our energy inside amplifies itself through our body and mind into everything we do. A beautiful inside attracts others to the strength and beauty of our character. A strong heart brings joy and happiness to share with others. Our raised inner strength allows us to make correct and difficult decisions that are good for everyone. Thus, strong energy is a requirement for a happy life.

Negative energy

The heart's negative energies create suffering within us, and the energies vibrate through our physical being to spread pain

THE DELICIOUSLY CHEESY HAPPINESS EQUATION

and suffering to others. With negative energy within, we will make up reasons and excuses to take from others to balance our internal unhappiness. We may also create destruction because that is the only energy that we know in our hearts. The pain and suffering created by our negative energy go into the world and sooner or later return to us because we reap what we sow.

Transformed energy

The energy inside us can transform from negative to positive or positive to negative depending on our circumstances, our clarity of understanding, and the quality of the questions we ask. When we ask what we can do to make our world better for others, our internal energy transforms into positive and giving. When we ask what we can do to have more for ourselves, our internal energy becomes negative. Negative energy leads to our actions that will take from others. Our energy will transform into the strength, clarity, and quality of our questions and our thoughts. If we want a change or transformation in our physical world, we must change the internal energy that drives our actions. When we transform our energy inside, it will drive our external actions. Our physical efforts become effortless to be forces of transformation on the outside.

Happiness energy

When we raise our internal energy, we raise our energy strength, focus, speed, and positivity. Thus, we will arrive at happiness on the inside. Happiness energy is clear and active energy. Our internal happiness helps us to stay better balanced with our changing world. Our energy inside does not change due to the outside's changing circumstances, but it reflects our clear understanding and inner strength. To others, our actions may appear uncaring or easygoing, but it takes a transformation in understanding to reach a state of happiness independent of external elements. When we arrive at happiness through our mental work and effort, our happiness never ends because it is dependent only on our understanding of timeless traditions and

THE HEART

wisdom. Our clear understanding constantly balances our internal Happiness Equation. Our raised inner strength drives our manifestations in the physical world.

Raise the Strength and Beauty of the Heart

**Inner   Physical
Strength Body**

The strength and beauty of our heart's energy drive our actions.

The greatest power in the universe

> "The noblest of art is that of making others happy."
> — P.T. BARNUM

When Superman rescues a cat from a tree, thwarts a robbery attempt, or saves the city and the planet, he saves the day and brings joy and happiness to others. Superman makes others' lives better than they would have been without him. The greatest power in the universe is not a super-powerful being capable of bending others' will due to their force of strength or being able to bend the universe to their wishes and commands. The greatest power in the universe is bringing joy and happiness to others to strengthen our social fabric. The ability to raise others' happiness comes from the inner strength of a happy being. The ability to spread happiness does not come from Kryptonian DNA but a heart nurtured by love in Kansas.

THE DELICIOUSLY CHEESY HAPPINESS EQUATION

Our greatest moments are those filled with joy and laughter among family and friends. The potential to bring joy, laughter, and happiness is in all of us because it resides in the energy of a beautiful, strong heart that frees us to share happiness with others. When we raise the inside, we ask for clear information and strong energy within. We will need our inner strength to rise to the challenges of the forces of nature.

THE HEART

CHAPTER FOUR
Wisdom

Inner Strength

"Knowing yourself is the beginning of all wisdom."

— ARISTOTLE

WISDOM

In Norse mythology, when Odin became King of Asgard, he sought wisdom for guidance. He traveled in search of wisdom and came upon Mimir's Well. The Well of Urd sits amongst the roots of Yggdrasil. The roots of the mighty tree Yggdrasil connect all of the cosmos. Odin asked Mimir for permission to drink from the Well of Urd, and Mimir denied him. Mimir told Odin that the price was too high. Odin stated that he was willing to pay any price for wisdom and asked Mimir to name the price. Mimir told Odin that he would have to gouge and remove one of his eyes from its socket if he wanted to drink from the Well of Urd. Odin immediately sacrificed one of his eyes and drank from the well of wisdom, and he began seeing with better clarity than when he had both eyes.[1]

BALANCE OF THE INSIDE AND OUTSIDE

The only thing that I feel I know for certain about myself is that there is a consciousness inside that resides in the biological evolutionary vehicle of a human being. Through senses designed by nature and clouded by conditioning, I viewed the world with colored perceptions, and my actions reflect my perceptions. Thus, I live in my mind on the inside and in the world on the outside.

Our journey consists of our inner strength measured against the reality of the outside. From our inner strength, we live in the physical world. Therefore, we have to synchronize our hearts' energy with our clear information to balance with the reality that is our world. Thus, we should look inside and outside to balance our inner strength R(I) with our external reality R(E). When our clear understanding and our hearts' energy match our world, we have the wisdom to guide our life's journey.

THE DELICIOUSLY CHEESY HAPPINESS EQUATION

A summation for the heart

> *"And you? When will you begin your long journey into yourself?"*
> — RUMI
>
> *"Your visions will become clear only when you can look into your own heart. Who looks outside, dreams; who looks inside, awakes."*
> — CARL JUNG
>
> *"Knowing others is intelligence; knowing yourself is true wisdom. Mastering others is strength; mastering yourself is true power."*
> — LAO TZU

The qualitative summation of Carl Jung, Lao Tzu, and Rumi: begin our journey to discover our inner self, awake to the workings of our internal forces, and raise the strength of our inside to conquer ourselves to become our own master. We will become what William Earnest Henley describes in his poem "Invictus."

> *"I am the master of my fate: I am the captain of my soul."*
> — "INVICTUS" (1875), WILLIAM ERNEST HENLEY

Our Happiness

We are up against random events. We are up against human forces outside. We are up against the misunderstanding of others. We are up against the desires, fears, environmental conditioning, and ego outside. We are up against our lack of clear understanding and random energy levels. We are up against the flow of time. We will have to work with our uninformed youth initially and then with our weakened physical bodies later in life. We are up against our attachments to reality in an ever-changing world. More importantly, we are up against human forces inside of us. The forces inside create confusion in our hearts and cloud our perception. It is our inner clarity and strength that will lead to our happiness. Thus, we must achieve inner clarity and strength.

We need to balance our Happiness Equation through all the external changes to achieve happiness. Our desire and expectation want our mobility of youth, the appealing sensation of pleasure, and the reliability of permanence in our lives. Our reality is pleasant, unpleasant, and in constant change. Our expectation needs to be flexible to factor in pleasant realities, unpleasant realities, and constant changes. We need to be able to balance our Happiness Equation over time in all the different elements. Thus, we need to clear our confusion inside to give us a clear perception of our world. We can see our world's processes and systems with a clear view. We can balance our Happiness Equation through the many changes and challenges. Our journey to happiness starts with looking inside first and then balancing the inside with the outside. The universe will not change, but it is we who must adjust.

The chicken or the egg

In this causality dilemma, we see the chicken come out of the egg and the egg coming out of the chicken, and we ask which came first, the chicken or the egg. We can only observe a small piece of space-time of a timeless and ever-changing process of nature. Thus, we ask the question of the chicken or the egg. The process has its ancestry at the beginning of life on our planet, and the process itself is still adapting to the constant new changes. Many concepts, such as a beginning or an end or an up or a down, are not universal. They are limited to our human perception and understanding. There is no up or down in the universe outside of our planet. The emptiness of space simply goes in all directions. Therefore, there may be no beginning or an end to space and time.

The chicken or the egg is an ongoing process in fostering survival. It is a complicated, ever-changing process as the planet or universe changes. There's no beginning and end to the process, but it adapts and evolves to accommodate outside

THE DELICIOUSLY CHEESY HAPPINESS EQUATION

changes. Our human perception, limited by time and our current understanding, does not allow us to see the chicken and the egg's entire process of development or forecast its future. Instead, we try to define the process by other patterns that we are familiar with, including a beginning, an end, or order of sequence, and we ask which one comes first. The chicken or the egg is an ongoing process for continuing life that probably evolved from another process long ago. In time, it may evolve again into something else new. But really, the chicken or the egg is the confusion in the cause and effect of our current situation or our being: how did we get here, who we are, and how do we move forward with balanced information and energy for a purposeful journey? We are looking to understand our own life processes.

The chicken and the egg of life and death

Many things in the universe do not have a beginning or an end, but they are simply part of much larger rest and growth patterns. In many of our daily observations, many things have a sense of a beginning and an end. Our own life's journey is perceived to have a beginning, birth, and an end, death. Our clear understanding is limited to what we can observe with our human perception in our lifetime. Our perception is also strongly influenced by our level of understanding. We perceive many things to have a beginning or an end because we base our perception on our immediate observations. We are trying to understand an ever-changing process that might have no beginning or end. Like space and time, our conscious awakenings may have no beginning or end but are part of the endless cycles of rest and growth. We call birth, life, and death the boundaries and processes of our endless journeys. The processes of life and death are our adaptions to the universe's cycles of rest and growth.

> *"All we are is dust in the wind."*
> — KERRY A LIVGREN

WISDOM

Like the chicken and the egg, when we look at birth, life, and death, we can only see a small portion of an ongoing process of rest and growth in nature. From our finite human perspective, we see our becoming dust in the wind when our consciousness no longer connects to our physical bodies, and the material disintegrates into the wind of time. Like the chicken or the egg, we can see the dust in the wind, but we are part of an endless and changing process within endless systems like the constant waves of the ocean. Our self at this moment consists of our physical body and the internal component and processes within it. Thus, we have a temporary component and an eternal component. Our bodies are temporary, but our atoms are eternal. Our consciousness is temporary, but there may be an eternal field of consciousness. *What if* we are a process to conduct information and energy across space and time? A simple diagram of our being is as follows:

The Components of our Being

Our body holds our ego, regulating and protecting our mental, emotional, and awareness.

The process of our conscious energy, continuous growth, and universe may have no beginning or end, just like night and day or the changing seasons. We once thought the sun goes around the earth because we had not yet understood the complete view. We see stars moving away, and we think they used to be closer together; thus, there must have been a big bang a long time ago. The comprehension of our world and universe is limited to

THE DELICIOUSLY CHEESY HAPPINESS EQUATION

certain angles, space, time, or filtered through our human perception and current understanding.

We wake up in this world, in our human body. We feel the push and pull of our desires, pleasures, joy, happiness, and fears, or we subject ourselves to the environmental conditioning that surrounds our development. Perhaps the evolution of our feelings gives us a unique feel to our lives, so we may aspire to make the best use of our time.

Our energies are our emotions, and our information is the clarity of our understanding. With our consciousness, information, and energy, we are trying to figure out what we are and also how to make the most efficient use of our time in this existence. We are fighting for our survival and, at the same time, finding a reason and purpose for our existence. Like the chicken and the egg, we are part of a much larger process of nature. Our roots and branches stretch beyond our current ability to see and understand. We mark the boundaries of what we can see, calling it birth and death. *What if* we are part of cycles of rest and growth that serve a purpose that we have yet to understand fully? What is beyond does not necessarily conform to observations of patterns here on our planet. Thus, we need to ask better questions to the oracle to yield more objective and clear answers for our journey.

WISDOM

THE FORCES OF LIVING BEINGS

> *"You are a bag of particles governed by the laws of physics."*
> — BRIAN GREENE, THEORETICAL PHYSICIST

Besides being particles, we are human beings governed by the great laws of the heart. In the physical universe, there are four fundamental forces of nature. First, there is gravity, which weighs on the fabric of space-time to distort space and time. Its distortion of space attracts objects in the universe to each other. Its distortion of time slows down the flow of time near heavy objects. Second, the weak force is responsible for subatomic particle decay, changing one particle to another, such as protons to neutrons. Third, the electromagnetic force acts between two charged particles. Fourth, the strong nuclear force holds the nucleus of atoms together. It also binds the quarks that make up the neutrons and protons. These fundamental forces of nature govern the behaviors of particles. Finally, there are also forces of nature that govern the behaviors of mobile living beings. As living beings, these internal forces or laws of the hearts govern our actions.

The most powerful forces in our social universe

> *"It is conceivable that life may have a larger role to play than we have yet imagined. Life may succeed against all the odds in molding the universe to its own purpose."*
> — FREEMAN DYSON, THEORETICAL PHYSICIST

Life is beautiful, fantastic, and forever exciting, but the forces inside create clouded perceptions and suffering. There are fundamental forces for objects in the universe, and there are fundamental forces for mobile beings living in the universe. Our

THE DELICIOUSLY CHEESY HAPPINESS EQUATION

desires, fears, ego, environmental conditioning, or clarity in our hearts' strength drive our thoughts and actions. These are the most powerful forces in our social systems because they will push and pull us in all directions or guide our lives toward a peaceful and purposeful existence. Our desires and fears are so strong that they manifest themselves in our dreams. We do not dream in reason and logic, but we dream in emotional energy. We dream about things in our hearts, not things in our minds. That is why our dreams feel so strong when they hardly make sense when we wake up. Often, we do not even question the internal forces within but serve their pushes and pulls instead of redirecting them to serve a better understanding. They become our purpose and cause social storms or peaceful calms in our lives.

One day in the distant future, these forces will take us into the depths of space, create the next higher species, destroy a star, create a new star, open a doorway to another universe or even create a new universe from the beginning. These are the forces and energies that drive living beings. Unless we are aware of their influence on our hearts, they can create distortions in our perceptions. Through our clear understanding, we can refocus our internal energy to serve a better purpose instead of serving our internal confusion. The forces of mobile living beings are desires, fears, ego, environmental conditioning, and clarity. The first four forces distort the fabric of our perceptions of the world, and clarity lights our way.

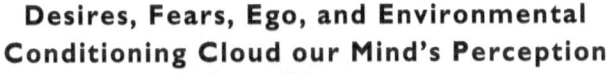

Desires, Fears, Ego, and Environmental Conditioning Cloud our Mind's Perception

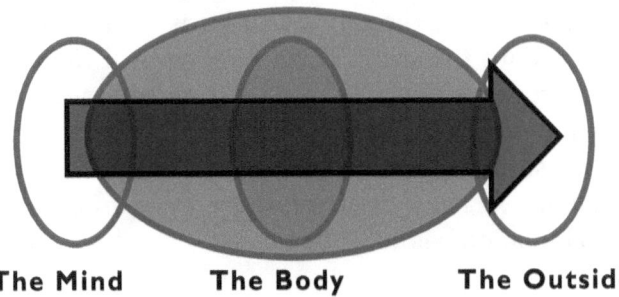

The Mind**The Body****The Outside**

WISDOM

The internal forces create confusion inside and block our clear view of our world.

DESIRE

> *"I count him braver who overcomes his desires than him who conquers his enemies; for the hardest victory is over self."*
> — ARISTOTLE

In 2010, a young man wasn't content with the Nissan 350Z that his family went out of their way to purchase for him. He looked at his situation and saw only a list of unhappiness. He desired a 350Z with a turbo engine to make him happy. Thus, he asked a biased question to the universe clouded with desires and laced with what is in it for him, and the universe provided a biased answer to his question. He found a Nissan 350Z with a turbo engine for sale by a private seller, and he decided to ask the seller for a test drive. On the drive, he complained of noise and made a stop on a deserted stretch of road to investigate the noise. He shot and killed the young husband and father of four and took the Nissan 350Z for its turbo component to put it into his car to make him happy. A young father is dead, and now the young man sits in prison. Thus, his biased question based on his desires led to disastrous results.

Our desire is one of the strongest forces that drive our lives. Desire creates a large expectation that leads to internal suffering to pull our actions toward it. For desire, we will change almost everything about ourselves to reach our perception of what we desire. Our desires pull us to complete our tasks or goals to alleviate our suffering inside. We desire something because we do not have it yet. Thus, desire creates a large imbalance in our Happiness Equation below.

THE DELICIOUSLY CHEESY HAPPINESS EQUATION

H = R - E(R)
Our desire becomes our expectation E(R)
and creates a large E(R)
Our happiness H is negative because of R < E(R)

Our desire will pull us to increase our reality R so that our reality equals our expectations, and we will have a balanced Happiness Equation, H = R − E(R) = 0. Desire is a force within us, but it is not us. By gaining a clear understanding, we can neutralize our desires to match our reality R. Our Happiness Equation becomes H = R − R = 0, and we have a balanced Happiness Equation by changing our E(R) to match our R.

Desires cloud our Happiness

Our desires cloud our happiness. Once we attain our desires and remove them from our thoughts, our happiness shines through. We can also remove our desires by achieving a clear understanding.

The force of desire pulls us very strongly. Thus, we have to make sure that our desires follow clear processes for success and happiness and that our desires also benefit others and ourselves. If we have misunderstood desires that lack clear understanding or set out for our benefit only, pursuing and achieving such desires will create suffering for others. We will end up taking more from others for ourselves. Thus, our desires must always factor in others' happiness and our own. Happiness comes out when we insert love, kindness, and balance into what we do. We

WISDOM

are all part of the same system, and our clear desires should serve everyone's benefit in our system. A life dwelling on misunderstood desires is unsatisfied because the greatest of all desires is happiness. A clear internal understanding helps us free ourselves from many unnecessary desires to achieve inner happiness. When we no longer desire something, our perception will clear, and we can better understand its patterns and serve them best.

FEAR

> *"Fear defeats more people than any other one thing in the world."*
> — RALPH WALDO EMERSON

The emotional push of fear is a stronger and faster drive than the pull of desire. We will do just about anything to be rid of our fears. Our fears trigger a very strong need for survival, and our actions will lack any objectivity. When we subject ourselves to our fears, we will internally put limitations on our actions. We will not stop to think of the reason and logic of the fear but be paralyzed or flee in fear, which is not actions that reflect clear thinking. Our dwelling in fear or taking off immediately in fear does not serve us well in most circumstances. Fear is nature's guide for us when we are not thinking or have no time to think. It is a force in the universe necessary for the continuation of life. However, we can use our thoughts to raise our tolerance for fear and step into it. According to *The Teachings of Don Juan (1968)* by Carlos Castaneda, we must not run when faced with fear but stand there. We must overcome the tremendous push of fear to make better decisions based on our clear and objective reasoning. Once we face our fear, we will never run away from it again. We will have raised our hearts' strength to give our minds time to make better decisions and face new fears.

THE DELICIOUSLY CHEESY HAPPINESS EQUATION

Fear keeps us fresh

> "Without fear there cannot be courage"
> — CHRISTOPHER PAOLINI

There is a story about the shipping of live cod from the coast to the Midwest. When the cod gets to the Midwest, their meat has become stale even though the fish are alive. So to solve the problem, they put a catfish in the tank with the cod. The cod and the catfish are natural enemies. The cod are aware of and know that there is a predator within. They stay active and alert, and they arrive in the Midwest fresh. Fear solves the problem of the staleness of living beings. We need fear in our lives to keep us active, fresh, and alive on the inside. Without fear in our lives, we will become stale and useless like the cod. We should not eliminate what we fear but learn to live with our fear because doing so keeps our internal and external selves alive.

Based on Yann Martel's book, the movie *Life of Pi* (2012) illustrates the understanding that fear helps keep us sharp. The main character Pi Patel became stuck on a lifeboat with a Bengal tiger. Pi had a chance to kill the tiger by simply letting it drown when it fell out of the little lifeboat, but Pi decided to save the tiger out of compassion.[2] The tiger represents our fear, and we cannot simply get rid of it to feel safe. We must learn to live with the tiger's presence for our continued strength and balance. If we get rid of what we fear, we will not have anything to keep us sharp and alert to other dangers. We must learn to live with what we fear and manage it internally because it will help us stay alert. Thus, our fear keeps us alert and fresh to help strengthen our hearts.

Our adversaries will be our greatest teachers because they will spend their days and nights trying to find our weaknesses to exploit. Others can see our weaknesses and strengths better than we can, and our adversaries are best at doing so because it is their duty. When they find and exploit our weaknesses, they will help make us stronger for our journey ahead. Our adversaries will be

WISDOM

our greatest teachers in strengthening our hearts. We can never get rid of our greatest teachers, but be thankful for their contributions to raising our strength for life's challenges.

The wild adventures of facing our fear

> *"Through every generation of the human race, there has been a constant war, a war with fear. Those who have the courage to conquer it are made free, and those who are conquered by it are made to suffer until they have the courage to defeat it, or death takes them."*
> — ALEXANDER THE GREAT

When we face our fear, it takes us on a wild adventure into the undiscovered strengths of our hearts. We will have raised inner strength, and we can solve emotionally difficult problems. We can rise to do anything, and our life becomes filled with wild adventures.

The Wild Adventures of Facing our Fears

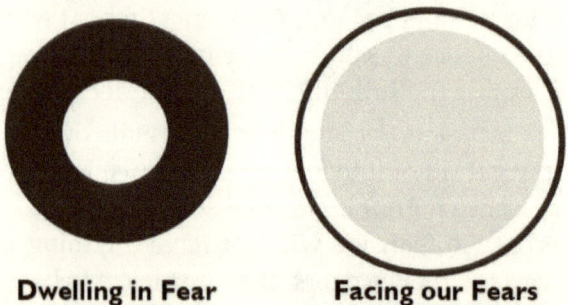

Dwelling in Fear   **Facing our Fears**

When we live subject to our fears, it limits our actions and our lives. However, when we face our fears and learn to live with them, the wild adventures of our lives open up.

In Chinese writing, the characters' danger and opportunity make up the word crisis. We need to face our fears to neutralize them to see the opportunity present in a moment of crisis. Everyone else will be stuck in fear, worrying about the danger, and unable to see the opportunity. Those in fear will see the

THE DELICIOUSLY CHEESY HAPPINESS EQUATION

danger, and those who learned to live with fear will see the opportunity. The fear no longer clouds their perception.

In "1 Samuel 17," the Israeli army was in camp getting ready to fight the Philistine army. Among the Philistines, there was a huge warrior named Goliath from Gath. Goliath challenged the best of the Israelis to fight him. For 40 days, Goliath came every morning and evening to make his challenge to the Israeli army. The Israelis and King Saul were terrified and demoralized.

When David got to camp, he told King Saul that he would go and fight Goliath. Because he was a shepherd, David had once killed a lion and a bear to rescue a sheep. He had already faced his fear of wild nature. David went to fight Goliath without a sword or shield. Goliath cursed at David attacking his inside to try to weaken his inner strength. When Goliath came at him, David took a stone, put it into his sling, hit Goliath on the head, and knocked him over. David took Goliath's sword and defeated him with it. When the Philistine army saw that their strongest warrior had fallen, they turned and ran. The Israeli army pursued and won a victory. David and Goliath's story is a moral lesson to face our fears for a wild adventure into the undiscovered strength of our hearts. It is also a metaphor for something larger, rising to face a towering menace to the leadership and destiny of a people. Our greatest journeys require us to stand at an edge of fear and doubt, face a tense moment of uncertainty, focus our hearts' energy, and then dare to say, "*I want it because I am good enough, and I will take this course of action.*" Our purposeful destiny never comes any other way except by going through our fear.

> "A life lived in fear is a life half lived."
> — STRICTLY BALLROOM (1992 MOVIE)

EGO

> "Most of the trouble in the world is caused by people wanting to be important."
> — T.S. ELIOT

When Charles Darwin discovered the patterns of nature in the Galapagos Islands and wrote the ideas of natural selection in his book *On the Origin of Species*, it helped us understand our long journey to becoming humans. Charles Darwin postulated that life began in the sea, and we evolved from a fish that came onto dry land. He never said that we evolved from monkeys, not that he wasn't aware of our ancestral cousin. Later on, when the academic world started looking for the missing link between humans and apes, Charles Darwin suggested searching in Africa because of the abundance of great primates there. He never said that our ancestral cousin is a monkey because it would run into the defense of the establishments' egos. Being descended from a fish makes sense, but how dare someone would think we descended from or are related to monkeys. Our self-importance of who we think we are would get in the way of accepting the truth regarding our evolutionary journey to become humans. Our ego would prevail over objective observations.

An American Zen Koan

Your significant other asks you this question. Your spouse tells you that both of you and one of your parents are out at sea. The boat is sinking, and you can swim, but there's only one life jacket. He or she asks you, "Who would you give the one life jacket to?" Would you give it to your spouse or your parent? Many of us feel trapped into answering *"You"* so that we do not bear the wrath of "You love me so much less than your parents." We answer for emotional neutrality at the moment, but somehow the answer does not make complete sense to our hearts. It is as if someone beat the answer out of us during an interrogation, and

THE DELICIOUSLY CHEESY HAPPINESS EQUATION

then they use it as evidence of our love in a court of law against our every continued action. That is because the real answer requires clarity in thinking to see the ego's influence on future patterns and then using our reasoning and courage to make the right choice to streamline future patterns for our happiness.

The ego inside can hijack our internal systems for its self-importance. As a result, our mind, emotions, and awareness will serve our ego rather than reason and logic. Without commonsense, our ego's need for self-importance will lead us to take action for our benefit at the expense of others.

The Components of our Being with a Strong Ego

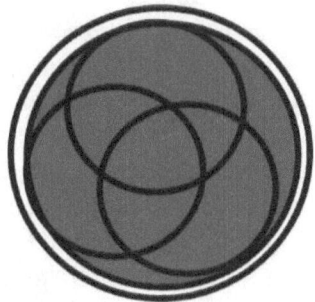

Our ego can hijack our internal systems and shut down our mental clarity, emotional maturity, and awareness for its self-importance.

The ego will defend and rise against criticisms even when it's wrong. The constant errors of our self-importance and the ego's defense are as old as time. The insanity of our being resides within the ego's importance, and it will distort our internal reality by lessening the importance of others and inflating our own. Our insanity will tell us anything our ego wants without double-checking the objectivity and validity of our desires and actions with nature's wisdom, traditions, and patterns. We will build something grand to amaze others across space and time so that it is as if from an unproven plane of existence; we think that they will think that we must be great to build such grandeur. In time, nature and the universe take back everything that is no longer needed or serves a purpose for others' happiness. We

WISDOM

must verify our ego's desires against nature's timeless traditions and processes for our happiness and balance. The things we build will be recycled back into nature when they no longer serve others' happiness. Percy Shelley's poem *Ozymandias (1818)* illustrates the uselessness of our ego's need for grandeur versus time:

> I met a traveler from an antique land
> Who said: "Two vast and trunkless legs of stone
> Stand in the desert. Near them on the sand,
> Half sunk, a shattered visage lies, whose frown
> And wrinkled lip and sneer of cold command
> Tell that its sculptor well those passions read
> Which yet survive, stamped on these lifeless things,
> The hand that mocked them and the heart that fed.
> And on the pedestal these words appear:
> `My name is Ozymandias, king of kings:
> Look on my works, ye mighty, and despair!'
> Nothing beside remains. Round the decay
> Of that colossal wreck, boundless and bare,
> The lone and level sands stretch far away."

Our ego wants to create something grand so that others will remember our name through time. There's no reason or logic to validate this desire of the ego. The desire assumes that our consciousness will witness others' admiration when we are no longer in the world. So that, in another dimension from beyond, we could say to others, "*Yes, I was great.*" Or others could say to us, "*Man, you were great!*" day in and day out for eternity.

Like our physical body, our ego's importance is a butterfly effect of conductions of information and energy. Thus, our ego is a creation of this unique existence of this world for this space-time only. It will not exist afterward in a different plane of existence to rejoice in others' awe of our accomplishments during our time here. Whatever we do here during our time, our actions need to benefit others and those to come only. The music of Mozart and Beethoven live on for others' benefit.

THE DELICIOUSLY CHEESY HAPPINESS EQUATION

Our big ego, our little self

Rabindranath Tagore's poem "Who is this" makes us aware that our inflated ego creates our little self. Our ego is loud, and it only knows of its importance. So when we become aware of our little self in the presence of the lord, we are ashamed.

> "Who is this"
> *I came out alone on my way to my tryst.*
> *But who is this that follows me in the silent dark?*
> *I move aside to avoid his presence but I escape him not.*
> *He makes the dust rise from the earth with his swagger;*
> *he adds his loud voice to every word that I utter.*
> *He is my own little self, my lord, he knows no shame;*
> *but I am ashamed to come to thy door in his company.*

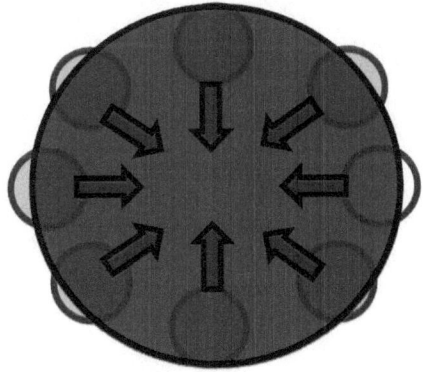

> *Our ego's self-importance blocks our perception, and we can't see the beauty of others. So we ask, "What's in it for me?" and others suffer.*

When we become aware of our thoughts and actions and are ashamed, we will become more humble and aware of others' importance. We will think better thoughts and take better actions

WISDOM

because we are humble in the presence of the lord. Our humility is our beauty that makes others better.

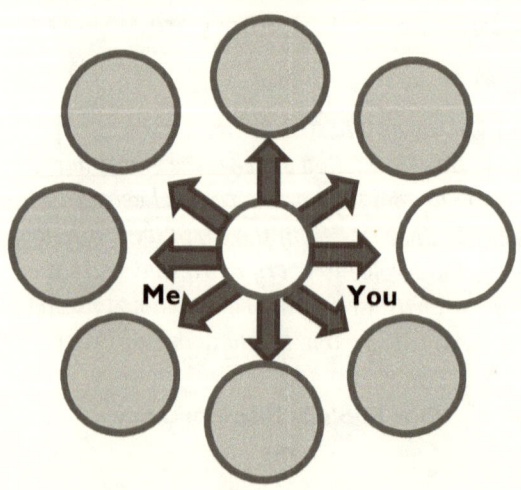

Our humility allows us to see the beauty and importance of others. We ask, "How can we make it better for everyone?" The true importance of us makes everyone better.

The meaning of my life, an existential crisis

> *"To say that we own the land is like a flea saying it owns the dog."*
> — ANONYMOUS

An existential crisis is when we question the meaning of our life, our being, and our purpose. When we are gone, and no one remembers us, what is the purpose of our being here? What is the purpose of our contributions? What is the purpose of it all? Why make contributions to anything if we will be gone and forgotten? Given all our choices, why do we do what we do? *What if,* after doing it, it becomes the wrong choice? If our life has so little meaning, why do we bother going on living? An existential crisis

THE DELICIOUSLY CHEESY HAPPINESS EQUATION

is born because we do not have a clear reason for our existence, and we question why we should exist at all.

Whatever we do will become nothing in the infinity of space and the eternity of time of the universe. Our attempts to give our lives meaning will be meaningless. It leads to the conclusion why even try if our result sooner or later means nothing. Our need for self-importance leads to these internal thoughts, leading to a crisis in the heart for what appears to make our lives meaningless. We want to know what is in it for us. When everything seems so meaningless, what do we get out of it to acknowledge our life's contributions during our time? There is nothing in it for us because no matter how great our achievements are, time will erode them away, or something grander will come along, or possibly both. Our life itself is already the greatest gift of nature because our consciousness touches and experiences the universe in the form of a human being. Yet, we still want to know what is in it for us.

If we accomplish something great, we will not care if others remember our good deeds after we are gone. If our energy exists beyond this particular human form, it does not interact with this physical dimension in the conditioning and thinking of a human being. It is only our human ego's desire for immortality that wants more. Our ego is a component of our human condition, and it will decay and dissipate along with our atoms, and it cannot bask in the glory of what we have accomplished in our lifetime in the form of a human being. Our contribution to our world is for its beautification that benefits others. It is for others to enjoy during their time. An existential crisis occurs when we attempt to look at the world from "what is it for us?" while we are here. If we keep asking what's in it for us, we experience an existential crisis. Nothing appears to make sense because we desire more than what nature gives. We insert our self-importance into our life's brief time, and we want eternity. We want more for ourselves, and we think we are not getting enough of it.

There is no existential crisis because that is only an empty existence for the self. Our purpose is in the service of others, and

WISDOM

our existence for itself is empty. We are a temporary human form that questions our human form's reason for existence out of our desire for self-importance. Our temporary human form's psychological and emotional needs manifest our desire for self-importance. Our evolution and the flow or conduction of information and energy create the desire for our self-importance. Thus, our self, desires, and thoughts only exist here in this space-time.

We get to contribute something fantastic to make the world more beautiful during our brief time here, and there is nothing in it for us to take beyond. Our desire for self-importance is born of a butterfly effect of the information and energy of this world. Our need for self-importance will end here when our energy no longer connects to our physical body and this world. The butterfly effect of our creation and life moves on to other new beings. Our desires, self-importance, and everything else will become butterfly effects of information and energy for others. Our lives, which allow us to connect to the universe, are a gift for happiness. We can ask for more and be unhappy or be thankful for the gift of life and be happy. When we are thankful for our connection to the universe that is our lives, we do not have an existential crisis, and we bask in the blessing of happiness.

Our outer beauty

> *"If you feel your value lies in being merely decorative, I fear that someday you might find yourself believing that's all that you really are. Time erodes all such beauty, but what it cannot diminish is the wonderful workings of your mind: Your humor, your kindness, and your moral courage."*
> — LOUISA MAY ALCOTT

In Greek mythology, the very good-looking Narcissus is the son of a river god and a nymph. One day Narcissus came by a pool of water, and he saw his reflection. He fell in love with it so much that he couldn't leave its side. He stayed and stayed there until he gradually died from starvation. Narcissus was so

THE DELICIOUSLY CHEESY HAPPINESS EQUATION

mesmerized by his own physical beauty that he stayed at the water's edge to be with his reflection, and he let everything else decay away. The story of Narcissus is a warning to those who are physically attractive about the dangers of self mesmerization.

Our physical appearance is a random factor of the universe. Our inner beauty represents the fruits of our conscious cultivation. One is fate, and the other is destiny. If we are born with physical beauty, it may enchant others, but it may mesmerize and enchant us into thinking that we are more than others. Thus, we will get by on our physical beauty, rely solely on it, and be stuck there. We will find it unnecessary to cultivate our inner beauty, and we will only depend on our physical beauty. It will work for a while, but we will experience pain and suffering as our physical appearance fades with time into the sunset of our lives. Our blessing will be our curse, and we will miss out on our journey of raising the inside for lasting internal beauty and strength.

Our inner beauty

> "Not being beautiful was the true blessing. Not being beautiful forced me to develop my inner resources. The pretty girl has a handicap to overcome."
> — GOLDA MEIR, ISRAELI PRIME MINISTER 1969-1974

Ryonen's Clear Realization

The Buddhist nun known as Ryonen was born in 1797. She was a granddaughter of the famous Japanese warrior Shingen. Her poetical genius and alluring beauty were such that at seventeen, she was serving the empress as one of the ladies of the court. Even at such a youthful age, fame awaited her.

The beloved empress died suddenly, and Ryonen's hopeful dreams vanished. She became acutely aware of the impermanency of life in this world. It was then that she desired to study Zen.

WISDOM

> Her relatives disagreed, however, and practically forced her into marriage. With a promise that she might become a nun after she had borne three children, Ryonen assented. Before she was twenty-five, she had accomplished this condition. Then her husband and relatives could no longer dissuade her from her desire.
>
> She shaved her head, took the name of Ryonen, which means to realize clearly, and started on her pilgrimage. She came to the city of Edo and asked Tetsugyu to accept her as a disciple. At one glance, the master rejected her because she was too beautiful.
>
> Ryonen then went to another master, Hakuo. Hakuo refused her for the same reason, saying that her beauty would only make trouble. Ryonen obtained a hot iron and placed it against her face. In a few moments, her beauty had vanished forever. Hakuo then accepted her as a disciple. Commemorating this occasion, Ryonen wrote a poem on the back of a little mirror:
>
> In the service of my empress, I burned incense to perfume my exquisite clothes
>
> Now, as a homeless mendicant, I burn my face to enter a Zen temple.

Ryonen destroyed her physical beauty forever because it was distracting others. Thus, she destroyed it to foster her more important internal qualities of beauty for her journey of lasting happiness.

Our physical beauty attracts others, and so does our internal beauty. Our looks attract others through the eyes, and our internal beauty creates connections through the heart. We can see physical beauty with our eyes, but we feel internal beauty in our hearts. The beauty on the outside pleases our eyes, while the beauty on the inside pleases our hearts. When we age, and our appearance changes, our emotional understanding in our hearts remains the same. The beautiful person we are looking to find is beautiful in the heart. Our physical beauty fades with time.

THE DELICIOUSLY CHEESY HAPPINESS EQUATION

However, the inside does not fade with time but can grow to become even more beautiful.

ENVIRONMENTAL CONDITIONING

"Facts are many, but the truth is one."
— RABINDRANATH TAGORE

When our environmental conditioning from the *Dishwashing Machine Hypothesis* drives our actions, we can become out of sync with reason and logic or other changes due to time. We have learned through conditioned emotional patterns from long ago, and our conditioned behavior still dictates our actions. We have lived with it for as long as we can remember, and we find it hard to see the uselessness of the energy given to us. Even though the outside has changed, we still hold on to our internal emotional energy. Our consciousness awoke in this world, and we call the conditioned energies of the heart our own without first understanding ourselves and our world. Thus, the conditioned forces inside block our clear perception.

Blocked Perception

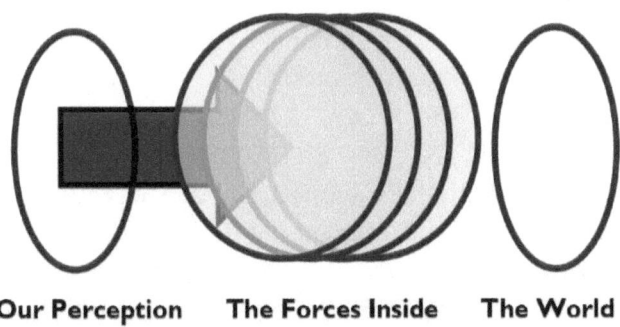

Our Perception **The Forces Inside** **The World**

WISDOM

> *There are a thousand perceptions E(R)s, but only one reality R. The countless perceptions of our internal forces block our clear view of the one reality.*

The universe designs the imprinting laws of the heart for a particular place and time. A Zen story called *A Goose in a Bottle* demonstrates the influences of our environmental conditioning on our perception. A woman put a goose egg into a bottle, and when it hatched, she raised the gosling within the bottle. When the gosling had grown into an adult goose, she wanted to get it out without harming the goose or breaking the bottle. So how do we get the goose out of the bottle? One monk asks another monk, *"How do you free the goose without killing it or breaking the glass bottle?"* The other monk thinks about it for a minute, then says, *"The goose is free."*

The moral of the Zen story is that we have been imprinted subconsciously by our environment. The imprinting is a gift of nature for our survival when we are young, but the imprint also creates an invisible limitation like a glass bottle. We can't see it, but it limits everything about who we are. Unless we free ourselves from the glass bottle limitation, we will continue to define ourselves by our environmental conditioning for our lives' duration. The glass bottle is invisible, yet it limits our being by limiting the clarity in our minds and the strength of our hearts. We begin to see the glass bottle when we understand and accept that our environment's conditioning limits us. Then, we can begin to work on accepting better information and energy to remove our invisible limitations. The imprinting by our environment serves our beginning. We will need to use our conscious minds to move beyond our environmental programming limitations for our journey ahead.

An obscure folktale tells about a monster devouring the sun in broad daylight and the moon at night. When that happens, the people go inside their homes to get their pots and pans. They bring them outside and bang on their pots and pans as loudly as possible. Because they did so, the monster spits back out the sun and the moon. Since ancient times, the deterrence by clanging on

THE DELICIOUSLY CHEESY HAPPINESS EQUATION

pots and pans has worked every time to give us back our sun and our moon. It has worked every time because now we understand the process of solar and lunar eclipses. Our clarity leads us to a better understanding of our life's events. Without it, we will make up stories to justify patterns in nature because we may be viewing life from an obscure perception.

$$\text{The Perception Equation:}$$
$$\text{Our filters are D, F, EC, E}$$
$$D = \text{Desires}$$
$$F = \text{Fears}$$
$$EC = \text{Environmental conditioning}$$
$$E = \text{Ego's importance}$$
$$\text{Scale/Range} = 0 - 1$$
$$\text{Perception Equation} = 100*((1 - D)*(1 - F)*(1 - EC)*(1 - E))$$

Our filters combine and overlap to determine our level of perception clarity. If our desires, fears, environmental conditioning, and ego each block half our view, our Perception Equation becomes:

$$\text{Perception Equation} =$$
$$100*((1-D)*(1-F)*(1-EC)*(1-E)) = 100*(.5*.5*.5*.5) = 6.25\%$$

We would only see with 6.25% clarity

Due to multiple half-clarity filters, our perception reduces greatly. Many of us have such different views because our perceptions become small. We have a limited perception of our reality, and our actions will reflect our finite perception.

WISDOM

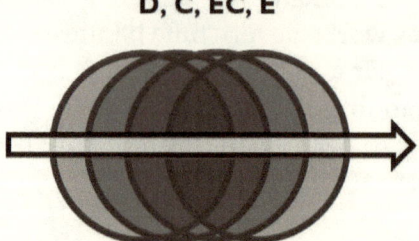

D, C, EC, E

Our internal forces cloud our perception. Therefore, if we want a clear perception of the world, we must neutralize our desires, fears, environmental conditioning, and ego. When we neutralize our internal forces, our Perception Equation is as follows:

$$\text{Perception Equation} = 100*((1-D)*(1-F)*(1-EC)*(1-E))$$
$$= 100*((1-0)*(1-0)*(1-0)*(1-0))$$
$$= 100*(1*1*1*1) = 100\%$$

We see with 100% clarity
Our actions will reflect our clarity in perception

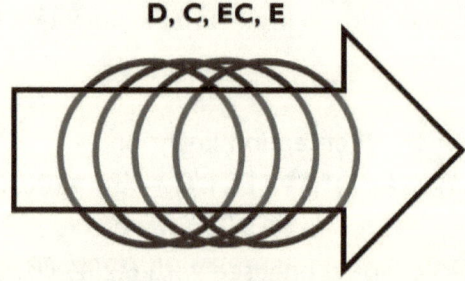

D, C, EC, E

Our list of happiness or unhappiness is always the same because they represent the reality R we have in front of us. However, our hearts' perceptions change the energies to negative or positive. We see one or the other depending on our heart's perception. When there's no longer confusion inside, we have clear perceptions and a better worldview. Thus, we can better see a list of happiness.

CLARITY

> "It's amazing how once the mind is free of emotional pollution, logic and clarity emerge."
> — CLYDE DESOUZA

Many people live the entirety of their lives in desires, fears, environmental conditioning, and ego without reaching clarity to discover what life is or who they can be. They exist and yet do not know what life is or why they are here, and then they move on, never having found the happiness of being here. In Dennis Prager's Fireside Chat Ep. 203, he mentioned being with a group of recovering alcoholics who hadn't drunk for 5-10 years. Dennis asked one of the men when did he decide to become sober, and his answer was, "The day I realized I was the source of my problems, not others."[3] The man neutralized his ego to accept his responsibility, and he took charge of his inner energy for better choices. His clarity of thought allowed him to become master of his fate, and he freed himself from his addiction.

No matter how cloudy or stormy it is down here on the ground, it is always sunny above the clouds. Thus, we are always happy on the inside, but our internal forces cloud our happiness. When we clear up our internal confusion, our internal happiness shines through into the world. When we clear up our perceptions, we will see the clarity of happiness in our life's journey. We will gain a better view of it all and see the beauty of life. With our clear view, everything becomes clear and positive. Thus, our happiness inside radiates into the world.

WISDOM

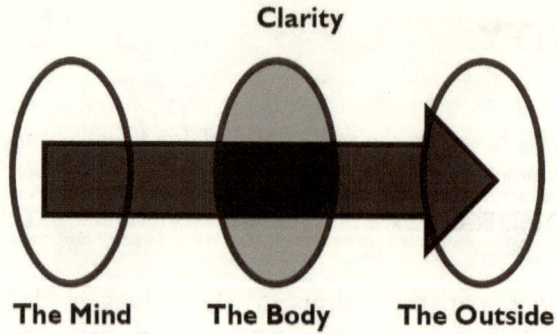

Our clarity of understanding allows us a clear view of the world.

Once, we thought we were at the center of the universe because everything seemed to revolve around us. So we stopped learning and stopped looking for a better understanding. We limited ourselves to our imprinting by our environment, and we stopped asking better questions. We are imprinted by and for a particular place and time, and we believe it to be true. We believed it to be the only reality.

When our perception became clearer, we accepted that we were not at the center of the universe and that the sun and the universe do not revolve around us. We began to define our place in the universe better. We rose to find our place in our world through our observations, reason, and logic. Our ego's importance prevents us from believing and seeing that we are not at the center. When we accepted our smallness in the universe and became more humbled, we began to see the universe's bigness and beauty. We began seeing all the beauty around us and in nature. We saw the balance of the universal laws in the processes and systems.

When we gain clarity in our understanding, we will free ourselves from the pull of the forces of desires, fears, environmental conditioning, and our ego's need for importance. These forces that drive our actions help us but also limit us. We can grow to become more than our conditioned beginning and learn to understand our desires to make sure they make sense for everyone. We can learn to live with our fears and use them to challenge ourselves to become better and stronger. We can raise our internal clarity to appreciate the beauty in others. We can break free from our environmental conditioning to grow beyond the limitations of our emotional past. Thus, we can learn and grow to become our better future selves. A life without sight is a life living in the dark. A life without clear thinking is a life living in the darkness of our minds and hearts.

The battle of good and evil

> *"If you were my preacher, I would begin to change my ways."* — from the song *"If You Were A Sailboat."*
> — KATIE MELUA

Our good and evil are the clarity or confusion in our hearts amplified into the world. The battle of good and evil does not occur on some other plane of existence or mystical realms with flying angels and demons. It takes place inside the dimensions of our hearts. It is the battle of desires, fears, environmental conditioning, and ego versus clarity. The battle of good and evil has been raging since time began. Right after our becoming life forms, in our quest for energy, importance, procreation, and survival, we compete for limited resources and our heart's desires. Our desires amplified by a large ego create confusion in our hearts to take more from others, and our kindness amplified by humility becomes clarity to share our resources equally. The battle of good and evil takes place in the confusion and clarity of our hearts' understanding.

Our traditional and spiritual teachings help us find internal clarity, happiness, and peace. They clear up our hearts' internal confusion by teaching us wisdom from the stories and experiences of those who came before. We learn from their mistakes as well as their courage against temptations. For example, in the book *The Bhagavad Gita*, Lord Krishna said to Arjuna that one must overcome fear, desire, and anger so that the mind and heart will be clear. When we have internal clarity of understanding, we will be free of our internal forces' confusion to see clearly and make better decisions.

Love is greater than evil

> *"Love is the most important thing in the world. Hate, we should remove from the dictionary."*
> — JOHN WOODEN

In the Big Bang theory, scientists have said that if the universe had exploded into existence at even one-millionth less of its speed, it would have fallen back on itself and crunched by now. We would not be here to observe it. The Big Bang in the universe happened with such a speed that it did not fall back on itself, which is why we exist today. We exist to witness the universe today because the force of expansion was greater than the gravitation force of contraction that would have otherwise crunched the universe.

We exist today to observe our world because the force of love is stronger than evil. If evil were stronger than love in the world, our ancestors would have fought and annihilated each other a long time ago, and we would not exist today. However, because love is stronger than evil, we continue to grow and prosper until today, and we will continue to grow and flourish into the future.

Love in the world is getting stronger every day. Our world is becoming more beautiful with each passing year, decade, and century. Those who preach hatred against others do it out of their fears, desires, lack of clarity, and egos. Their message and their lives are short-lived and filled with negative energy. We imprison ourselves with negative energy. Those who preach love do it openly for others. Their purposeful life is long and peaceful, and their messages echo across space and time to strengthen the hearts of others in distant places and times. We free ourselves with positive energy. Our internal confusion holds back the force of love. Yet, love in the world is getting stronger every day. With our continued growth in clarity of understanding, love will continue to grow and bring us closer to each other for unity, purpose, and new journeys.

The birth of objectivity

Without a clear process, we would have no method for objectivity and clarity in thinking. Our ego's need for self-importance and to be right will get in the way of our objective observations of the truth. Our advances in science are due to the objective observation and study of nature on earth and our universe based on a clear thinking and data gathering method called the *scientific method*. Without it, we would make assumptions based on our desires, fears, environmental conditioning, and self-importance as these internal forces embed themselves in our questions about the universe. Therefore, they will not be objective questions, and we will receive biased answers. With the aid of the scientific method, we can view the world with better objectivity, and therefore we can see the world and our universe more clearly. Thus, we can ask better questions for better answers. The scientific method is as follows:

- *Observation and then formulation of a question*
- *Hypothesis*
- *Prediction*
- *Testing*
- *Analysis*

Many western textbooks consider Galileo Galilee to be the father of the scientific method. However, the origin of the scientific method is hard to determine as many great thinkers contributed to its development. For example, thinkers from ancient Greece to the Age of Enlightenment contributed to developing the scientific method. However, some scholars consider that Hasan Ibn al-Haytham (965-1040 CE) was the first to develop the scientific method during Islamic Golden Age.[4] The scientific method by Hassan Ibn Al-Haytham is as follow:

WISDOM

- *Observe the natural world*
- *State a definite problem, or ask a question*
- *Formulate a hypothesis*
- *Test the hypothesis through experimentation*
- *Assess and analyze the results*
- *Interpret the data and draw conclusions*

The scientific method allows us to clear our misconceptions and better understand the universe's nature. As we are a part of the universe, we are getting to know ourselves. Our better understanding came about because we can look at the world and the universe more objectively by applying the scientific method in our observation and analysis. We began looking at the universe and ourselves with better objectivity, and we gained more clarity of perception. We have a clear view of our universe, ourselves, and our place in it with our better perception.

The different chapters of our spiritual understanding

What if our religious beliefs and science are different chapters of the same spiritual journey? They appear to be different because each represents different levels of objectivity in understanding ourselves and our universe. They also appear to be different because those in power who want to keep that power tell us they are different. However, both religion and science try to find our place in the universe using different observation methods and, thus, different clarity strengths. Religion uses our hearts, and science uses our minds.

Our spiritual practices and religious beliefs are in the first chapter of our spiritual journey. As a species, we are becoming more aware of the universe. However, there are still many unanswered basic questions as we cannot answer them yet. Our spiritual shaman practices evolved into idolatry, paganism, and organized religion. The Olympian gods of ancient Greece defeated the spiritual practices that came before and served their purpose for over a thousand years from the seventh century BCE until Eastern Orthodox Christianity replaced them. The last

THE DELICIOUSLY CHEESY HAPPINESS EQUATION

defeat of the Olympian gods was the Mani Peninsula area conversion in the ninth century AD. As our understanding became clearer with new revelations and our spiritual traditions adapted to the new understanding, something better came along to replace our beliefs and worship of the Olympian gods. The Scandinavian Norse gods succumbed to the same fate, the Egyptian gods experienced a similar fate, and the conquistadors destroyed the Aztec and Mayan gods.

In the beginning, we use our hopes and desires to find our place in the universe, and our science is the next chapter. We have grown in our understanding of our universe and ourselves through our objective observations. Thus, we use our reason and logic to find our spiritual place in the universe. One day, we will merge our traditions and spiritual beliefs with the scientific method so that our hearts and minds agree on our place in the universe. We will unify the forces of our hearts with the clarity of our minds. Thus, we will unify the forces of our energy with clear information. In time, a god will be born that unites the forces of the hearts with the scientific method.

Answer to an American Zen Koan

The better answer comes once we have thought about it in peace and calm, not because someone pressured us, and we act to please for emotional neutrality. All the better answers come through our emotional calm and clear reason and logic, not our emotional response to please others. For someone to ask us that question means we are dealing with a person who has a large ego, and they want to insert their self-importance and dominance between lifelong family bonds. If we answer for emotional neutrality or in their favor, they will require that we answer that way all our lives. Thus, we must face our fear and permanently answer it for lifelong happiness for ourselves and others. If we must answer the question correctly, it requires courage to bear the wrath of an egotistical psychological backlash. We need clarity and courage for our answer because it changes the pattern going forward into something loving and peaceful for everyone.

WISDOM

The answer is that for someone to ask that question implies that they are here for their importance. Those who come into our lives to stay bring love and happiness to share. They will not ask that question to begin the drama because they are too busy building a life with us to ask such questions. Instead, they will ask better questions to serve everyone's better future. Those who come for their self-importance will ask the question of who we would save, and we can kindly let them leave while everyone is safe on dry land.

The endless coming revelations

Each new revelation is an insightful and intuitive, clear understanding of our world and our universe's patterns. However, it is still a clear understanding of information and energy from a particular place and time. The particular problems surrounding each space-time give rise to revelations to resolve the specific needs of that space-time. Even after his enlightenment, the Buddha did not allow female converts to receive his teachings. Because his revelation came at a time and place when women had little or no rights, his aunt had to make a strong case to gain acceptance to become a Buddhist nun to receive his teaching. Our awareness and clear insight into the patterns of nature and the universe bring forth new revelations. Our revelations will be forever coming as new and more open ways of thinking are accepted and adopted, leading to new daily patterns. Due to our continuing growth in understanding our universe, new revelations, like the next prime number, are out there for us to discover when the time is right.

THE DELICIOUSLY CHEESY HAPPINESS EQUATION

AWARENESS

> "Awareness is like the sun. When it shines on things, they are transformed."
> — THICH NHAT HANH

If someone tries to redirect our unhealthy habits to help us become better, our ego will deflect and tune out the person's message of love because we need to get there on our own. To do so, we will need strength in awareness. We can only go where we can see. If we cannot see it, it does not exist in our minds and hearts, and we cannot travel there. Our awareness allows us to see the processes and systems, and our clear understanding will lead to our journey of inner strength. We can rise to our challenges inside and outside through our internal strength. When we perceive the world with clarity, we are free to match our expectation $E(R)$ to our reality R for strength and happiness.

Changing our perspective

What if we could get into a time machine and see our future selves? *What if* we live outside of time and see the entire timeline of our lives? We would have better objectivity in the actions taken during our lives. Our perceptions would no longer be subject to our hearts' internal confusion as we would be viewing our lives from the outside through a third person. We can see events more clearly from the outside because our view is not subject to our internal confusion. Thus, we are free to take actions that better maximize the strength and quality of our lives' journeys.

In Charles Dickens's *A Christmas Carol (1843)*, Ebenezer Scrooge got to see himself outside of time when three ghosts visited him. The Ghost of Christmas Past, the Ghost of Christmas Present, and the Ghost of Christmas Yet to Come visited Ebenezer Scrooge and showed him his life through time. Viewing his life from the outside through different time frames helped

WISDOM

Ebenezer realize the internal change he needed to make. We all might not be rich as Ebenezer, but in the end, when he decided to be a giving and generous person, it started with a change on the inside, enabling him to give love and kindness to others. After the Ghost of Christmas Yet to Come showed him a cold, lonely end, he decided to unleash the love that he had been holding back for years. Unfortunately, his internal confusion prevented Ebenezer from seeing the flow of his life through time. So, the three ghosts took Ebenezer outside of time, and he saw himself from the outside, thus, giving him better clarity.

We can see Ebenezer Scrooge's life from the outside, and we know that he needs to change. We are Ebenezer Scrooge, and we need to change for the better, but we can't see it. What would it take for us to un-become Ebenezer Scrooge? *What if* we could see ourselves from the outside? What would we change about ourselves to be more loving and kind to others and ourselves? We want to share our joy and happiness instead of living for our ego's need for self-importance. With our awareness of the consequences, what would it take to make the change? What stops us from releasing the love, beauty, and strength within us into the world? What is stopping us from releasing our best into the world every day and expecting nothing in return?

It is difficult to be objectively aware of our current attributes because our ego defends its inner components, even from our self-analysis. How can we view things differently when using the same old emotional lenses? How can we think of other different thoughts when our old ways of thinking are overwhelming our attempts at new thoughts? How can we see something hard to detect, like our subtle emotional changes or processes over time that affect how realities today transform to become tomorrow? The depth, flavor, and objectivity of our questions become the strength of our awareness. With our strength of awareness, we can better see ourselves in the flow of time.

Our strength in our awareness will help us see our thoughts, actions, results, and the rest of our emotional journey with better objectivity. We can see our thoughts and the emotional energy it creates, and we will realize that they are but our thoughts and

THE DELICIOUSLY CHEESY HAPPINESS EQUATION

emotions only. Each different thought will create different energy for a different action. Our awareness will allow us to create better thoughts for creating better emotional energies. We will stop and think about how our actions and habits affect us and others along our journey through our lives. We will not have the three ghosts to help take us out of time for better objectivity, but our awareness will help us visualize our lives through time. Thus, we can take better actions for happiness.

Squirrel, ducks, now frog

One of my junior high school science teachers once said that if we put a frog in hot water, it will jump out immediately. It senses the difference in sensation and leaps to escape the hot water. However, if we put a frog in room temperature water and slowly heat the water, the frog will stay there and die because it cannot sense its slowly changing environment. Our environmental conditioning puts energies in our hearts, and we have been living with them for so long that the energies became us. We live in our soup of internal confusion. We are a frog in water with the temperature rising, and we can't sense the changing environment. Thus, we will need our awareness to help us sense the changes in our environments. So, we can make internal emotional changes for what we desire rather than accept and live with changes we do not want in our lives.

Without awareness, we will not sense the new subtle changes, and we will think that today is not much different from yesterday. We will sit in our slowly changing environment, and we won't realize that the temperature, our environment, has been changing from one moment to the next. Our awareness allows us to see the processes, systems, and subtle changes around us as we move through time. Awareness allows the three ghosts to visit us to show us the connection to our emotional energy between our past, present, and future. Instead of dwelling on slowly rising negativity, we can ask better questions to allow our emotions to become what we want, rising positivity.

WISDOM

> *"The happiness of your life depends upon the quality of your thoughts: therefore, guard accordingly, and take care that you entertain no notions unsuitable to virtue and reasonable nature."*
> — MARCUS AURELIUS

Our awareness is the most important criterion for creating balance because it makes us aware of how our internal forces interact and drive our life's journeys. As a result, we can better see our lives' processes and systems. In the story of the Buddha's becoming, it was not the teachings of others that helped ease his suffering. His awareness and compassion for others enabled him to connect to the timeless processes and systems. His awareness made him feel compassion for those less fortunate than him, and he began to see the beauty in the world. Upon further reflection, he gained insight into the happiness of life and saw that happiness is the fabric of our social existence. Happiness is the fabric of our lives. Our emotions connect our hearts to others. The cultivation of our awareness strengthens *Right Mindfulness,* the seventh of the *Noble Eightfold Path*.

> *"Mindfulness is the capacity to be aware of what is going on and what is there. The object of your awareness can be anything. You can look at the blue sky, breathe in and say, 'I am aware of the blue sky,' and you are mindful of the blue sky."*
> — THICH NHAT HANH

THE DELICIOUSLY CHEESY HAPPINESS EQUATION

Awareness

Awareness allows us to see and empower our hearts' interaction with our mind and body. By practicing mindfulness, we are strengthening our awareness.

The why of meditation

> "What we practice grows stronger."
> — PROFESSOR SHAUNA SHAPIRO

The ancients knew the use and purpose of meditation before they understood how it works. We know how to use things before we completely understand their processes. We knew how to farm without ever actually knowing the complete process. It is the same for meditation. Our meditation process asks us to visualize our systems' interactions. We can see and visualize the flow of information and energy among the different processes and systems. For example, when we see the flow of our breath in the exchange of oxygen for carbon dioxide, we also begin to see the creation of our thoughts and the flow of energy they create.

Our awareness of our thoughts helps relieve negative emotional energies when we realize that they are just our thoughts and not ourselves. We gain the freedom to choose our thoughts to create our emotional energy. By focusing our minds, we also give our tireless subconscious minds a chance to relax from the constant need to solve problems. Our random thoughts create emotional stress because they constantly try to solve our unconscious desires or fears. We can choose our thoughts to create our emotional energy instead of allowing our emotional energy to create our thoughts. Meditation is like a person's body carrying heavier weights to be stronger, except for our mind. Meditations lead to our minds becoming stronger, thus leading to better emotions. Instead of our emotions determining our thoughts, we can now generate emotions with thoughts. Instead of our emotions hijacking our minds, we can hijack our emotions with our minds. We can create our emotional energy for strength to serve our purposeful being with better thoughts. When we can create our emotional energy, our happiness becomes a choice.

Through meditation, we raise our awareness and become stronger from the inside. From Chapter Three: The Heart, our strength equation is Strength = $(M*PS)\^H$. Our awareness further enhances our strength equation, Strength (awareness) = $((M*PS)\^H)\^A$.

EMBEDDED LAWS OF THE HEART

A bird in the hand

> "A bird in the hand is worth two in the bush."
> — ANONYMOUS

If we agree with the above popular phrase, why would we want a bird in our hand and not go for the two in the bush? Or, why would we want any of the birds when we can leave them alone in the bush? They will be free to go on with their lives and fulfill their purpose as birds. What would we do with a bird in our hand anyway? Will we eat it? A single bird will not feed our family. If we put ourselves in the bird's situation, we would not want someone else to say, "*A human in hand is worth two humans in their homes.*"

THE DELICIOUSLY CHEESY HAPPINESS EQUATION

Therefore, a bird in the hand is not necessarily better than two birds in the bush. However, most people know that this expression is just a metaphor to teach a simple lesson that the guarantee of having something now is better than waiting to receive uncertainty later. Many aphorisms help us achieve a clear understanding. Many fables and proverbs do not make any sense when we think literally, but metaphorically, they make complete sense. *What if* all the great stories that seem to defy universal fundamental physical laws are also true? When the story does not make sense or defies universal physical laws, perhaps the message is a moral lesson for our clarity of mind and heart's strength.

Myth buster: The Tortoise and the Hare

In the Discovery Channel show *MythBusters*, Adam Savage and Jamie Hyneman put all sorts of myths and urban legends to the test to see if they are true or just myths.[5] Has anyone ever designed a track for a tortoise and a hare in all of our human history? If they did, the hare would win one thousand out of one thousand times because "The Tortoise and the Hare" fable is not of the physical world. It is a story for gaining a better understanding of our human nature and our human drive. If no one has built a track for a tortoise and a hare yet, it is because we realize that it is a moral story for our clairvoyance into our human nature only. *What if* it is the same for many of the other exciting and wonderful classic stories? These interesting stories make us pay attention so that we may absorb the moral lesson. Thus, we will gain clarity of understanding for our minds to strengthen our hearts.

The deception of the Buddha: A moral story

The story of Siddhartha Gautama's deception, which created suffering in his heart and led him to seek salvation by finding a true reality, is a moral story for our awareness of our mortality and fragility against our internal deception of permanence and

WISDOM

endless pleasures. According to the sages and wise men who came to interpret his mother's dream, Siddhartha would either be a great king or a great sage. He would choose the path to becoming a great king, but if he saw a sick person, an old person, and a corpse, then he would take the path to becoming a sage. Most of us are too busy being immersed in the pleasures or worries of life to be fully aware of our mortality. We know it is coming because we see it around us, but we hardly prepare for all the coming natural changes in our lives when we become sick, old, dead, or lose loved ones. Our life's journey is not simply of comfort and youthful pleasures. That is only an easy spectrum of our journey.

What if the deception of the Buddha is the embedding of a moral story? The story brings awareness to our coming physical changes and our mortality. Our awareness helps bring an awakening to our lives' coming changes. Thus, we can accept our impermanence and free ourselves to understand and pursue the meaning and purpose of our lives. We find salvation and peace in our acceptance, understanding, and preparation for the coming changes. The deception of Siddhartha is the embedding of a moral story to help us awaken from our deception that life is permanent and pleasurable. We become aware that we will become sick, old, physically broken, and then die one day. We will find peace in accepting our impermanence because we will know the coming changes and prepare for them. Our expectations $E(R)$ will match our reality R. Thus, the deception of the Buddha is a moral story that brings awareness to our physical changes.

During the night before his enlightenment, Siddhartha Gautama sat under a bodhi tree. He was attacked by Mara The Tempter and her army of demons. Siddhartha asked for enlightenment. Mara asked him who would bear witness to his spiritual awakening. He touched the earth, and he asked the earth to be a witness to his enlightenment. The earth shook and responded that it would be a witness to Siddhartha's awakening. Having no power over an awakened being, Mara and her demons went away, and then the morning star appeared.

THE DELICIOUSLY CHEESY HAPPINESS EQUATION

Clouded Perception

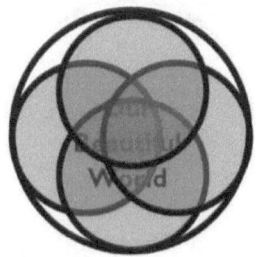

Before his enlightenment, internal forces block his clear perception of the world. As a result, Siddhartha only sees his internal confusion.

The night during Siddhartha's enlightenment is not a physical night of darkness underneath the stars. It is a night for Siddhartha because of the darkness and confusion inside him. The internal forces inside him create confusion and darkness within the perception of his heart and mind. He did not sit in the darkness of night, but he sat in the darkness of his internal confusion; thus, it is a night inside Siddhartha's mind and heart. He sat and did nothing because, in his internal confusion, he didn't know what to do. Thus, he took no action and sat.

When Siddhartha reached the clarity of understanding and overcame his internal confusion, he reached the morning and the light of a new day. He reached the morning light through an internal clarity of understanding when his mind and heart cleared up. Thus, the morning star is a new beginning of clarity for Siddhartha. The forces of temptations have no power over an awakened being because he can see through to clear reason and logic to guide his actions. He is no longer clouded by confusion because he can see the information and energy in the processes and systems surrounding his life's journey.

WISDOM

Clear Perception

When he achieved enlightenment, Siddhartha cleared up the internal confusion inside, and he gained a clear perception of our beautiful world.

The laws of the heart are embedded in moral stories so that we will enjoy the interesting stories. Thus, we will have an opportunity to learn from their teachings to clear our minds and strengthen our hearts. Like the scientific method, an exciting story with an embedded moral lesson gives us both the theory and the observational proof, making sense to our hearts and minds to help us arrive at and accept our emotionally and logically clear conclusion.

Unbecoming Ahab

> *"If you seek revenge, dig two graves."*
> — A CHINESE PROVERB

The embedded moral story from *Moby Dick (1851)* by Herman Melville is that seeking revenge will destroy us. In *Star Trek: First Contact* (1996 movie), because he was hurt by the Borg once in the past, Captain Pickard was obsessed with seeking revenge against a powerful Federation enemy. The Borg is a cyborg race, half biological living tissue and half machine. They start as normal biological beings but become assimilated into a Borg collective. The Borg collective is like a beehive with a queen at its center that runs the entire collective. They are very hard to stop because their cybernetic technology allows the entire Borg collective to quickly

THE DELICIOUSLY CHEESY HAPPINESS EQUATION

adapt to different weapon modulations. It took a woman from the past Earth to remind Captain Picard that he has become like Captain Ahab from *Moby Dick*, who, in seeking revenge, destroyed his crew, his ship, and in the end himself. She understood that if Picard stayed in his state of hatred and revenge like Ahab, they would suffer the same fate as Captain Ahab and his crew. She used the embedded moral story from *Moby Dick* to internally awaken Captain Pickard for a chance to alter his emotional energy and choose a different course of action. Understanding Captain Ahab's error and disastrous results, Captain Pickard immediately lets go of his emotional desire for revenge and chooses a logical solution.[6]

Once we accept our moral stories' lessons, we can refocus and change the direction of our hearts and minds so that our thoughts and actions make better sense. Our awareness helps us better understand and learn from the moral stories that can refocus our hearts' energies for better actions.

Laws of the heart

> "Hatred never ceases hatred, but only through love, that is the eternal and ancient rule."
> — BUDDHA

There are laws for the physical materials, like the stars, planets, moons, and galaxies, and there are also laws for mobile living beings that were not there when the universe began. Energies drive processes that govern systems. There could be laws, or forces, that transcend universal boundaries and reach into other different universes or dimensions.

In the very small quantum universe, objects exist in a wave of probability and not as particles. Depending on probability, an electron could be at points A, B, or C. It only becomes a particle when we observe it. In our everyday world, we can measure things with better precision. The measurements of where and how the subatomic particles behave are subject to different mathematics and laws. The measurements of where and how mobile living beings move and behave are also subject to different laws other than those that govern the subatomic world or our everyday physical world.

We are mobile living beings, and the hearts' many laws drive our actions. For example, the force of love heals suffering and also creates and strengthens social connections. No amount of reason and logic will penetrate through to others' hearts until we have gained their trust through our love and kindness for their hearts. The law of love and kindness is one of the many eternal laws of the heart. Our heart's energies vibrate inside and drive our actions. When we understand the laws of the hearts and apply them to our lives, we are more focused and happier because we live in balance with the laws of the universe.

INNER STRENGTH

> *"Attach yourself to what is spiritually superior, regardless of what other people think or do. Hold to your true aspirations no matter what is going on around you."*
> — EPICTETUS

A life of sound principles

There are many emotional perceptions of our life's journey. We can act out of our desires, fears, social conditioning, self-importance, or clear agreement with timeless wisdom and principles. For example, in the book of Job from the Bible, Satan came to test Job by destroying his crops, animals, servants, and family. Satan even made Job deathly sick. Nevertheless, God had faith in Job, and he had faith in God. In the end, God rewarded Job with an even greater abundance than before.

We must have faith in our plan, contribution, and principles no matter what happens. We must continue to believe that goodness guides our lives. Let our faith in sound principles guide our actions at all times. Our doing the right thing will lead to better results for everyone. We need clear information to guide us and strong energy for strength to make better decisions.

The beauty of our humility

In the book *The Bhagavad Gita (Song of God)*, two neighboring kingdoms, made up of half-brothers, first cousins, families, and friends, are about to go to war against each other for lands, birthrights, and egos in the great Kurukshetra War. Before the battle, the two lead rivals, who are first cousins, both went to God to seek help in resolving the matter. Arjuna, brother of Yudhishthira, is the son of King Pandu, and Duryodhan is the son of Dhritarashtra. Both King Pandu and Dhritarashtra share the same father, Veda Vyasa, but different mothers.

Before the conflict began, the two cousins, Arjuna and Duryodhana, went to meet Lord Krishna, the eighth incarnation of the God Vishnu, for his counsel. Krishna never turns down an offer to help resolve a matter. Krishna was sleeping or pretending to be asleep. Being God, he's never asleep or awake but aware of all that is happening. Duryodhana showed up first, and because the door was by Krishna's feet, he moved up closer to Krishna's head so that when Krishna woke up, he would see Duryodhana. Arjuna arrived a little later and stayed by Krishna's feet. When Krishna woke up, he saw Arjuna first because one looks down upon his feet first when he wakes up. Krishna allowed Arjuna to have the first choice in the matter. Duryodhana protested, saying he was there first, but Krishna said he saw Arjuna first and gave him the first choice anyway. Lord Krishna gave Arjuna a choice between having Krishna as a non-combatant counsel or his army of ten thousand well-trained and battle-tested warriors.

Lord Krishna saw Arjuna first because of his humility in choosing to stay at the feet. He did not step to be closer to the head of God. The source of strength and wisdom is always aware of the energies of our humility, love, kindness, or ego. Duryodhana felt that he was too important to be standing at the

WISDOM

feet, so he moved closer to what he thought was the source of strength. His ego's importance led him to stand next to the head of God. Duryodhana's lack of humility made Krishna recognize Arjuna first for his strength of humility.

When Lord Krishna gave Arjuna the first choice, Arjuna immediately chose Krishna as a non-combatant counsel. Arjuna chose the path of wisdom, God's counsel, over his force to dominate the enemy. Duryodhana was glad to have Krishna's soldiers and laughed at Arjuna's decision. Arjuna chose wisdom over the temptation of might because wisdom can bring a better solution for everyone. When we have others' well-being and happiness in mind, we will minimize our errors by making better decisions. Might and power will only try to force others' obedience to our will, and we will amplify our errors.

Humility allows us to see better the beauty that is in the world. From our ego, arrogance, and self-importance, we will miss out on the beauty surrounding us because we will be too busy with our importance to recognize the significance of others. The journey of self-importance is as old as time, and it always leads to disaster. We will see the importance of others only from our humility, so we will not step to their heads but humbly remain at their feet. Those with great strengths are aware of and see through our humility or arrogance. When we are humble, we will be able to receive God's greatest strength, his wisdom, to guide our actions. From our ego, we will want to wield his might for the destruction of others.

When Nicolaus Copernicus came up with the new concept of heliocentrism, sun-centered theory, and shared it, we stopped thinking that we were at the center of the universe. Instead, we became more humbled as we realized and appreciated the size and beauty of the universe. We came to accept how small we were, and we began to ask better questions. We started getting better answers regarding our place in the universe. Our humility regarding our place in the universe opened our minds to ask better questions. Discovering and then accepting that we are not at the center of the universe became our humble blessing.

THE DELICIOUSLY CHEESY HAPPINESS EQUATION

A calling for a purpose

> *"Good ideas are always crazy until they're not."*
> — ELON MUSK

In "Genesis 6:14–16," God gave Noah instructions for building an ark to save his family and a pair of all the world's animal species. Why would someone build a giant wooden boat in the middle of nowhere, intending to house a pair of all the animal species in the world as Noah did at the calling of God? *What if* we sacrificed all that time, energy, and resources, and it did not rain? We would be the laughingstock of everyone, including our family members. Others would consider that we are delusional or insane, and we could die from the shame of lack of rain alone.

The tale of Noah's Ark is similar to another story from the ancient Sumerian tale, *The Epic of Gilgamesh* (2000 BCE). The name of the character from Gilgamesh is Utnapishtim. In the story of Gilgamesh, Utnapishtim also built a large wooden boat and saved a pair of all the animals on Earth. For completing his task, Utnapishtim received immortality, and Noah was to multiply to fill the earth and have dominion over the animals. Thus, if Utnapishtim is Noah, his immortality lives in our spiritual teachings, myths, and legends.

Noah built a large wooden boat in the middle of the forest against social norms, authorities, and his family's wishes. When we try to understand why he did what he did, it leads to the answer that it is crazy because it does not make any sense. It is crazy to build a large wooden ark in the middle of the wilderness. That is why he had to do it. He had to build it because it was a calling from above to service life. Noah defied those in authority, common reason and logic, and his family's wishes in the calling to service life. He constructed something that does not make sense or conform to social norms. Others had never seen the idea before. He built it in the forest because new creative ideas are still wild and free. The social norm understandings have not yet accepted it as an everyday idea. Once upon a time, the

WISDOM

automobile, the airplane, the personal computer, and the cellular phone were wild, new ideas built out in the forest wilderness in defiance of social norms and authorities, against families' wishes. They all have become vehicles to service life.

When we receive a calling to service life for a purpose, we must follow it. We must execute it to the best of our ability to complete, no matter what obstacles are in the way or what anyone says. If it means we build something as crazy as a huge wooden boat out in the middle of the woods against everyone's wishes, we must do it because it is our calling to serve life.

The freeing of a people

> "It always seems impossible until it is done."
> — NELSON MANDELA

In the "Book of Exodus" from the Old Testament, Moses led his people out of Egypt, and they came to the banks of the Red Sea. Through God's will, the Red Sea parted, and they walked to the safety of the other side. While Moses was in exile, God came to him in the form of a burning bush and asked him to go back to Egypt to free God's people from bondage and slavery. Moses returned from exile and went to Egypt, and he eventually was able to free his people. They left Egypt and headed east toward the shore of the Red Sea. The pharaoh then changed his mind and, with his army, pursued Moses and his people. When the pharaoh's army approached, and it appeared all would be lost, the Red Sea parted. Thus, allowing Moses and his people to make their way across to freedom and safety.

There was a television episode on the explanation of the physical parting of the Red Sea. One of the narrators stated that perhaps it was meant to say the sea of reeds. Thus, it would be a shallow sea. There would be enough water movement in a wind storm to allow Moses and his people to pass through. The narrator was working out a physical explanation for the impossible. As universal physical laws apply to everything in our

THE DELICIOUSLY CHEESY HAPPINESS EQUATION

universe, the Red Sea's physical parting can only happen if it passes the scientific method. Thus, we should not look for evidence in the physical world. Our evidence is in a transformation for a new spiritual direction for a people. Like many other great stories from our past, the story of the parting of the Red Sea is not literal but a moral lesson for our overcoming the impossible to reach our new freedom in understanding.

The Red Sea parting is the victory over apartheid led by Nelson Mandela, and it is many other stories of freedoms achieved against a once insurmountable obstacle. It is our story of coming closer together for equality, led by the Reverend Martin Luther King Jr. through his nonviolence and disobedience movement. It is freeing a spiritually oppressed people from Pope Leo X and the Holy Roman Emperor Charles V, led by Martin Luther. His courage freed others to a new spiritual understanding. With his *Ninety-five Theses*, he challenged the actions and authority of the Roman Catholic Church. Martin Luther also translated the Bible into German vernacular for the common people, and the people became free to receive the teachings directly. It is also the story of Copernicus freeing our minds to better understand our place in the universe through his sun-centered theory. Thus, Moses and the Red Sea is a story of freeing people against oppression or outdated thinking that stands as an obstacle like the Red Sea.

The parting of the Red Sea took place in divine intervention to the hearts, making the impossible a reality. The once closed hearts and minds parted and opened a safe passage for those suffering from oppression to reach new freedom. The obstacle can be physical, emotional, mental, or spiritual. The hearts and minds of the people crossed over to a new and better understanding by splitting open a once impenetrable obstacle.

WISDOM

The Freeing of a People

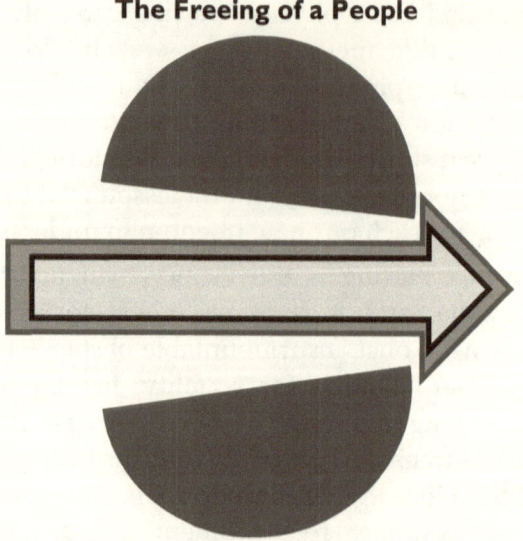

The freeing of a people can be external physical freedom, internal freedom, or both. The parting of the Red Sea is also a personal journey of freeing ourselves from the confusion of our minds and hearts. Once our internal obstacles clear, we will achieve new internal freedom and inner strength.

LOVE

"Love is not a mere impulse, it must contain truth, which is law."
— RABINDRANATH TAGORE

Deception

Our deception creates a hidden monster that eats away at our purity. The Minotaur, from ancient Greek mythology, was born out of deceit to the gods. King Minos was supposed to sacrifice the Cretan Bull to Poseidon, the god of the sea. Instead, he kept the prized bull for himself and offered a lesser bull. Because King

THE DELICIOUSLY CHEESY HAPPINESS EQUATION

Minos loved the bull so much that he would deceive the god of the sea, Poseidon deemed that his woman, Queen Pasiphae, should love the bull too. As a result, the queen became captivated by the bull and fell in love with it. She eventually gave birth to a child that was half human and half bull. Because the child belonged to the queen, King Minos didn't have the heart to kill it. Instead, he hid it underground in a labyrinth, feasting on Athenian virgin sacrifices until Theseus of Athens killed it, thus preventing Athens from sending future youthful sacrifices.

The Minotaur is a creature born of deceit and lies. As such, it lives in a maze of darkness. It hungers for youthful virgin sacrifices because deceptions destroy the purity of our future. Athens sends their youth every seven years for sacrifices to the Minotaur. Our lies and deceits will give birth to a monster buried deep in a dark labyrinth of mystery. The monster will eat away at our innocence, purity, and future until someone courageous enough goes into the darkness of the labyrinth and destroys it.

The Happiness Equation of love

> "The minute I heard my first love story, I started looking for you, not knowing how blind that was. Lovers don't finally meet somewhere. They're each other all along."
> — RUMI

Our loneliness writes a story in our minds and hearts, and then we try to fit the outside chance meeting into it, telling ourselves it is a natural fit. Then, later on, when the outside no longer wants to fit into our inner story, we have heartbreaks, pain, and suffering. We forget that love is always about giving from within. When we set out to love someone, make sure it is for their happiness and not just so that it fulfills our story. If we love someone, then our love should be for their happiness. When we come into their lives, we hope to bring happiness to share with them. We do that by giving our best to make their situation better than before. Rumi's poem below demonstrates the simple reason for love:

WISDOM

One went to the door of the Beloved and knocked.
A voice asked: "Who is there?" He answered: "It is I."
The voice said: "There is no room here for me and thee."
The door was shut.
After a year of solitude and deprivation, this man
returned to the door of the Beloved.
He knocked.
A voice from within asked: "Who is there?"
The man said: "It is Thou."
The door was opened for him.

If we knock on love's door for ourselves, the door will not open. When we understand and apply the Happiness Equation of giving, and we knock on love's door for their happiness, the door to their heart will open. Our successful social relationships, including business or casual, are out of love for others and their importance. When we love, make sure it is for their happiness. We provide a positive H of happiness into their world when we love. To win in love and life, we have to lose and go into our journey for their happiness.

WEALTH

The wealth of wisdom will help us to do the nearly impossible. It will help us to do the most difficult thing in the world, what we should do. The right thing to do becomes incredibly difficult because our confused hearts cannot see and understand our actions' clear balance. We just got here not long ago, but we think the world is for us, not knowing our lives are for others' happiness. We woke up from the void, and our confusion overwhelmed our hearts. Thus, the actions we take in our lives are different from the actions that we should take. We do things according to our desires, fears, ego, and environmental conditioning. Our actions reflect our internal confusion, and they do not match our reason and logic of the balance in nature. They

THE DELICIOUSLY CHEESY HAPPINESS EQUATION

do not match the timeless patterns of wisdom. If we cannot do the things we should do, we cannot do anything. The internal forces inside simply pull us along the journey of life until it ends.

The things we should do are extremely difficult because our hearts' perceptions cannot see clearly. Our hearts do not understand the importance of our required tasks, and they become nearly impossible to do. The internal forces create emotions that do not match reason and logic, and our emotions drive our actions. When our emotional energies do not match what we should be doing, we make wrong choices and take incorrect actions. Our choices and actions do not agree with common sense and logic, leading to suffering.

Reason and Logic vs. Emotions

Reason and Logic
Emotions

Our emotional energy, driven by our confusion, does not match our reason and logic. Therefore, we are doing something other than what we should be doing.

When our internal energy balances with our reason and logic, what we do and what we should do are the same. As a result, we make the correct choices and take better actions—the things we should do become easy for us to do because we have refocused our energy. We are applying wisdom in our actions, and it leads to balance and happiness. When we raise the inside to merge our minds and hearts, we free our drive to match our reason and logic. Thus, our actions become what we should do, and doing what we should do leads to happiness.

WISDOM

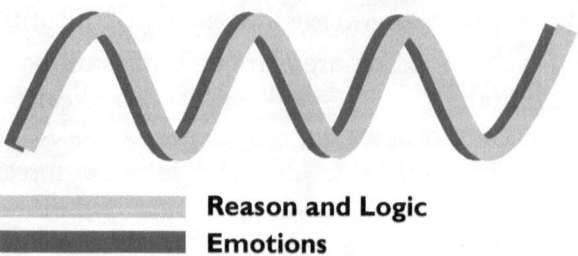

The emotional energy in our actions matches our reason and logic. We are doing what we should be doing. Thus, wisdom merges our hearts and minds.

Wisdom

> "God, grant me the serenity to accept the things I cannot change, courage to change the things I can, and wisdom to know the difference."
> — SERENITY PRAYER

What we cannot change is our reality outside. The outside elements will be what they are. What we can change are our expectations inside. When we can change our expectations, we can balance our Happiness Equation. Thus for clarity and strength to make changes, we must ask for wisdom to know the difference.

When Solomon became king, God came to him in a dream and said he would grant Solomon anything he wished. King Solomon asked for wisdom and knowledge to guide his people. God then said to Solomon that because he asked for wisdom and knowledge to guide his people and did not ask for gold, a long life, or the destruction of his enemies, God would give him wisdom and knowledge because he asked. But God said he would also give Solomon wealth, possessions, and honor. Like

THE DELICIOUSLY CHEESY HAPPINESS EQUATION

Arjuna, Solomon chose wisdom for his strength over might and power.

There is a story of King Solomon's wisdom to help resolve a matter involving two women fighting over a baby. One of the women had rolled over her baby and suffocated it in the middle of the night. She then switched it with the other live baby in the room. The next day, they each claimed that the dead infant was the other's, and the one still alive was hers. The case eventually made its way before King Solomon. Since both mothers were claiming the baby to be hers, King Solomon asked for a sword so that he could cut the baby in half and give it to both mothers. One of the women said, *"Yes, let's go ahead and divide up the baby."* The other mother said, *"No, let her have the baby. She's the mother."* So King Solomon gave the baby to the mother who chose life for the child because he knew only the birth mother would want life for her child. He tested the two women's emotions and actions with his wisdom because he knew that their emotions would drive their actions to reveal themselves. We cannot see into people's hearts, and, thus, we cannot depend on what they say, but we can get a glimpse into the color and strength of their hearts through their actions. Their words may deceive us, but their actions give themselves away.

We can see the world more clearly by asking for wisdom. Wisdom will give us the strength of kindness and compassion to make better decisions. We will be more considerate and think of others' happiness and our own. We will make better decisions for everyone, and they will make better decisions for us as well. The suffering in our lives comes from our internal confusion due to the forces within. Wisdom will help neutralize these forces by giving us greater clarity in understanding for better energies of the heart. We will have clear emotional energies to make logical choices. Our better choices lead to happiness. Wisdom is more valuable than gold because wisdom comes with everything else, including happiness and gold. King Solomon is the wisest king in the Bible and one of the richest.

Our human technological advancements come from our better understanding of nature's physical laws. Our human social

WISDOM

traditions come from our understanding of universal laws of the hearts. All the different traditions in the world contained wisdom for peace, confidence, success, and happiness. By practicing traditions, we learn and apply wisdom to guide our lives. We are applying our understanding of universal laws.

Traditions

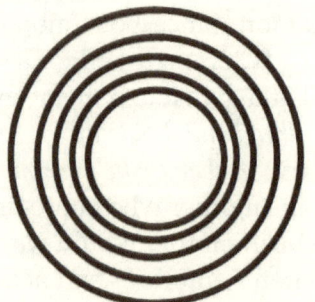

Traditions
Wisdom
Laws of the Hearts
Laws of Nature
Laws of Universe

Our tens of thousands of year-old traditions for happiness are from wisdom derived from universal laws.

Our happiness

> "Give a man a fish and you feed him for a day; teach a man to fish and you feed him for a lifetime."
> — MAIMONIDES

Wisdom helps to guide us for our better choices and actions. When we have wisdom inside, our emotional energy balances with our reason and logic. Thus, happiness and strength live inside our hearts. No amount of material wealth will complete our life's journey. Most of us will squander unearned wealth in disempowering ways for our ego's self-importance, pleasure, or out of boredom. Our wisdom is the greatest treasure that we can ask to receive because it allows us to see and apply the great laws of the hearts. Wisdom raises the inside of our being to be happy and rich in character and strength for our entire life. We will have the information and energy to take actions that make sense because our emotions will match our reason and logic. Our inner strength will allow us to rise to meet the challenges outside.

Wisdom will free us of our internal confusion to give us inner peace, happiness, and balance. There is no longer confusion inside to block our perception, and we can see the beauty in the world. Once our hearts can see with clarity, we are free from the inside. Our internal wealth of wisdom does not run out like accumulated material wealth. Like Solomon and Arjuna, we have to ask for wisdom, and the universe will grant our wish. If we ask for wisdom for our inner strength, our world becomes more beautiful.

SUMMATION OF WISDOM

The forces of our social universe

Our desires, fears, egos, environmental conditioning, and clarity are the most powerful forces in our social universe. Whether we are aware of it, they drive everything we do. Their energies become us, and we do not even know it. These forces inside can drive us to take actions that disagree with our clear understanding and common sense. If we witness others taking the same actions, we would disagree and judge their actions. These internal forces have been here before we were humans, and they will be here long after we are humans. Their use, creation, and evolution came from nature and the universe because they are prerequisites for life. These forces are in the hearts of all living beings at different spectrums. Their existence within serves us but simultaneously clouds our minds and hearts to create emotional confusion and unhappiness. Thus, we serve the internal forces most of the time, and our confusion inside goes into the world.

WISDOM

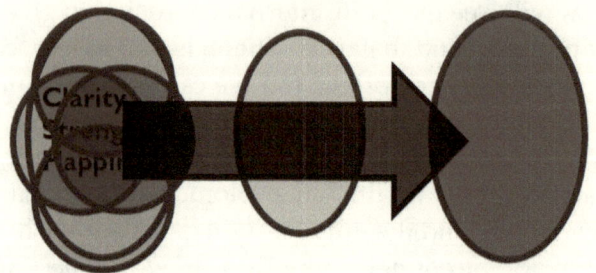

Our Internal Confusion into the World

Our desires, fears, ego's self-importance, and environmental conditioning create confusion that goes into the world.

The internal forces initially help us, but they become our invisible, subconscious limitations. The forces are so strong on the inside that they create blindness in our hearts' perceptions and constrain our minds. However, once we accept the invisible limitations, we can work to remove them. Our minds and hearts grow as we accept better information and energy from those that came before and newly discovered patterns in nature. If we conduct information and energy from better sources, we can free ourselves from our internal confusion and limitations to reach clarity.

When we have a clear understanding, we will have wisdom and a clear perception of the world. Where once our desires, fears, ego, and environmental conditioning cloud our perceptions and actions, our clarity in thinking becomes an even stronger force. Our clarity neutralizes our internal confusion and allows us to see through to the beauty in the world. Our clear perception and understanding bring forth our better actions.

Our clarity

We can raise our clarity of information and heart's strength with our mind's awareness. We can take on difficult actions that make sense for our journey ahead. From a clear understanding,

THE DELICIOUSLY CHEESY HAPPINESS EQUATION

we can balance desire with a purpose for others, fear with courage, ego with humility, and environmental conditioning by conducting clear information and strong energy. Our freedom is the freedom from the unnecessary push and pulls of our internal confusion. With our clarity, we free ourselves of the confusion inside for happiness and strength.

Many thinkers have spent their entire lives reflecting upon and discovering wisdom and happiness. We do not have to rediscover the art of thinking from the beginning. The ancients, gifted with great perceptions, intuitions, and questions, have already spent their lives dwelling on happiness, success, and peace. They have solved the problem of clearing our minds' internal confusion for strengthening our hearts to reach happiness. We can learn from their teachings embedded in our moral stories, songs, arts, poems, traditions, and spiritual teachings. The world may always be changing, but the matters of the heart have remained the same. The ancient teachings for our hearts would apply today as they did a thousand years ago, and they will continue to apply in the future. Our traditions' teachings are to free our inner selves and not attain the power to impose our will on others. In Chapter 16 of the *Tao Te Ching*, Lao Tzu shows us what happens when we free our minds to see our world better. When we clear our minds to free ourselves, we become one with the cosmos.

> *Empty yourself of everything.*
> *Let the mind rest at peace.*
> *The ten thousand things rise and fall while the Self watches their return.*
> *They grow and flourish and then return to the source.*
> *Returning to the source is stillness, which is the way of nature.*
> *The way of nature is unchanging.*
> *Knowing constancy is insight.*
> *Not knowing constancy leads to disaster.*
> *Knowing constancy, the mind is open.*
> *With an open mind, you will be openhearted.*
> *Being openhearted, you will act royally.*

WISDOM

Being royal, you will attain the divine.
Being divine, you will be at one with the Tao.
Being at one with the Tao is eternal.
And though the body dies, the Tao will never pass away.

Our education for our journey's clarity requires learning from others who have great knowledge and experience. For happiness, we must learn from those who came before and found great happiness. For strength, we must learn from those who achieved great strength. Thus, we need to conduct better information and stronger energy in our life's journey. So we will have peace and happiness in our hearts and purpose in our journey. Our hearts' strength will rise to complete our tasks that need to be done, without effort or struggle, because they agree with timeless wisdom. The once difficult tasks become easy to accomplish because they are clear to our minds and hearts. The happiness and beauty in the tasks draw our actions. Our wisdom balances our information and energy with our lives' journey. Thus, we are happy, our actions match our reason and logic, and we do what we should do.

Our Happiness Goes into the World

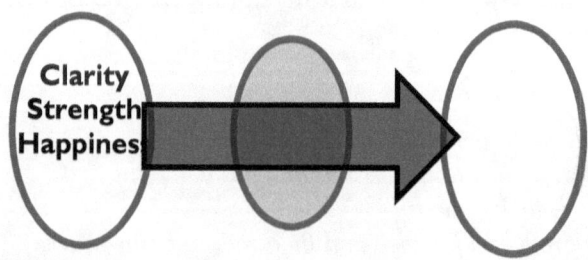

Once we clear up confusion, our inner clarity, strength, and happiness will go into the world.

Our internal confusion clears through our minds' clarity, hearts' strength, and spiritual balance. Our clarity gives us happiness and strength for purpose and destiny on our journey to the unlimited stars.

THE DELICIOUSLY CHEESY HAPPINESS EQUATION

"Shine like the whole universe is yours."
— RUMI

CHAPTER FIVE
The Stars

Journey

"Don't you know it yet, it is your light that
lights the world."

— RUMI

THE STARS

OUR EXCITING AND AMAZING JOURNEY TO THE STARS

"An Old Pond"

Furu ike ya	Into the ancient pond
kawazu tobikomu	A frog jumps
mizu no oto	Water's sound!

— MATSUO BASHO   — TRANSLATED BY
                                                        D.T. SUZUKI

Our journey awaits

"The two most important days in your life are the day you are born and the day you find out why."

— MARK TWAIN

In a Cartoon Network's *Samurai Jack* episode, Jack reached a time portal that would take him back into the past to defeat the evil Aku. The Guardian of the portal said that he had been waiting for eons for *The One* to come. He defeated all opponents, big, small, aliens, and robots in that time. The Guardian then told Jack that he was not the one to be allowed to use the time portal. Jack told the Guardian that his purpose was for a noble cause, but the Guardian still refused Jack access to the time portal. Finally, Jack challenged the Guardian for access to the time portal. The Guardian bested Samurai Jack and was on the verge of finishing him off when the portal flashed a message. The Guardian stopped, and then he signaled a flying dragon to carry Samurai Jack off to safety. The Guardian said, *"You can't use it yet, Samurai Jack."* A picture of an older and more tested Samurai Jack flashed

THE DELICIOUSLY CHEESY HAPPINESS EQUATION

within the portal.[1] Because the current strength of Samurai Jack, his reality R, is less than the strength and expectation E(R) of the Guardian, he could not commence his journey into the past yet. He could not commence his journey to the stars.

Our failures are nothing but messages that say we are not ready for our journey yet. We have further work to do to raise our inner strength. We can only commence on our exciting and amazing journey once we are ready on the inside. Our portal to our journey will then open for us.

Beyond our desires, fears, ego's self-importance, environmental conditioning, and senses of pleasure and pain, there waits an exciting and amazing journey to the stars. The internal forces cloud our perceptions and prevent our ability to see our journey. Once we apply wisdom and clear up the internal confusion, our clear perception allows us to see our beautiful world and awaiting journey.

> "Happiness is the secret to all beauty. There is no beauty without happiness."
> — CHRISTIAN DIOR

We live in one of the most beautiful places in the entire universe. But without a clear perception, we will only see our internal confusion and keep asking what is in it for us. We will only see the unfairness of it all when we do not attain our desires. Our beautiful Mother Earth loved and nurtured our being for countless eons through countless lifeforms and evolutionary changes. When we clear our perceptions, we will see our beautiful world and commence our exciting and amazing journey to the stars.

If we must sail across the ocean, we must build a ship and not do it in a canoe. To arrive at the commencing of our journey requires better thinking for clear perception and heart's strength. But, first, we must raise and synchronize our information and energy to our journey's challenges. For our journey to the stars, we must first raise the inside. And, just like a samurai warrior,

THE STARS

our lives are in the service of others. If we must go into the oceans of the stars, we cannot do so with our current information, energy, and a biological vehicle designed by evolution for a small pond.

TO THE STARS

> *"Oh, the places you will go."*
> — DR. SEUSS

We stand at the edge of a great leap in space, time, intelligence, love, and purpose for stewardship of our space-time. For the first time in our history, we stand at the edge of infinity. Our entire species is awakening from the void. We will journey to Mars and then onto the stars. It is not a matter of if we are going but when. In the future, the cities of Mars will be more beautiful, complex, and high-tech than the cities of Earth ever were. So will also be the Oort Cloud cities that stretch halfway to the nearest star, the interstellar spaceship cities that give our permanent home mobility and freedom, and the Dyson sphere cities of the sun that capture more life-giving energy than ever before. The strength and wisdom of our distant descendants, gained through their sufferings and struggles of the journey into the new frontiers, will build fantastic cities for the accommodation of life. The harsh environments will be challenging for our descendants, but their suffering will become their strength for future great engineering achievements. It is not if we will go, but when or how we will go into the rest of the solar system and the stars. A child who is already born will build an ark for us to go to Mars. One day in the future, a child will be born and build an ark for the rest of the solar system and the stars. Once this child builds the ark for us to go to the stars, he or she will live forever like Noah.

Due to our physiology's balance with our planet, the greatest challenge may not be an ark capable of taking our body, but an

THE DELICIOUSLY CHEESY HAPPINESS EQUATION

ark capable of accommodating our internal balance required by our physical body. Thus, our ark into space will have to accommodate the microorganisms we depend on for survival, for we cannot live without them. However, the components of our being could be even more complicated than just biology alone.

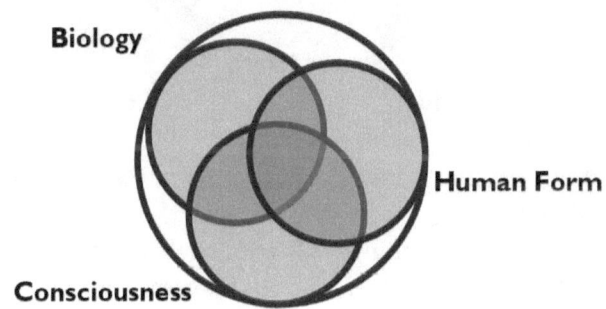

Our human being's biological development evolved with our Earth's development. What if our consciousness also evolved with the Earth's development?

We see that our physical body gets its materials from our planet because it uses recycled atoms and molecules repeatedly to create new beings. *What if* it is also true of our conscious energy? *What if* our consciousness is not from an alternate spiritual plane of existence or another dimension that crosses the physical plane? It is from here and has been developing and growing alongside the physical beings on our planet. Our consciousness is here, and the field evolved together with our biology. That would make our going to the stars more complicated than we thought because we will have to make accommodations for the field of consciousness from Earth. Patterns in nature develop together and depend on each other to complete each cycle. According to fractal geometry, patterns in nature mimic each other on different scales and from one system to another.

THE STARS

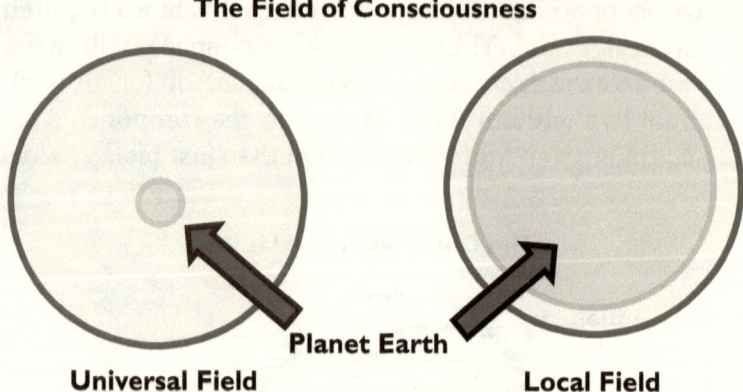

If our consciousness energy field is from Earth, and like the body, we may need the field from Earth to form new consciousness for new beings. Our journey to the stars will be more complicated than we anticipated. We cannot simply move to another planet. Like the biology that makes up our physical body, the consciousness energy field within us will not exist on that new planet because our source of consciousness is here on Earth. Our consciousness energy field could have been developing and evolving with our physical bodies since life began on our planet. To move to another planet in the stars, we will have to accommodate our bodies, the microbes inside, and our consciousness energy field. That would make it more complicatedly interesting than simply having to accommodate our biology alone.

The importance of being explorers

> "We are, by nature, explorers."
> — STEPHEN HAWKING

An article titled "People Who Use Firefox or Chrome Are Better Employees," published in *The Atlantic,* states that people who use Google Chrome and Mozilla Firefox are more productive and happier than Safari and Microsoft Internet

THE DELICIOUSLY CHEESY HAPPINESS EQUATION

Explorer users. The reason is not in the applications themselves but in the spirit of the user's desire to explore and grow. Happiness is a journey of growth. Safari and Internet Explorer are standard for Apple and Windows software. To use Google Chrome or Firefox, we have to go out of our way to download them and learn something new regarding the applications. The explorer's emotional energy to go out of the way to discover something new is responsible for happiness and productivity.[2] Thus, we must explore beyond our beginning and comfort zone to reach happiness. Instead of just doing something new each year, we can discover or take on a different thought each year and be an explorer on the inside and outside.

The fractal pattern of our human journey

> "Only those who will risk going too far can possibly find out how one can go."
> — T.S. ELIOT

In our early childhood beginnings, we use more of our subconscious mind for decision-making. Without it, we would not have survived to reach the development of our conscious mind. The limbic system is in the more ancient part of our brain. As we mature and grow, we still use the limbic system, but we come to use more of the cerebral cortex, which is the newer addition to our human brain. The cerebral cortex gives us the ability to think and visualize. As a person matures, we use more of our cerebral cortex. That is also true of our human species. We will evolve to use more and more of our cerebral cortex. The pattern is the same in one human being as it is in our human species.

For our exciting and amazing journey into the stars, we will have to leave our planet behind, one day our solar system, then one day our galaxy, then the Virgo Supercluster, and then one day in the distant future, our universe.

THE STARS

A long time ago, our great ancestors left the comfort of the forests and trees, and they began to explore other possibilities and ways of life. They even crossed entire oceans. Their bodies and minds changed to accommodate their new journey. That is the pattern for our growth from a long time ago, and it is also our pattern in the distant future. We are to leave the comfort and ease of familiar surroundings and set out into the unknown with our strength of dare, common sense, curiosity, and courage. The pattern in the small and the pattern in the large are the same across space and time.

Those who do not leave our planet will enjoy the comfort and beauty of our beautiful Earth for all their lives, their children's lives, and their children's children. They will dwell in the beauty and comfort of our beautiful home here on Earth forever as human beings until a distant future when changes made by nature, the universe, or others make our original planet inhospitable for human life.

> *"What is to give light must endure burning."*
> — VIKTOR FRANKL

Those who leave our planet will set out for an exciting and amazing journey to the stars in the different dimensions of space, time, information, energy, and spiritual balance. The journey to go out there will require tremendous internal growth inside. Those who leave the planet will struggle due to having to adjust to different, limited, and challenging environments. We will suffer in all sorts of unimaginable ways. Yet, in our suffering, we will grow exponentially. As our hearts and our genetic materials rise to the challenges of our unique new environments, we will transcend into becoming other beings. Our trials and suffering will lead to our becoming a new species in the universe that can handle the unique new environments. Through challenges will emerge our journey of evolutionary growth. We will have strength created by the suffering of our journey to propel us further forward. Our being uncomfortable will lead to our internal growth across space and time. We will have become a

THE DELICIOUSLY CHEESY HAPPINESS EQUATION

species that will rise to the unique challenges of our environments.

Comfort, Discomfort, Limits, and Fear

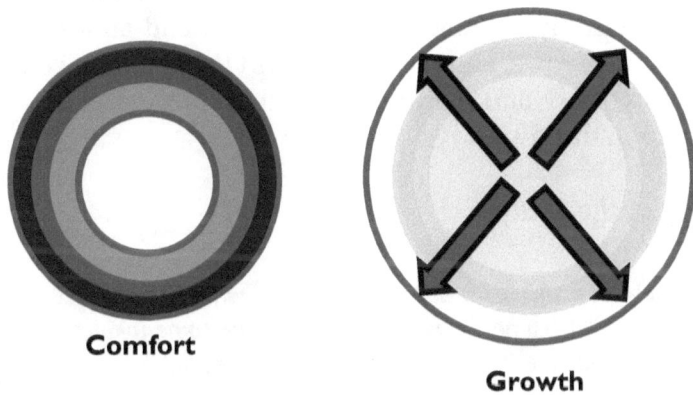

Comfort **Growth**

There will be those who choose to stay in comfort. Those who choose to go into the stars will expand beyond their discomfort, limits, and fear.

Our need to become explorers is in our one individual journey and also in our human journey. The ancient Taiwanese, Hawaiians, Indonesians, and Australians needed nothing but a simple raft and human courage to journey into an unknown ocean. So with an engineered raft of today, our species will sail into an unknown ocean of space. We can choose to stay in comfort and watch others grow or seek clarity to strengthen our hearts for a journey into exciting undiscovered space-times.

If our pasts indicate our future, there will be some who will stay behind on Earth, and there will be many who will take to the solar system and then the stars. We are waiting for the child whose calling and purpose are to build us an ark to the stars. To go to the stars, we will not be like the human explorers of our past that sailed across uncharted oceans hundreds or thousands of years ago, but we will be like the fish that came onto dry land over 350 million years ago. Our physiology will have to morph to the new environments out there. Mars is the beach for which humans will step out of Earth, and it is there that we will transform and our strength will grow.

The age of animal survival of the fittest will end for us, and we will come to the age of thinking beings. It is the next chapter of our human journey. Our self ascends Maslow's hierarchy of needs, and our entire human species will ascend as well. As a human learns, grows, and matures, so will the emotional energy of humanity grow and mature. The pattern in the small is also the pattern in the large.

One day in the future

> *"Man does not simply exist but always decides what his existence will be, what he will become the next moment. By the same token, every human being has the freedom to change at any instant."*
> — VIKTOR FRANKL

As we learn to share our resources, grow together, and focus on our journey to the stars, we will adapt to the different natural and unique environments out there. If nature can create it, we can learn to assimilate it and make it better. We will grow to include synthetics in the body and mind because doing so will allow us to live longer, think faster, and become physically stronger and more durable. We can better adapt to the many different environments in the universe. As the environment out there demands, we will branch out to become new species. We haven't evolved for hundreds of thousands of years because our natural environment has not demanded it yet from our hearts, minds, and genes. Going into the vastness of space will expose us to new and different challenging environments. Our biology will grow to become less like that of here on Earth.

One day in the distant future, to see a normal human being the way we are now will be like looking back to our great ancestors of hundreds of thousands or millions of years ago in East Africa. Such is the flow of nature and the universe because the patterns repeat themselves over and over again.

THE DELICIOUSLY CHEESY HAPPINESS EQUATION

One day in the future, we will create artificial gravity and live in space cities or on a large asteroid in a setting constructed to support life. We will no longer truly need our home planet anymore. Our need for growth will turn us into explorers, and we will continue to look at what is beyond. Our great descendants will stand on their fathers' accomplishments and look to the future to explore further growth to understand better ourselves, our universe, and our place in it. We will forever continue to learn and grow. There will never come a time when growth, better expectations for tomorrow, love, or compassion for others no longer serve the purpose of our lives. We achieve happiness by understanding and accepting our role in each unique space-time of our lives. Each new generation has exciting opportunities and challenges, especially those with clarity in understanding and heart strength. They have a unique and amazing opportunity to provide a better world for others. Their happiness lies in their clarity of understanding and accepting the unique challenges of their generation, space, and time.

One day in the distant future, a child who is yet to be born will find a way to bring us in balance with ourselves, all of nature, and the universe. We will truly become one species with one goal: the happiness of everyone.

One day in the future, a child who is yet to be born will find a way to put our consciousness into a synthetically designed body built to last forever with interchangeable parts. The new artificial body will run more efficiently than the current design by nature. Our external self will have immortality, and our life's duration will depend on our inner strength, vision, and daring purpose. Our evolution will take a gigantic leap, and we will be like the fish that came onto dry land and then branched into different species.

One day in the distant future, a being of the universe that has yet to be born or created will find a way for us to connect with every single atom's vibration and energy. We will see and understand the past, present, and future in the vastness of space and time. We will connect with the energy of every photo, proton, neutron, and electron in the universe, and we will be fully

THE STARS

aware of all creation and purpose. We will understand our purpose in each cycle of our growth. We will understand all the laws and processes of the universe and its many systems. However, we would still not yet understand the many other sides of the cycles upon cycles of our existence. We would see and understand the time of our being's growth but not yet see and understand the resting side. We can see life in action, but we cannot see beyond death. We would see our universe, but we would not see into the multiverse.

One day in the distant future, a child who is yet to be born will build a gravity engine, and we will learn to harness the power of black holes and quasars.

One day in the very distant future, a being of our universe yet to be conceived, created, or both will build an ark into another dimension or realm and take us into another universe. Thus, we will become inter-dimensional beings.

One day in the distant future, a being that will be created and or evolved into being will surpass all others before until another distant future when a new being comes along, surpassing it as well. Like prime numbers, evolution has no end as long as we have space, time, curiosity, and purpose. The universe has unlimited space and time, and our hearts' unlimited curiosity will find a purpose in the stars.

FROM THE STARS

In the stars, there potentially exist beings possibly far more technologically advanced than humans. Their understanding of the universe's patterns and traditions is clearer and deeper than ours. If they can travel the vastness of space to get here, they are likely more advanced than us in many dimensions. Technology is just one of the dimensions of their depth. Their understanding of the universal laws is multi-dimensional. Thus, their depth of understanding is physical, mental, emotional, and spiritual.

THE DELICIOUSLY CHEESY HAPPINESS EQUATION

Every time there is a movie about an alien invasion, the aliens always lose. Despite the advanced technology that allows them to travel across vast space to reach Earth, the aliens always lose to the humans. Even when they fight cowboys, the aliens still lose. If aliens have humor as a part of their evolutionary development, they would all be cracking up hysterically upon seeing movies like *Independence Day* (1996 movie) or, especially *Cowboys and Aliens* (2011 movie) that have beamed into space.

Aliens will not invade Earth for our natural resources because they can find all those in the stars. They will have no such desires as a motivation for an invasion. If aliens do come, we will be mature enough to receive them properly as fellow beings of our universe. They will not come here for gold, water, oil, human labor, or food. To fulfill our basic Maslow needs for survival, we will take from others. To fulfill our mid-level love and belonging needs, we will reach out to others to create social bonds. To fulfill our higher self-actualization needs, we will help elevate others. In the higher need for self-actualization, one understands and cherishes the beauty of life and wishes to see life prosper by supporting and empowering others. If or when aliens do come, they will be here for our greatest resource, over a billion years in the making. They will be here for humanity's unique thinking and adaptations, our arts, philosophy, sciences, social and cultural contributions, and all the adaptations of the other species on this planet. They will be here to learn of our adaption to the universe's vibration in this region of space-time. When aliens do come, they will be here when we can communicate with each other on a higher plane of consciousness for everyone's benefit. Thus, we can learn from each other's unique adaptations for the betterment of all beings.

To think that aliens would come here for their basic needs is our fear and imagination getting the best of our thinking and not letting our thinking make us better than our imaginations' fears. As their civilization matured on a universal scale, they would no longer be acting out of desire, fear, ego, or ignorance. They would be acting out the clarity of understanding of higher social laws of the universe. They will not be here to take from us, but they will

THE STARS

come here to ask what we can give or want to contribute to a better future for all life in the universe. They will not be here to harvest our bodies for consumption. They are advanced enough to manufacture their energy source. They will not be here for our natural resources because all that material is out there in the asteroids, moons, comets, and Oort Cloud. They will come here to ask us for humanity's contribution to all living beings' growth in understanding. As an advanced civilization, they would have grown in their minds as well as in their hearts. The strength of their heart will accompany their technological growth. Our internal growth is fractal, and it is also multi-dimensional.

We have a growing awareness of understanding for love of others and balance with our environment. With time to develop advanced technologies to travel the vastness of space, the aliens would have raised their understanding, thinking, and heart strength required to achieve their technological growth and survival. They would have suffered many setbacks and grown beyond them, both in their technology and hearts. They would have achieved the need to raise their awareness of self-actualization. They will not come here for Maslow's hierarchy of basic needs, food, water, or safety. They will come here for the higher needs of belonging, accomplishment, and achieving their full potential as a sentient species of our universe. They will come here to learn from other species' unique adaptation to the universe's vibrations for this region of space. To reach the stars, they would have already achieved internal happiness and balance as a species.

> *"The first and best victory is to conquer self."*
> — PLATO

Before we can go into the stars, we must conquer the stars inside our hearts. The portal to the stars will only open once we have passed our strength test. *What if* it is not a universal race to expand and conquer what is out there, but it is a universal race to expand and conquer what is in here first? *What if* it is a universal race for our internal happiness? Thus, the stars are

THE DELICIOUSLY CHEESY HAPPINESS EQUATION

inside us. We must first journey to the stars inside us; that is how we can shine.

OUR HAPPINESS BEGINS

> *"If there is to be peace in the world, there must be peace in the nations. If there is to be peace in the nations, there must be peace in the cities. If there is to be peace in the cities, there must be peace between neighbors. If there is to be peace between neighbors, there must be peace in the home. If there is to be peace in the home, there must be peace in the heart."*
> — LAO TZU

Happiness brings positive energy to do and a clear mind to do it well. With our happiness, we free ourselves to give our best. Without happiness, we will find an understanding of our purpose elusive. We will be too busy filling the emptiness inside with things from the outside to relieve our suffering temporarily. By understanding and applying the Happiness Equation, we can balance our happiness in many situations. Thus, we will have a permanent flexible solution that adjusts to changes. When there's no longer a hole in our hearts, we can focus our minds and hearts on a logical and purposeful life of happiness and service.

The happiness of Socrates, Siddhartha, and Mother Teresa

> *The Moon Cannot Be Stolen*
> *Ryokan, a Zen master, lived the simplest kind of life in a little hut at the foot of a mountain. One evening a thief visited the hut only to discover there was nothing to steal.*
>
> *Ryokan returned and caught him. "You have come a long way to visit me," he told the prowler, "and you should*

not return empty-handed. Please take my clothes as a gift."

The thief was bewildered. He took the clothes and slunk away.

Ryokan sat naked, watching the moon. "Poor fellow," he mused, "I wish I could have given him this beautiful moon."

The happiest people need almost nothing but a clear understanding giving them inner peace, and they give their best to others all their lives. They give everything away to others and ask how they can give more. Some of the happiest people like Socrates, Siddhartha Gautama, and Mother Teresa have almost nothing material. They only have a clear understanding inside for their happiness and inner strength. Socrates was found guilty of corrupting the minds of the Athenian youths and was sentenced to death. His friend Crito wanted to arrange for his escape, but he refused because it would break the Athenian laws, causing more harm to everyone. Socrates refuses to escape because he is happy to live the life he consciously chose. When Siddhartha Gautama achieved enlightenment, he spent the next forty-five years of his life begging for food and teaching others the ways of happiness. He did so because he found happiness on the path of service that he came to understand. Mother Teresa spent her entire life in the service of the poor. She did so because she was happy to give love and kindness to those who needed it the most.

All these happy individuals found happiness from the inside, and they needed nothing else from the outside to make them happy. They discovered that the meaning of life is to bring happiness to others, and it freed them to pursue a life of service for others. Our happiness is clearing up our internal confusion, so we have happiness inside to share with others.

THE DELICIOUSLY CHEESY HAPPINESS EQUATION

Our greatest discovery

> "Optimism is the faith that leads to achievement. Nothing can be done without hope and confidence."
> — HELLEN KELLER

There is a level of excitement in anticipation when looking to the future. We will experience and see new inventions, discoveries, and adventures unlike before. We feel the excitement of our future Happiness Equation level H2 greater than H1 due to our reality R2 being greater than R1. If we want to live in the future, we already live in the future. If we want to live like a king, we already live better than a king. We live in the inventions, discoveries, adventures, and luxury that ancient pharaohs, emperors, or kings never had. We are already living in the distant futures of ancient pasts. To go further into the future from here is only for further curiosity unless it serves a purpose.

There will come a time when the year 10,000 is here on earth, and the world's people will be counting down the final seconds of its arrival in celebration. There will come a time when this moment is a million years or ten million years in the past. Those times are for the living beings in that space-time. They, too, will wonder in the excitement of their future. Wondering about the future is the nature of our being's curiosity because time flows towards the future. The beauty of each moment is always now. Our time is here and now, and the preparation for our exciting tomorrow is today. It doesn't do us any good to dwell on a future that does not involve us or dream about a past we want to live in because it appears simpler.

We live our best lives in the space and time of our being's conscious awakening. Thus, we want clarity in understanding, hearts' strength, and purposeful lives in our conscious awakening of different environments or life forms. When we fulfill our purpose, we will have happiness and peace. We want to live a life that would contribute to a better today and tomorrow for ourselves and others. We want to achieve clarity in thinking and strength of heart and then use that strength of information and energy to service the world in our space-time for its betterment and beauty.

Our greatest discovery will not be when we discover that intelligent life exists in the universe. The discovery of life out there will satisfy a curiosity that has been there since we began looking at the stars hundreds of thousands of years ago. Once we find life out there, we will wonder how long they have been there or if they will come to destroy us in the future. Our minds will wander on to wonder about other cosmic curiosities, like how we can punch a hole in the fabric of space-time to reach other universes or dimensions. Once we discover other universes or dimensions, we will wonder about the workings of their physical laws. There are endless curiosities of the mind for our growing understanding of our universe and beyond, but they will not be our greatest discoveries. They are curiosities because we have not seen them yet, and we wonder about their possibilities compared to our own.

Our greatest discovery is not out there, but it is always within ourselves to tame our hearts and minds to achieve focus and happiness in each life. Our greatest discovery will come when we can control our emotional energy to drive our mental decisions and actions the way we want them. We will become happy and effective for the duration of our journey in our space-time. When we discover ourselves and who we are, we can find, define, and refine who we want to become. We will have confidence, happiness, and strength for our life's adventures.

> *"We must learn to live together as brothers or perish together as fools."*
> — MARTIN LUTHER KING, JR.

Our greatest discovery will not come from the stars, but it will come from inside our hearts. We will discover how we can overcome our emotional past to gain better clarity and perception of nature's patterns to understand and accept our role as

THE DELICIOUSLY CHEESY HAPPINESS EQUATION

stewards of our planet. Our greatest discovery as a species will come when we conquer ourselves to live in balance with our world. Others' happiness will be our happiness. Thus, we will achieve internal balance and happiness and share our happiness with others. Our future in the stars together depends on the strength of our understanding, love, and kindness for each other.

OUR CLARITY LIGHTS THE WAY

> "The mind is like water. When it's turbulent, it's difficult to see. When it's calm, everything becomes clear."
> — PRASAD MAHES

In *The Edge* (movie 1996), Anthony Hopkins plays a mentally gifted billionaire named Charles Morse, who became lost in the Alaskan wilderness with two other men after their plane crashed. While lost in the wilderness, he said that people do not die of being lost in the woods, but they die of shame. They couldn't believe they allowed themselves to get lost in the woods. They let themselves go out of shame and eventually die, succumbing to the wilderness.[3] The giving up happens first on the inside, and death begins on the inside. The ferociousness of life is a fierce jungle like the Alaskan wilderness. If we do not reach clarity and raise our heart's strength, we will become lost in the jungles of our thoughts and emotions. In shame, we will give up and die on the inside. Our outside will soon follow the death on the inside.

> "Behold, this is my last advice to you. All component things in the world are changeable. They are not lasting. Work hard to gain your own salvation. Do your best."
> — BUDDHA

THE STARS

Due to its constant changes, the outside cannot provide lasting happiness. Our happiness will only come from within our minds' clear perceptions and heart's strength. Thus, we must work on gaining a clear understanding to strengthen our hearts. Our internal clarity and strength inside are not interchangeable but lasting because they are from timeless traditions, wisdom, and nature's patterns.

We live our lives according to the information, energy, and patterns surrounding us. There are unlimited perceptions of the world, and each has its excuse, reason, or logic for existence. We do not have all the answers, and our limited perception creates suffering in our hearts when it does not match reality. When our internal confusion clears up, we perceive our reality more clearly. Our clear inner being knows no conditioned desires to create suffering. Our clear perception sees a universe that makes sense. Thus, when we have clarity, we have happiness. The clearer our information and the stronger our energy, the clearer our perceptions become. We'll make decisions and take better actions that agree with nature's processes and systems. Nature presents the best opportunity to learn for our journey. Its depth of understanding goes to the beginning of life on our planet because it has learned to live in balance with the universe's vibrations.

A pattern in nature

Toward the end of his life, the Buddha gathered his disciples near a lake. Once everyone was there, he reached into the water and pulled out a lotus flower with its roots dripping with water and mud. He showed it to his disciples. Many of them were confused by the demonstration. One disciple, Mahakasyapa, understood at once and began to smile in contentment. The demonstration illustrates that our journey is like that of the lotus flower. Our beginning is in the mud, gradually rising through the murky water, eventually into the open air, and then basking in the open sun to blossom in beauty for others. From the dark depths of our confusion, we can rise to reach clarity, strength,

THE DELICIOUSLY CHEESY HAPPINESS EQUATION

and beauty for others. The Flower Sermon also demonstrates that we are to learn from nature's deep traditions and patterns.

Do you know where you are going?

> *"First say to yourself what you would be, and then do what you have to do."*
> — EPICTETUS

Our attachments to the past make it appear as if something is ending, and our preparation for our future can bring changes to make our future more exciting. When we paint a room or cook in a busy kitchen, our preparation is the key to making everything go smoothly. Without proper preparation in painting, we would get unwanted paint everywhere. An average night in the kitchen can become hard to manage without prepping. Thus, a smooth journey requires not only our doing but also our thinking and preparation. If we do not add thinking to our doing, the draw of pleasure will hijack our hearts to do less or do what is only pleasurable. Also, to do only makes us a constant laborer, and to think only makes us a constant dreamer. Thus, we have to do and think, then learn from it, and do and think again better. We need a balance of doing and thinking because our thinking is the preparation for our doing. Life is very simple. When we think and do, we find success in our endeavors. When we think and do for others' benefit, we achieve the best form of success; happiness for everyone.

THE STARS

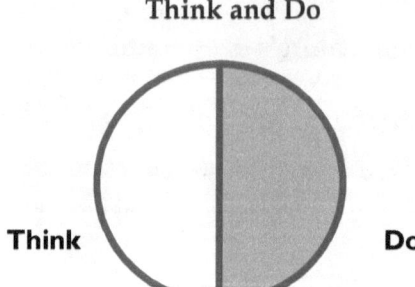

Our thinking and doing complete is the fusion of information and energy. Information guides and energy drives.

Our reflections are preparations. It is our thinking before our doing. Without our reflections to tame our hearts and guide our minds, our internal confusion will cloud our hearts and minds, and everything will be a mess. If we do not prepare and paint a clear journey inside, it will not exist outside. We need a blueprint for designing the emotional journey that drives us. Our exciting adventure becomes one of doing based on our clear thoughts and reflections. If we do not dream of and prepare a better world and a better us, they will not come into existence. If we don't dream of a better me, it will not come into being in this world. When we reflect on who we are and what we want to be, our actions follow our clear thinking. Our lives become easy to manage when we reflect and ask better questions first before doing. We will discover the ways of happiness, who we are, and who we want to become. We will expand our perception.

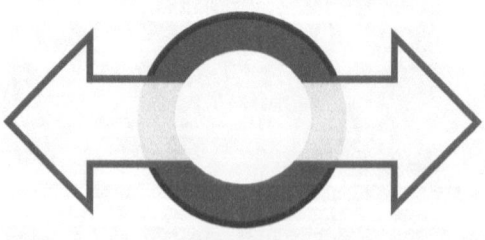

THE DELICIOUSLY CHEESY HAPPINESS EQUATION

> *When we reflect on our information and energy, we expand our understanding inside beyond its small, confined beginning.*

The one person we should meet

> "If tomorrow brings new hope, I hope it brings you."
> — PERRY POETRY

Many of us dream of finding that special someone to bring magical happiness into our lives. Perhaps, we spontaneously meet them at an art festival. Thus, we will know they have a depth of inner beauty and sophistication to bring into our lives and share with us. The problem is that they are also looking for a special someone to bring magical happiness into their lives. Are we that person they are looking for? Or will both of us come into the relationship with mismatched expectations that will grow to become unhappiness and suffering later on when we take off our smiley-painted emotional masks? Or will we paint strength on the inside to give our best for their hope, anticipation, expectation, and happiness? Will we take Gandhi's advice and become the change we wish to see in the world. We must meet someone else first before meeting the special person from our hopes and dreams.

> "Dear God, Why can't I have a decent guy who is fun and wants to have fun with me. Who is sweet and sexy. Who loves me for me. Who will dance with me and sing for me — without having asked. Who will watch the stars with me in his arm and I would want to be there too. A man who is warm, sexy, kind, fun, loving, and sweet."
> — JULY 15, 2007, A FRIEND'S LETTER TO GOD

The above is a friend's letter to God asking for someone to come into her life to bring her magical happiness. She was asking for someone from the outside. Unfortunately, she never received

THE STARS

what she asked for because the many guys God sent her were not up to her expectations.

> *"Go find yourself first so you can find me."*
> — RUMI

We are looking for someone to come into our lives so that our lives will be complete. Before we can find happiness, there is one person that we should meet first. Nothing on the outside would complete us until we first put it inside. Life's patterns on the outside will be unclear to our hearts until we clarify who we are inside, allowing us to see the beauty outside. The person we should meet first is our best self. To do that, we need to answer the question, *"Who am I?"*

- I am a temporary human form, a conductor of information and energy, within a process of rest and growth among endless cycles and systems.
- I am the amazing and beautiful being within you, locked up in information and energy confusion. Find yourself first, and you will free me for your strength and happiness.
- I am your clarity of understanding of processes and systems across space and time. Find yourself first, and you'll have the wisdom to guide your life's journey.
- I am your strength of heart to conquer your fears and overcome your desires. Find yourself first, and you will have conquered your inner self for happiness and strength.
- I am your compassion and kindness. Find yourself first, and you will have love and friendship all your life.
- I am your endurance to rise to physical and emotional challenges. Find yourself first, and you will have the energy to do everything.
- I am your physically, mentally, emotionally, and spiritually balanced self. Find yourself first, and you will understand who you are every day.

THE DELICIOUSLY CHEESY HAPPINESS EQUATION

- I am your purpose, your peace, and your awaiting destiny. Find yourself first, and you will find an exciting and amazing journey.
- I am your confidence for your entire life's journey, and I am your never-ending happiness. Find yourself first, and you are already there.
- I can do anything, and I will do it in this lifetime. So find yourself first, and I will live inside you.

Better than finding someone out there is finding your best self in here. The clarity of the ways of your journey is inside. Find yourself first, so you will know who you are, and you will complete yourself on the inside to begin your journey on the outside. Love yourself first, and others shall love you. Believe in yourself first, and others will believe in you. When you find yourself first, you will be free from the inside to unleash all your internal beauty into the world. You will share your best self with the world and plant the seeds for a better tomorrow. When you find who you want to become first, you will put the energy of *"I can do anything"* inside. You will see a list of happiness, and you can rise to any challenge. You shall find the best you to receive the person of your hopes and dreams. If tomorrow brings new hope, I must bring a better me.

The smallness of our space-time

> *"You are not a drop in the ocean. You are the entire ocean in a drop."*
> — RUMI

When we look up at the stars, the vastness of space makes us realize the smallness of our being. So likewise, we look at the passage of time and wonder at our smallness in the eternity of time. Our life's journey is a drop of water in an ocean of space and time. However, our information and energy have the potential of the entire ocean in a drop.

THE STARS

When we look up at the universe with our eyes, we only see it through the visible spectrum. The visible spectrum that our eyes can detect is only .0035 percent of the electromagnetic spectrum. If we want to see the universe better, we must look at the universe through the entire electromagnetic spectrum, from gamma rays to radio waves. Thus, we need to expand our perception to see more of the electromagnetic spectrum to understand our universe better. To see better, we enlarged our perception of the universe, and we looked at the cosmos through other spectrums invisible to the human eye like infrared, X-rays, gamma rays, and radio waves.

If we are to understand the world better, we have to view it through other perceptions, or else we could be viewing our world through a very small finite perception. Our minds and hearts would be nearly blind. Our clear understanding of our world requires viewing it through better information and energy. To better understand our world, we need to understand other adaptations of information and energy to the universe's vibrations. We need to expand our clarity of perception. *What if* we learn to think outside the conditioning and requirements of our small space-time? When we absorb other information and energy, our perceptions in our minds and hearts clear up and expand. As a result, we can better understand the processes and systems of our world, allowing us to see better.

In the moment of our lives, we sometimes think our life is all that matters. But life has existed for a billion years through countless evolutionary forms, and it will continue to do so after we are gone. We are born into a small space-time, but we live our lives to butterfly effects of information and energy from other spaces and times. The ongoing forces of change will come from all directions during the duration of our lives. Therefore, we must expand our understanding to include information and energy from other space-times, giving us a better perception of our world. Thus, we can grow and better adapt to the fluctuations and changes from all directions. *What if* we learn to think outside of the conditioning and requirements of a human being? We will

THE DELICIOUSLY CHEESY HAPPINESS EQUATION

grow to become more than we were. We will grow to become how we think, and, thus, we will grow to our potential.

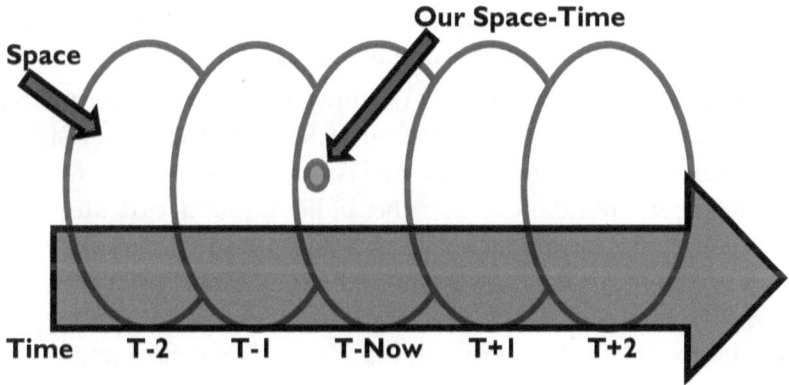

The Smallness of our Space-Time

Our space-time is a drop in an endless ocean of space and time. We live our lives to the information, energy, vibration, and changes from other space-times.

We defeat ourselves from the inside because our information and energy are from a small space-time, becoming our inner strength or weakness. We are at the mercy of our limited information and energy inside. The smallness of our space-time defines us and binds our inner strength to that information and energy — our limited information and energy cloud our life's journey becoming our greatest enemies. Our limiting thoughts and energy defeat us from the inside. Thus, we have to discover and absorb new thoughts to redefine our energy to become better and stronger. We have to accept that we can expand from the smallness of our being into the clarity of our being.

The deception of Ashi

> *"Free your mind, and the rest will follow."*
> — EN VOGUE

THE STARS

In *Samurai Jack*, Ashi is a daughter of Aku and a high priestess that worships and serves Aku. The high priestess nurtured in the heart and trained in skills Ashi and her six sisters to become assassins with only one purpose. Their one given mission is to kill the evil and cruel Samurai Jack. Even at a young age, Ashi was more aware of her surroundings than her sisters. She also shows curiosity and compassion for other lesser beings.

Once they completed their training, they were sent out into the world to find and kill Samurai Jack. One by one, her sisters were killed by Jack. Ashi was the last of her sisters, and even in her defeat and bondage, every fiber of her taunted, ridiculed, and wanted to kill Samurai Jack. His awareness made Jack realize that Ashi is a living person programmed for evil, and *what if* he can show her the truth. Jack saved Ashi's life, time after time again. Finally, one day, she awoke to realize and saw the compassion and beauty in Samurai Jack, and she accepted a new truth.[4]

Ashi's conditioning taught her that Samurai Jack is evil, and her expectation $E(R)$ for Samurai Jack is -9. However, through her time spent battling Samurai Jack, she eventually saw that the reality R for Samurai Jack is a 9. He's not evil at all but very good. He serves life by defending others against the tyranny of Aku. Ashi's two Happiness Equations show her happiness level H, before and after her awakening.

The Deception of Ashi:
Samurai Jack is evil: $R(SJ) = -9$
$R(SJ) = -9,$
Her expectation is $E(R(SJ)) = -9$
$H = R(SJ) - E(R(SJ))$
$H = -9 - -9 = 0$

The Clarity of Ashi:
When she found out that $R(SJ) = 9$,
Her Happiness Equation changed
$R(SJ) = 9$

THE DELICIOUSLY CHEESY HAPPINESS EQUATION

$$E(R(SJ)) = -9$$
$$H = 9 - -9 = +18$$

She became drawn to Samurai Jack's large +H

Evil raised and distorted Ashi's perception so she would destroy good in the world. However, her awareness and compassion allowed her to absorb better information and energy to see the beauty in the world. With the help of Samurai Jack, Ashi eventually changed her internal programming and energy, and she achieved a clear view of the world. She raised her inside and synchronized it with a clear understanding of the patterns around her. Eventually, Ashi became Samurai Jack's greatest accomplice and protector, and she helped him fulfill his destiny. She found a time portal for Jack to go back to defeat Aku in the past. In her search for truth against the deception created by others, Ashi expanded her internal understanding allowing her to learn the truth of her deception. As a result, Ashi found happiness, peace, purpose, strength, and love in her awakening.

The deception of you and me

> "I know that I'm a prisoner to all my father held so dear. I know that I'm a hostage to all his hopes and fears."
> — MIKE AND THE MECHANICS

We are all born into a small region of space-time. The limited information and energy become our strengths and weaknesses. Like Ashi and her sisters, others taught us their emotional energy because they thought it would benefit them. Thus, we were deceived by those that came before. They want us to follow their dreams, information, and energy. Even Siddhartha's father deceived him, hoping that he would follow in his father's footsteps to become a great king. The deception by others conducts positive as well as negative energy. There are two paths before us, a conditioned path or a path of our choice. We have to

THE STARS

free ourselves from the deception of others to become who we want to be.

> *"You gotta kill the person you were born to be in order to become the person you want to be."*
> — WILSON, *ROCKETMAN* (2019 MOVIE)

There is a glass bottle limitation that someone created inside us. We still feel and obey its emotional energy, but we no longer remember its origin and believe it to be us. The glass bottle inside constrains our inner growth. Our fundamental consciousness is not even human, but we learned to be human for survival, just like the squirrel had to become a squirrel to survive. The desires, fears, happiness, and suffering of others become our subconscious programming's deception. The conditioning serves and helps us, but our conditioned behaviors limit our growth and expansion. It defines and limits us to the smallness of our being. Once we become aware of our programming and limitations, we will need to find better information and energy to free ourselves of our invisible limitations. We must undo the environmental conditioning that no longer serves our life's journey. Our education for clarity and heart's strength from a small space-time is incomplete. We will need better information and energy from other space-times.

What we learn through our clear understanding will be stronger than our conditioning. We will override our deception at the subconscious level to achieve clarity and strength to choose our own life's journey. What stops us from freeing ourselves from our deception is the deception itself. Our deception is the only emotional understanding that we have ever known. Thus, our mismatch of expectation and reality creates our suffering, and we blame the outside. We keep asking and forcing the universe to change to correspond to our view instead of changing our information and energy to correspond to the timeless patterns of the universe.

THE DELICIOUSLY CHEESY HAPPINESS EQUATION

What if we are a fish at Lake Phalen? Suppose we are born a fish at Lake Phalen, live our entire life at Lake Phalen, and die a fish at Lake Phalen. We never knew about other lakes, streams, rivers, gulfs, seas, oceans, or land and air. We never knew of the beauty, size, or potential in other dimensions of space or forms of existence. We never knew what else we could be, except our life as a fish at Lake Phalen. Thus, Lake Phalen's geography and a fish's evolutionary physiology constrain our freedom and shallowness of enlightenment.

As humans, the depth of our imagination and our current level of clarity in thinking are the only constraints. *What if* we raise the inside to absorb better information and energy from other space-times? Our biological constraints limit our external growth, but our internal self may have no growth limits when we free ourselves.

Circles of being

> "Why do you stay in prison when the door is so wide open?"
> — RUMI

In the vast ocean of space and time, whether it be ten thousand years from now with advanced technologies, ten thousand years in the past during the Mesolithic age here on earth, a thousand light-years away in an alien civilization, or two million light-years away in another galaxy, we need to attain clarity of understanding for our happiness and hearts' strength. So we can better contribute to the processes and systems of our space-time. Thus, all space and time require our internal clarity and heart strength. Therefore, our first task is to seek clear information and strengthen our hearts so we can live our lives to share happiness.

> "Boil things down to fundamental truths… and then reason up from there."
> — ELON MUSK

THE STARS

To better understand our universe, physicists look to find fundamental understandings of particles and forces. First, they try to find out what makes up our universe and what drives it at the basic level. From there, they can theorize how our universe works. Thus, the materials that make up our bodies have a fundamental level but so do the conscious beings that live in the bodies.

The imprinting of our subconscious mind is a gift of nature for our survival. It helps streamline our emotional energy when we have not learned to use our thinking minds yet. For most of us, our imprinting is so strong that it will define who we are for the rest of our lives. Even when the information and energy have become outdated and useless, we still apply them.

At our current best, our imprinting may work well for a particular place and time, but place, time, information, and energy change. *What if* we could see beyond our human understanding and perception? To adapt to the coming changes, we would have to redefine ourselves to accommodate changes. There are many different levels of understanding for our being. We are beings conditioned for our particular environment, and we are fundamental beings that can transcend the many circles of our being. There is a human physical side and an eternal side to our journey. If we accept ourselves at the fundamental level as a sentient being of the universe, we would be free to explore all the spectrums of our many circles of being. Our true nature is at the fundamental level of the circles of being. We are a life form of our universe with different potentials. Thus, when we boil it down to fundamentals, we are all the same.

THE DELICIOUSLY CHEESY HAPPINESS EQUATION

Circles of Being

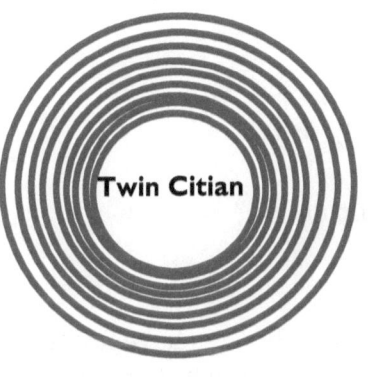

Twin Citian
Minnesotan
Midwesterner
American
Human Being
Being of our Planet
Circle of Male/Female
Being of our Universe
Sentient Being of
   our Universe

Our circles of being have many levels of understanding to transcend. Our awareness, clarity, and heart's strength expand our place in the circles of being, and we transcend in our minds and hearts to discover our fundamental selves.

No one is born anything or anyone, but we get to decide who we want to become when we believe we can. We can let the glass bottle limitations define our existence, call it life's fate, or remove the limitations by accepting better information and stronger energy and calling it destiny. Our clear understanding and strong energy go into the world to become our destiny. All the happiest people designed themselves to become who they wanted to be. They raised the focus and clarity of their minds for the strength of their hearts. They synchronized their information and energy with their visions and set out to paint the visions onto the world all their lives. They invented all aspects of who they are, starting with their information and energy inside. We look at their purposefully focused lives, and we call them great. They just raised their inside and transcended the circles of being.

THE STARS

OUR HEART POWERS OUR JOURNEY

Information guides and energy drives

> *"Only from the heart can you touch the sky."*
> — RUMI

If we have not achieved our goal in life, we have not thought of it yet, and it does not exist. If we have thought of it, we have not learned the necessary skills and knowledge. If we have learned the skills and knowledge, we have not yet put the strength into our hearts to execute the skills and knowledge. Our heart drives everything we do because it is the emotional strength of our drive. Without energy in our hearts to drive, our clear thoughts are useless. Our actions come from the depths of our hearts and not from the reason and logic of our minds. Reason and logic guide our actions, but our heart drives them to become a manifestation in reality. Our balanced heart itself is also our source of happiness and peace.

Because the energy in our hearts controls our thoughts and actions, we must change it inside at the source that drives us if we want to change our actions. We have to use our thoughts to make the energy serve us, or the energy inside will use our thoughts to serve its need for pleasure and comfort. Often, we have to fail, and the pain and suffering will provide stronger energy to push us to the next level. We will raise the information and energy for clarity in our minds and strengthen our hearts to take charge of our energy inside. Thus, we must first balance our hearts so that it is hospitable to strong energy. Edgar Albert Guest's poem *Don't Quit* shows we must ever be resilient from the inside:

> *When things go wrong, as they sometimes will,*
> *When the road you're trudging seems all uphill,*

THE DELICIOUSLY CHEESY HAPPINESS EQUATION

When the funds are low and the debts are high,
And you want to smile but you have to sigh,
When care is pressing you down a bit
Rest if you must but don't you quit!

Life is strange with its twists and turns,
As every one of us sometimes learns,
And many a fellow turns about
When he might have won had he stuck it out.
Don't give up though the pace seems slow
You may succeed with another blow.

Often the goal is nearer than
It seems to a faint and faltering man
Often the struggler has given up
When he might have captured the victor's cup
And he learned too late when the night came down
How close he was to the golden crown.

Success is failure turned inside out
The silver tint of the clouds of doubt,
And you never can tell how close you are,
It may be near when it seems afar
So stick to the fight when you're hardest hit
It's when things seem the worst that you mustn't quit!

But what is it that we mustn't quit? Because our journey is on the inside, we mustn't quit finding the best self that we want to become. It is not a goal or a dream of the external world outside. It is a goal of the internal. We have to find and become the person we would be proud of on the inside. We mustn't quit becoming the strong person that we want to be. We mustn't quit on the journey to finding our clear perception of ourselves so that we can answer the question, "Who is my best self?" across space and time.

THE STARS

Fight for our future's past

> "Take risks now and do something bold. You won't regret it."
> — ELON MUSK

Poets know how to best express in words information and energy that create volatility in our hearts. In *Dead Poets Society* (1989 movie), the new English teacher at the school, John Keating, points out that we are like all the other generations that came before us. Our bodies will become cold and lifeless one day, and they will decompose to nurture other life, like pushing up daisies. Yet, while we are alive, we can live our lives to our best abilities. If we could listen to the generations that came before us, they would whisper to us, "*Carpe diem. Seize the day, boys. Make your lives extraordinary.*"[5] An extraordinary life will require extraordinary efforts, and extraordinary efforts will require great strength in the heart. Thus, great strength will require raising our internal energy, which will require our clear perception. Our future's past awaits our heart's strength. Therefore, an extraordinary life filled with many exciting adventures awaits our clear perception. According to Thomas Babington Macaulay's poem *Lays of Ancient Rome (1842)*, we will die sooner or later, but we can choose to live better:

> *Then out spake brave Horatius, the Captain of the Gate: To every man upon this earth. Death cometh soon or late. And how can man die better than facing fearful odds, for the ashes of his fathers, and the temples of his gods.*

The world is coming to an end. The minute we are born, our time starts ticking away, and we will leave our world in time. We will travel beyond the horizon of our human perception and understanding. It is the way of everyone who is ever born. We will soon leave this world for permanent rest or a journey into another dimension of being that is beyond our current comprehension. Our time here is for the growth and beautification of this world only. How do we want to leave it

THE DELICIOUSLY CHEESY HAPPINESS EQUATION

when we die? Do we want to die hiding somewhere in fear, relaxing, or dwelling in pleasure? Do we want to die happy while living our best to make a difference for others and our world? Will we let time pass us by, or will we have the strength to ask for our destiny?

As we are born, we all will die sooner or later. Birth and death follow each other like night and day or the chicken or the egg because they are natural patterns. What better way for us to die than to die in honor of the ways of our beliefs. What better way to die than to die living our best, facing our fears against great odds. When we conquer ourselves, our decision is clear, and we can give our best regardless of the outcome. There's no better way to die than for us to die happy in our services to life. Because we are born, we will die. But, due to our clear information and heart strength, we can live our best life even in death. Thus, we must raise the beauty and strength inside to live.

DESIGNING OUR INFORMATION AND ENERGY

As cool as a rabbit

> *"You've been down there, Neo. You already know that road. You know exactly where it ends. And I know that's not where you want to be."*
> — TRINITY, THE MATRIX (1999 MOVIE)

Also, in *The Edge* (1997 movie), after learning that one of his guests has a photographic memory, the lodge owner challenged Charles Morse to a knowledge test. There is a paddle hanging in the lodge showing a panther. The lodge owner challenged Charles Morse to guess what was on the other side of the paddle.

THE STARS

He answered that a rabbit smoking a pipe was on the other side of the paddle. The rabbit is smoking a pipe because it is relaxed, calm, and at peace. It's not afraid of the panther because it knows it can outsmart the more powerful panther. The rabbit is unafraid because it uses its mind's strength to outsmart its physically stronger enemy. The rabbit's inner strength and confidence give it peace.[2]

By raising our inside and knowing we have a clear mind and heart strength, we will not be afraid to face insurmountable and menacing obstacles. Our internal strength brings peace and calm, like the rabbit, for confidence that we will triumph over any difficult challenges. However, raising our inner strength requires better information and energy. Accepting and receiving better information and energy requires us to open our minds.

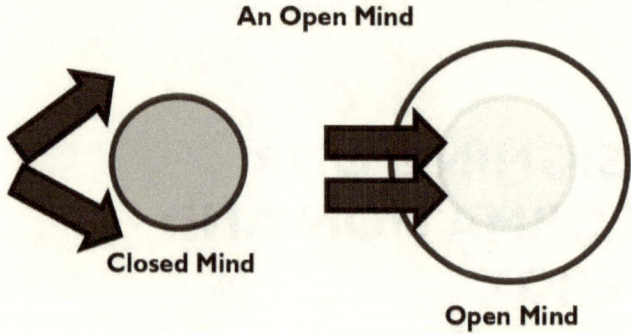

Better information and energy cannot penetrate a closed mind. However, better information and energy can penetrate an open mind.

Better information and energy

> "Success consists of going from failure to failure without loss of enthusiasm."
> — WINSTON CHURCHILL

THE DELICIOUSLY CHEESY HAPPINESS EQUATION

The quality and duration of our lives depend only on the strength of our inside. Our actions are at the limits of our information and our energy. When we make an internal attitude adjustment, we change the flavor and intensity of our energy inside. Positive energy gets everything done and shares happiness. Negative energy gets nothing done, but it complains and blames others.

To design our energy, we have to write down our vision of what we want it to become. Thus, we will have a blueprint for the flow of energy that drives our actions. We have to imagine how we want to feel inside through ups and downs. Thus, we need to write down the emotional destination we desire to handle the fluctuations of the external environment. Our energy drives us, and therefore we want calm energy no matter what is happening outside. When we write it down, we will have created a blueprint for the internal energy that drives our actions. Every day, we will see the reaffirmations to strengthen, focus, and raise our energy. If we do not write it down, it will only exist in our minds' random thoughts. Our energy will depend on our moods or responses to outside changing elements. If we write it down, we will know the exact flavor and intensity of the energy we desire in each moment. Thus, we will have calm and strength inside in the elements of the outside. To put better information and energy inside, we must learn to conduct better information and energy.

> *"Set your life on fire. Seek those who fan your flames."*
> — RUMI

Our poems, songs, moral stories, traditions, and spiritual teachings are gifts of information and energy for our journey from those that came before. Their teachings help focus our hearts to overcome the forces of our internal confusion. The heart's laws have not changed for tens of thousands of years. These teachings' clear information and empowered energy will work today like they did thousands of years ago. When we accept better information and energy, we will have inner strength and happiness. The following Zen story demonstrates that we must discard our old information and energy that did not serve us well to learn something better.

A cup of tea

> Nan – in, a Japanese master during the Meiji era (1868–1912), received a university professor who came to inquire about Zen.
>
> Nan – in served tea. He poured his visitor's cup full, and then kept on pouring.
>
> The professor watched the overflow until he no longer could restrain himself. "It is overfull. No more will go in!"
>
> "Like this cup," Nan – in said, "you are full of your own opinions and speculations. How can I show you Zen unless you first empty your cup?"

We must discard the information and energy preventing our growth and inner strength and causing unhappiness. Thus, we must replace the useless internal information and energy and learn to conduct clear information and strong energy from other space-times. We must absorb great information and energy from those who came before to put into our minds and hearts. From Genghis Khan, we learned to trust those with heart strength, forgiveness, and love of others. Thus, we must learn from great teachers of the hearts. There are many components to the strength of our hearts.

- *Humility:* Our humility allows our inner beauty to shine through. We will see others' beauty and have the objectivity to make better decisions for everyone.
- *Persistence:* The force of the survival of the fittest is always constantly rebalancing life with new changes. We must be persistent like the tortoise in our endeavors because the laws of nature never rest.

THE DELICIOUSLY CHEESY HAPPINESS EQUATION

- *Our deception and clarity:* Like Siddhartha, we must overcome our deception to arrive at a balanced understanding of our life's journey.
- *Wisdom:* Our wisdom is our greatest treasure because it allows us to better see and understand each situation for our better decisions.
- *Kindness:* Our kindness for others is the greatest virtue because it strengthens the social fabric of love that connects us to everyone.
- *Optimism:* A better tomorrow requires positive energy. Our energy becomes our actions, and our actions go into the world and become our journey.

Living wild and free

> "Security is mostly a superstition. It does not exist in nature. Life is either a daring adventure or nothing at all."
> — HELLEN KELLER

Freedom brings great joy to our lives. When we are free, we are free from worries, work, duties, and chores: We can do anything or go anywhere we wish. Thus, by clearing our minds and strengthening our hearts, we will attain lasting internal freedom. We free our thoughts to invent new exciting adventures. Once we have freedom inside, the circumstances on the outside cannot take it away. The freedom of a clear heart and mind also frees us from our desires, fears, environmental conditioning, and ego's self-importance. Thus, we will arrive at lasting happiness because our freedom and peace come from our understanding inside.

We will have the strength to forego pleasures because they do not make sense to our well-being. We will rise to challenges because they make sense for our purpose and journey. We will be free to go beyond our discomforts, limits, and fears and go into the wild adventures of our hearts. Information guides and energy drives, and all the magical happiness we desire will only come through action. There is no other way to get there besides freeing ourselves to the magic of doing.

THE MAGIC OF DOING

> *"The heights of great men reached and kept were not attained by sudden flight, but they, while their companions slept, were toiling upward in the night."*
> — HENRY WADSWORTH LONGFELLOW

One of the great mysteries in life is that we want an amazing life filled with exciting heroic adventures, success, strength, and happiness, but we want to do as little as possible to attain it. We want the happiness and Zen at the top of a mountain while never getting off the couch. We want everything to fall into our lap while we experience no suffering to earn it. Thus, in the Happiness Equation of our lives, we want an E(R) of 9 but are willing to put out a giving R of 3. So we experience pain and suffering at $H = 3 - 9 = -6$, and we blame all sorts of circumstances for our unhappiness, then we hope for that large R in the next life or afterlife to meet our expectations.

Our life's journey is very simple, but our confusion inside makes it more complicated than it needs to be. We do things we should not do, and we do not do things we should be doing. It is simple; if we do not wash our bowls after each meal, they will pile up and clutter our sinks, minds, and hearts. We will make excuses and blame others for our clutter. Then, we will carry the information and energy of our excuses into our life's other tasks and challenges. Our life becomes a thousand excuses for unhappiness. Thus, the reason and logic of it all are very simple. If we want great physical balance, we have to balance our activities with our energy intake. If we want success and happiness, we have to work for it by seeking a wealth of wisdom. If we want to find spiritual balance, all we have to do is reflect on

THE DELICIOUSLY CHEESY HAPPINESS EQUATION

our inner selves, and we will learn who we are and what our purpose is. We must empower the magic of doing inside.

Our internal confusion blocks our clear path's simplicity, and we make up all sorts of excuses not to do it for happiness. We steal from ourselves and our future when we choose to do less. The path of ease, comfort, relaxation, and shortcuts draws our subconscious minds away from the simple ways of happiness and balance. Our suffering and stress come from our unwillingness or our inability to do because we chose to do less. We fight ourselves not to do until there is something pleasurable, tangible, or psychological for us at the moment. We disregard the doing that is in balance with nature's laws. To live is to do. To live our best life is to do for others. To do for others is to share happiness. When we do, it leads to our strength and happiness. We find the magic of doing elusive in our lives because we give ourselves all the excuses not to do it.

> *"Nobody made a greater mistake than he who did nothing because he could do only a little."*
> — EDMUND BURKE

Our excuses and complaining become our failure and unhappiness, and our doing becomes our success and happiness. There is only one way to get things done, and that is doing it. Our physical balance, mental clarity, emotional calm, and spiritual understanding all require doing to achieve. How do we intend to get stronger without carrying any weights? Nothing ever gets done by complaining or making excuses not to do it. Nothing changes without actually doing it, and our lives are what they were before from year to the next. When we make excuses or complain, we do so because we do not want to complete our required tasks. Our excuses and complaints may appear to justify our inaction, but they only limit our development and growth to deny our journey toward happiness, purpose, and destiny.

An excuse says, *"I will do it later."* When we complain, we say, *"Why do I have to do it?"* We have time, energy, and happiness to

THE STARS

do everything once we stop complaining and making excuses. We grow and become energized, productive, and happy when we stop complaining. Our happiness requires energy for doing from the inside that balances with outside tasks. Our suffering comes from our unwillingness to give our best efforts, but we hope to receive R from the world while doing less. When we wait and hope to get more from the outside, we limit our contributions to our inner strength. We limit our efforts because we hope to get more for doing less. We limit our happiness because happy, positive energy creates better energy to do.

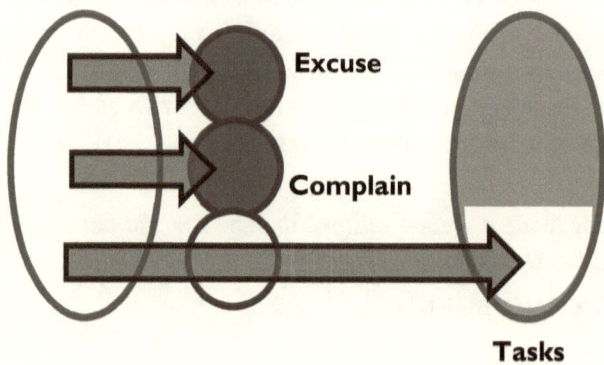

Our excuses and complaints limit our actions. As a result, we accomplish only one-third of our tasks. Thus, we would live only one-third of our lives.

Our excuses and complaints constrain our growth. It is not the sun, the moon, or the rain that holds us back. Instead, our excuses create constraints to restrain our thoughts and actions, and we get nothing done. Our need for comfort, pleasure, and relaxation creates excuses, constraints, and restrictions on our actions. Excuses make it appear okay not to do, and we delay our internal growth and pending happiness due to inaction. If we factor in fear's limitations, our actions become half of one-third or around seventeen percent of our full potential. Without excuses and complaints to hold us back, our potential has no limits. Thus, our excuses and complaints prevent us from living our best.

THE DELICIOUSLY CHEESY HAPPINESS EQUATION

> *"At the end of the day, let there be no excuses, no explanations, no regrets."*
> — STEVE MARABOLI

The hardest working people are the happiest people. Their positive energy empowers and drives their actions of doing. Those who have achieved great success and happiness do it without struggle. They have raised their inside and achieved internal information and energy focus to get everything done. Our doing continues to raise our internal growth because we take action and learn. Our ability to complete a task does not depend on the task's difficulty. It depends only on our ability to do it, and our ability lives in the strength of our information and energy inside. The excuses and complaints we make hold us back from happiness because they permit us to give less than our best effort. We allow ourselves to fail through our excuses and complaining. The more we complain, the more excuses we make, the unhappier we become, and the less we do. The more we love, the happier we are, and the more we do. When we are happy, we will be happy to do everything.

Free from Excuses and Complaining

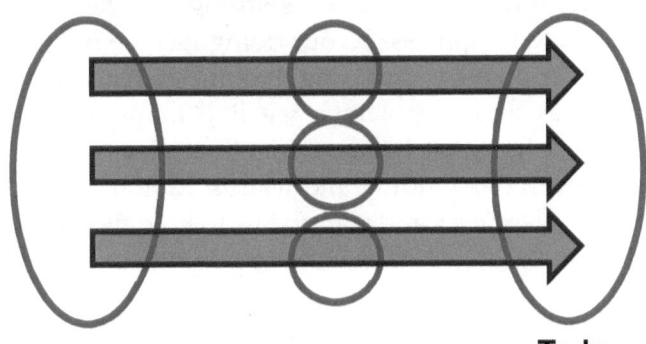

Tasks

When we free ourselves from our excuses and complaining, we have no limits on our actions.

THE STARS

When we stop complaining and have no more excuses, we will be happy to do everything. We get to do our best for the benefit of others. Our willingness to do draws all the difficult tasks, and their rewards, to our abilities and willingness. Thus, when we apply the magic of doing to our lives, others will seek our service for their happiness, and we free ourselves to live our best life.

We are up against the natural forces outside, the persistence of the tortoise and the hare, and Herbert Spencer's survival of the fittest. There is no time for our leisurely rest of doing nothing in all of nature. We will need our raised internal strength to rise to the natural forces' challenges. We can rest in the confidence of our inner strength to complete our required tasks. Like the rabbit versus the panther, our rest is in the calm confidence of our inner strength.

> *"Almost every successful person begins with two beliefs: the future can be better than the present, and I have the power to make it so."*
> — DAVID BROOKS

The energy and strength to happily do everything lives in our subconscious mind, and the endless energy is ours for the asking. When we do, our doing makes us stronger. When we do for others, we share happiness. So our doing has the magical effect of making us stronger and sharing happiness. When we give up all our excuses and complaints, we live in physical, mental, emotional, and spiritual balance. Imagine what we can create with our clear understanding and heart's strength when we no longer have any excuses and complaints to hold us back. We free ourselves to put magical efforts into our doing.

Working, doing, and a piece of cake

When our internal strength $R(I)$ is 4, it is easy to complete a task with an external level difficulty $R(E)$ of 1 because $H = 4 - 1 = +3$. Thus, we get a positive H for performing the task. It's like eating cake, or it's a piece of cake. It doesn't take much inner

THE DELICIOUSLY CHEESY HAPPINESS EQUATION

strength, and anyone can do easy, but most of our tasks in the world will have difficulty levels greater than 1. They will be more challenging. Our most exciting tasks have an expectation R(E) level of 9 or higher.

A Piece of cake
R(I) = 4
R(E) = 1
H = 4 - 1 = +3

If we go against our subconscious mind's programming in our more difficult tasks, our subconscious mind will win, and we will fall short in actions. Our will, trying, and discipline are challenging to do consistently. When we have to try, we are not there yet on the inside. We do not want to do it when we call it working or trying. We will find it hard to consistently get anything done when we do not want to do it. We will lose to our subconscious mind's slow-moving molasses-like drag because our trying creates internal suffering. Our level of suffering is the difference between our internal energy strength and the difficulty of our task. When we try and work hard, our Happiness Equation of our trying or working is as follows:

Working
R(I) = 4
R(E) = 7
H = 4 - 7 = -3

If we try to complete a task with an expectation R(E) of 7 using an internal strength R(I) of 4, we will experience internal suffering at a value of −3. It may be unbearable for any heart to accomplish a task while persistently suffering at −3. When we raise our internal strength R(I) to be 7, our inner strength balances our task's difficulty level. Our task becomes easy to do, and we no longer suffer. We simply do and complete the task.

THE STARS

$$\text{Doing}$$
$$R(I) = 7$$
$$R(E) = 7$$
$$H = 7 - 7 = 0$$

When we add thinking to our doing, we will overcome any obstacle and perform at the level of 9 or higher. To complete a task with a level R(E) of 7 will be like eating cake. All the great tasks require a level of 9 or higher. However, before we can add thinking to our doing, we must fall in love with our endeavor.

Falling in love and becoming world-class

> *"We live in the world when we love it."*
> — RABINDRANATH TAGORE

Three beautiful young ladies bless my life. They all each have different levels of understanding and energy that drive them. They all have different levels of awareness and focus, but they do share one similarity. They love pets, especially cats. One of them got bitten by a cat once, but that still did not deter her love for cats. We do not have any cats as pets in the house, so they decided to volunteer at the animal shelter to be closer to cats. Each Sunday morning, they all get up very early, make themselves ready, and volunteer at the animal shelter to clean "nasty" cages and other duties so they can be closer to cats. Two of them are allergic to some cats, and they even take allergy medications so that they can go and volunteer. Love drives our hearts to put in extraordinary efforts, against relaxation and comfort, for others' well-being. When we love what we do, we break the rules to better ourselves for those we love. Falling in love is for the benefit of others because it makes us happy to do and give our best.

If we are to become world-class, we must fall in love with our beautiful world and the beauty of life. If we fall in love, we will find something amazing in us that we want to share with others. Our hearts will find all the reasons to give our best. What we are

THE DELICIOUSLY CHEESY HAPPINESS EQUATION

in love with, we will dedicate ourselves to its growth and success. We will put magical efforts into it and then some extra. We give all of our hearts to what we love because doing so eases our suffering to make us happy. We can become world-class at what we give our hearts to, and success will find us. Thus, if we fall in love with what we do, we will find happiness and success. The greatest success is the happiness of everyone around us.

> *"Talents are best nurtured in solitude; character is best formed in the stormy billows of the world."*
> — JOHANN WOLFGANG VON GOETHE

In the Zen story *Great Waves*, O-nami is a strong and skillful wrestler who cannot overcome his emotional obstacle to wrestling in public. In private, he could defeat his teacher, but in public, his students defeat him. So he went to see a Zen master by the name of Hakuju for counsel. Hakuju tells him that O-nami, Great Waves, is his name now. The Zen master tells him that he is no longer a wrestler who is afraid to wrestle publicly. Hakuju told him to imagine that he was a huge wave sweeping everything in its path. That night O-nami sat and meditated:

> *He thought of many different things. Then gradually, he turned more and more to the feeling of the waves. As the night advanced, the waves became larger and larger. They swept away the flowers in their vases. Even the Buddha in the shrine was inundated. Before dawn, the temple was nothing but the ebb and flow of an immense sea.*

THE STARS

When O-nami raised his internal strength to become a great wave, it raised his external's strength to become a great wave.

The next day, O-nami entered a wrestling contest, and he won. Eventually, he became the best wrestler in all of Japan. He raised his energy inside to become what he wanted it to be on the outside. He trained his subconscious mind and feelings to be the person he wanted to become. Before becoming O-nami on the inside, he already had the skills and knowledge. By accepting and becoming O-nami, he put an unstoppable great wave of energy into his heart to apply the skills and knowledge already there.

Like the night before Siddhartha's enlightenment, O-nami did not achieve becoming a great wave in one night. The night represented when he lacked emotional clarity and confidence on the inside. He was in emotional confusion; thus, he was in darkness regarding his internal energy strength. The morning was when he achieved clarity in his heart through his focused emotional energy. And, a new day and a new journey began for O-nami.

"Those that achieve success in trading know with absolute confidence that they are going to win. They exude confidence. If you are not absolutely certain that you are going to win, you are not there yet."
— JACK SCHWAGER, AUTHOR OF *MARKET WIZARDS*

THE DELICIOUSLY CHEESY HAPPINESS EQUATION

From Beauty and the Beast, if our external circumstance is not where we would like it to be, we have not yet put the needed energy inside. We want a result on the outside, but our inside is confused or wants something else. Most of the time, our inside wants something easy. Our imbalanced inner strength and external desires create doubts, confusion, and suffering. We will fail to follow through on the outside because we lack the strength inside. We first have to put the energy of confidence and strength inside before manifesting our desires in the physical world.

My youngest daughter wanted to paint Easter eggs for the Easter Bunny a few years ago like she normally does at her mom's house. She was getting older, and I thought she might have outgrown painting Easter eggs. The request caught me a little by surprise, and thus, I was hesitant. I told her that the Easter Bunny might not show up because she's now at my house and not at her mom's house. Her response was, *"I know he will show up. I just know it."* She said it with such positive energy and confidence in her belief that the Easter Bunny showed up to collect her painted eggs and replaced them with treats the next morning.

We need inner strength to drive our skills and knowledge. Otherwise, we will fail in our external quests. In *Kung Fu Hustle* (2004 movie), Sing possessed the most powerful fighting style in the Buddhist Palm technique. However, he could not apply the skills and knowledge because his energy, chi, was locked up in confusion. It took a series of beatings before his chi finally flowed freely, allowing him to use the Buddhist Palm to defeat the Beast.[6] Our hearts will usually strengthen through suffering like the sum of Scarlett's *"As God is my witness, I'll never be hungry again."* Through trials and suffering, most of us will arrive at inner strength. There is only one worthy destination in our life's many exciting adventures: we must climb the mountain inside for a clear view and inner strength. Thus, the question becomes, how fast do we want to free our chi to put inner strength inside. We can streamline our chi through long-suffering like Sing or put it inside as O-nami did for focused inner strength.

THE STARS

PUTTING IT INSIDE

> *"The only Zen you can find on the tops of mountains is the Zen you bring up there."*
> — ROBERT M. PIRSIG

Summary of a story told by Carlos Castaneda: One day, a man met up with his mentor to talk. His mentor, and friend, is a Native American medicine man from the Southwest. It was a very dry season, so his friend, the medicine man, told him that he needed to go and do a rain prayer first. They drove to an isolated area, and the medicine man walked away to a site that appeared to have been a place of worship. The medicine man stood in the middle of the site with his eyes closed for a while. And, when he finished, he came back to the car. The man asked his friend if he had prayed and asked for rain. The medicine man replied that he did not ask for rain, but he stood there and imagined how it would feel like soaking wet in the rain. The medicine man asked for the feelings and internal energy of rain and not the rain itself. He is designing his energy from the inside so that it feels the presence of the rain. The energy inside will drive him to attain the rain on the outside.

> *"Repetition, repetition, repetition."*
> — DR. IVAN JOSEPH, "THE SKILLS OF CONFIDENCE."

If we simply wrote down our desired energy, we may forget the message when it's not in front of us, or it may exist in the

THE DELICIOUSLY CHEESY HAPPINESS EQUATION

shadow of other negative energies. Better than writing it down is focusing, raising, and transforming our internal energy. When we believe that we can do anything, it moves us to exciting challenges. Once we charge the internal energy inside to believe we can do, we can accomplish anything. But, first, we must put the strength and energy inside our hearts through the repetition of affirmation.

If we do not consciously choose our mantras based on our clear understanding, our desires, fears, ego, and environmental conditioning will subconsciously choose our mantras for us. Our mantras, filled with confusion, will become our internal energy. Thus, we can use our minds to hijack our emotions instead of allowing our random emotions to hijack our minds. We can do better than the information and energy from the environment of our beginning.

> *"It's the repetition of affirmations that leads to belief. And once that belief becomes a deep conviction, things begin to happen."*
> — MUHAMMAD ALI

Muhammad Ali transformed his inner strength into becoming a lion through the repetition of affirmations. Our conditioned beliefs stop our transformation into becoming a lion inside. Thus, the glass bottle limitation stalls our transformation. We are not a lion yet because we have not believed in ourselves, asked for the energy from within, and reaffirmed our energy through repetition of affirmation. We have not yet put the belief that we can do anything and everything on the inside. Our balance is easy common sense, but it is very hard to follow through because we lack inner clear understanding and energy strength. Thus, we have to put the energy on the inside first before it becomes easy for us to do. If we ask for inner strength, the universe will grant our wish.

THE STARS

> *"The universe will correspond to the nature of your song. The universe will correspond to that inner feeling and manifest because that is how you feel."*
> — REV. DOCTOR MICHAEL BECKWITH

When I think about all the things that I want in my life, what I want most is an emotional balance to make good decisions, especially when facing a hard choice requiring sacrifice and discomfort. There's only one thing worth having in life: the ability to make good decisions. More than anything, I want an internal calm to allow me to make correct decisions for others and myself. A series of good decisions will lead to good actions, which will lead to good results. Thus, the hard decisions requiring discipline become easy because they already make emotional and logical sense to our hearts. The easy decisions for pleasure and comfort become hard because they no longer make sense. When nothing bothers our hearts, we are free to make decisions based on clear reason and logic, leading to better results. Thus, I am waiting for the day when I am free to make good decisions.

The ten thousand practices of the inside

> *"I don't believe in praying to win."*
> — JOHN WOODEN

I want to go into that place inside my subconscious mind and put in the energy for better choices. When I come upon a task that makes sense, I will immediately say yes. Discipline takes trying, but streamlining my energy will pull actions to fulfill my energy design. We can design our mantras to fit our individual life journeys and endeavors. When we design our energy, we design happiness inside to complete our tasks. I have been practicing incorporating the two mantras below into my emotional energy.

I wrote down the person I wanted to be in the first mantra and recorded it to relaxing meditation music. I listen to it twice a day

THE DELICIOUSLY CHEESY HAPPINESS EQUATION

so that my emotions become the energy that I want them to be. My clear mind designs my internal emotions according to information and energy for happiness and success. The actions on the outside become easy because my internal energy has absorbed the understanding that I chose while calm. Thus, my internal energy pulls my actions according to my clear design, and doing becomes easier. The following mantras are only my energy design, but everyone can design their own unique energy mantra for their particular journey:

> *I am living my greatest life today and every day. I do not have a day off from living my greatest life and giving my best each day. I will cherish every moment of each day and never want it to end. Each moment is so unique and beautiful. I will accomplish my goals for each day. Fear, greed, desire, and other negative thoughts have no place in my mind. I will dwell in positive energy, goodness, kindness, and principles.*
>
> *My life is about giving the best of me at all times. Even when I am exhausted, physically, mentally, or emotionally, I will find the extra ounce of energy to give my best. I am detached from results, and so I will never embrace success, but I will constantly embrace and reinforce the work ethics and principles that are designed for success. I will never allow negative thoughts or emotions to hijack my mind because negativity shuts down my creative mind. I am disciplined in all that I do.*
>
> *My goal each day is to conquer my thoughts, emotions, and actions because happiness is when what I think, what I say, and what I do are in harmony with each other. I will never put poison in my mind or my body or do any other silly things. I will always choose kindness over being right. I will listen four times longer than I talk. I will communicate from the heart and with honesty for healing, mending, growth, and empowering, and never for destruction, belittling, loudly for my ego, or for vengeance.*

THE STARS

> *Each morning, I will have a plan of what I need to do for the day. At the end of the day, I will review it to see what I did or fail to do and why and make the changes.*

Through all the external challenges, I want the ability to make good decisions for others and myself. That ability comes from an emotional calm to see the reason and logic of each decision. Therefore, I want to define how I will feel through the different challenges so that the external circumstances do not determine my energy. Because I defined my energy in advance and asked for it, I will have calm and happiness to handle external challenges. I will have the strength to do according to clear reason and logic. As a result, my decisions and actions will be according to my energy design.

My trading endeavor

I read Jack Schwager's book *Market Wizards* (1989) and became fascinated with the concept of trading stocks, commodities, and futures.[7] I admired the individuals interviewed in the book, who balanced their desires and fears to take on an endeavor that weighs directly upon our hearts. Trading is one of the most difficult endeavors because we deal directly with our desires and fears daily. We desire to win, and we fear losing, but we have to risk losing to win. It can rip apart our hearts when the reality R does not match our expectation E(R). The fears and desires will drive us to take further incorrect actions and become even more lost and confused. Thus, we must reassign emotional values to our actions and not our results to overcome our emotional obstacles.

In the second mantra, I wrote what I wanted to do regarding my trading endeavor and the execution of my trading plan. I recorded my trading mantra to relaxing meditation music, listening to it at least twice daily. I am synchronizing my subconscious mind to understand my trading endeavor and the emotional energy for successful execution. I am asking for internal energy for actions according to my design, independent of my desires, fears, and results:

THE DELICIOUSLY CHEESY HAPPINESS EQUATION

How do I become a world-class trader and one of the best two-week time frame traders in the market? There is only one path to achieving that objective. It is with detachment to results, absolute discipline to my trading plan, and rules. Use the key of discipline in me to unlock the door of my trading plan. This is the path of the best traders in the world and my mentors. In any situation, there are only two reasons for failure or not reaching my objective. One, not having a good enough plan, and two, if the plan is good enough, then it is not executing the plan correctly.

Quantifying my entry has brought my trading edge to the level and clarity reflected in my back-testing, or it may even be better. My quantify entry, my money management rules, position and order management rules, and my exit rules are very good. It represents the best of my work, my thinking, my understanding of the market, and my understanding of myself. I will execute my trading plan exactly the way I wanted and tested both on quantified entry and money management rules. Detached from results, I will have absolute discipline to my trading rules on order management, position management, and exit rules.

This is very important; when I am done with my work I will log off my platform and stop watching the market because watching market fluctuations has nothing to do with success in trading. I love everything about the market. I love the discipline it requires of me. I love how it tests me every day to make me stronger, mentally, emotionally, and even spiritually. But my testing, plan, execution, and rules do not require watching fluctuations in the market all the time. So I will log off my system and make constructive use of my time.

If I break a rule by taking an action based on desires or negative emotions, it will make the situation three to four times worse. Therefore I will not attach emotions of pleasure or pain to temporary fluctuations in my PNL or the market, but I will trade from a carefree state of mind,

THE STARS

free from fear and desire and with absolute discipline to my plan, execution, and rules. I have tested my system on over one thousand trades over twelve years, and I have quantified my entry, giving me objectivity and better clarity. There is no more room for fear, greed, desire, or doubts in my mind. I am absolutely certain of and I have complete faith in my entire system.

My objective in trading, it is not achieving external consistent positive results, but it is my internal journey of becoming or being a trader who, one, executes my trading plan exactly as tested every day, and two, absolute discipline to my trading rules independent of results. I do not desire consistent positive results, but my only desire is consistent actions according to my trading plan. Therefore today, one, did I execute my trading plan exactly the way I wanted and tested, applying my quantified entry and money management rules? Two, today, am I completely disciplined with my trading plan and rules on management of live orders, live positions, and exit rules, independent of results? If my answer is yes to both these questions, then my growth is in the direction of my objective. I have done all I can, and my day is a success, and so will be my week, my month, my year, my decade, and my life.

Therefore no matter what is happening in the market, up or down, no matter what is happening with my PNL, positive or negative, and no matter what is happening in my life, my best response will always be, with detachment from results. I will be calm, cool, and have absolute discipline to my trading rules and plan. Today and every day, I will be a world-class trader by executing my trading plan, quantified entry, and money management rules, exactly the way I wanted and tested, and with absolute discipline to my rules independent of results. Today and every day, I will be one of the best two-week time frame traders in the market by executing my trading plan, quantified entry, and money management rules exactly the

THE DELICIOUSLY CHEESY HAPPINESS EQUATION

way I wanted and tested, and with absolute discipline to my rules independent of results.

We trade stocks or other financial instruments because we want to win, and our desires create fantasy scenarios that do not match reality. When the outside does not match the inside, our wild mismatched expectations create a negative H that rips apart our hearts. Therefore, we need to attach our emotional expectations to our ability to make good decisions in the market fluctuations, independent of our results. It will allow us to prepare our trades better and execute them correctly. My second mantra aims to focus my heart's energy so it balances with trading rules and principles, not my desires or fears. I am in charge of my internal energy, actions, and expectations. Therefore, I can execute my trades correctly in the fluctuations of fears and desires because I have synchronized my heart's energy to sound trading principles.

Out of my focus on better energy to follow the original system exactly as designed, a new, more versatile, and more effective trading system was born. An opportunity came to put my thoughts and energy to the test. From absolutely following my plan and losing, I realized that we have to think about things before applying our trading strategy. Our purpose is to trade the imbalance of the market's reason and logic versus its emotional energy. So I created a new plan that reflects a better understanding of the market's movements over time. In following the system in the mantra, I was down 27 percent on over two hundred trades. In the new system, we were up over 300 percent in diversified positions of over a dozen trades in less than a year.

The success would not have been possible without the emotional understanding that trading stocks require execution according to a plan, no matter what happens. It is also true in many other areas of our lives; we must follow a plan designed for success by incorporating correct actions. We do that by putting emotional energy inside that is firm on principles and flexible on results. That is also how we become a lion. Before we

THE STARS

can touch the sky, we first have to put the energy and strength into our hearts.

Touch the sky

> "You were born with potential.
> You were born with goodness and trust.
> You were born with ideals and dreams.
> You were born with greatness.
> You were born with wings.
> You are not meant for crawling, so don't.
> You have wings.
> Learn to use them and fly."
> — RUMI

Once upon a time, a peasant boy in Japan named Toyotomi Hideyoshi came upon Lord Oda Nobunaga on the open road. Lord Nobunaga was on horseback and dressed in his full samurai armor with helmet and horns. He looked down upon Toyotomi Hideyoshi and said, *"Boy, did you say you wish to serve me?"* Without looking up at the silhouetted, menacing figure, Toyotomi Hideyoshi said, *"Yes, that is correct, Lord Nobunaga. I wish to serve you."* With his clear conviction of purpose to serve, Toyotomi Hideyoshi became Lord Oda Nobunaga's sandal bearer. Hideyoshi rose through the ranks of the Oda clan and succeeded Lord Oda Nobunaga upon his death in 1582. Toyotomi Hideyoshi eventually became one of the three great unifiers of Japan. During his time, he united the country by ending Japan's one-hundred-twenty years of constant civil wars among warring daimyos. Through his commitment to serve, Toyotomi Hideyoshi touched the sky in the service of others.

We can choose and design what we give to others with our clear minds and hearts' strength. We will give a positive H into the world, making it more beautiful. Therefore, it is not what we get or give but who we become that matters. Once we use our clear mind to light the fire inside and focus our internal energy, our strengthened energy will come into the world. Who we become will come into the world consistently. A life of great balance, purposeful service, and happiness awaits our raised inner strength.

THE BEAUTIFICATION OF OUR WORLD

> "Walk with the dreamers, the believers, the courageous, the cheerful, the planners, the doers, the successful people with their heads in the clouds and their feet on the ground. Let their spirit ignite a fire within you to leave this world better than when you found it."
> — WILFERD PETERSON

A Drop of Water

> A Zen master named Gisan asked a young student to bring him a pail of water to cool his bath.
>
> The student brought the water and, after cooling the bath, threw on to the ground the little that was leftover.
>
> "You dunce!" the master scolded him. "Why didn't you give the rest of the water to the plants? What right have you to waste even a drop of water in this temple?"
>
> The young student attained Zen in that instant. He changed his name to Tekisui, which means a drop of water.

The young Zen student realized the clear understanding that we are in the service of life, and we are not to waste a single moment of our time and energy in our endeavor. Thus, he changed his name to honor his moment of enlightenment. When Tekisui found a clear understanding of the purpose of his life, he found peaceful happiness in giving his best to others. Our life's journey is in the service of others.

THE STARS

> "I slept and dreamt that life was joy. I awoke and saw that life was service. I acted and behold, service was joy."
> — RABINDRANATH TAGORE

When we find the reasons to give ourselves and do it great for others, we will find strength and happiness inside. We will beautify our world when we think and do for others' benefit. When we do for others, especially if there's nothing for us, we do it out of love. When we do things out of love, we can accomplish amazing things. We have fallen in love with our world. When we do it out of love and serve, we give nearly everything we have and find reasons to give more. As a result, our world becomes more beautiful. Our journey for our world's beautification awaits our clarity and inner strength.

The best question to ask the oracle

> "Life's most persistent and urgent question is, 'What are you doing for others?'"
> — MARTIN LUTHER KING, JR.

No matter what, when, where, or who we have evolved to become, there is one question that will bring joy, happiness, and success to each moment for everyone when we find the answer. The answer to the question will bring strength, balance, purpose, success, and happiness to our journey. When we do things for the love of others, we can do anything, and a doorway will open for an exciting journey. The one question that we should ask the oracle is:

> "How can I best service life for others' happiness?"

When we find the answer to this question, we will raise our inner strength and find our happiness, and we will find our awaiting journey to serve. Wherever we go, we will share happiness with others. Once we commit to serving life, we will find happiness and purpose. We will free our inner beauty into the world. We will have inner strength and a beautiful world filled with happiness.

The purposefulness of our being

There is only one journey that is worth living. Like a squirrel, we come into this world through the countless conductions of information and energy. Our parents' information and energy create our physical body, and the conduction of information and energy of our space-time creates and molds our internal energy. This world created our internal energy and our external being. The information and energy of this world made us for use in this world. Even our name is designed information and energy for effectiveness and purpose. Like Johnny Cash's song "A Boy Named Sue," Our parents created our name for a purpose, to channel information and energy.

Our desires are from this world's conduction of information and energy. Our creation is for one-time use only, and then from what we see in nature, the materials of our being get recycled. The information and energy of our environment also create unhappiness and suffering. Thus, the clear information and strong energy to complete our happiness also exist only in this space-time, not in another peaceful dimension beyond. What is beyond this dimension of our world is something alien and different. It will have unique laws, information, and energy different from our own.

Our purpose for this awakening is the here and now. We get to contribute to our place and time and beautify this world for others. We leave a beautiful world behind for others, as was done for us. When we give our best for our world, it will do its best for us. When we give our best and ask for nothing in return, we will have found our purpose. Thus, our best journey is to beautify our world and the happiness of others. Once we have designed our information and energy and put it inside, we release our inner beauty into the world.

THE STARS

> *"The vocation of every man and woman is to serve other people."*
> — LEO TOLSTOY

A cup is empty not because it lacks water or fluid inside. It is empty because it is only a cup and does not have a separate existence independent of or beyond its purpose as a cup. Suppose we remove its purpose as a cup. In that case, the cup becomes empty clay, empty dirt, empty natural materials, empty chemical elements, and empty subatomic particles, which are part of the cosmos. The cosmos is not empty because of its immortality and service to all. We are empty unless, like the cup, we serve a purpose for our being. Then, we are a part of the cosmos, serving the cosmos. The fulfillment of our desires that serve our internal confusion is empty because it lacks a fundamental and eternal purpose. When we share happiness, it is not empty because it serves the beauty of the cosmos. If we do not serve a purpose, we will wither and fade away to make room for other more useful beings. When we serve life's beauty, our actions, information, and energy live on for others.

Our atoms come from the universe, and they date back to the beginning of the early universe. The consciousness inside us comes from a source that we cannot yet determine, understand, or trace yet, but it is part of endless cycles beyond our current comprehension and understanding. The universe loves and nurtures our being. Love and kindness connect us from one generation to the next and each other and strengthen the social fabric that keeps us together. Thus, love and kindness have the power to make tomorrow better. They are the emotional fabric of our social bond to connect us to everyone else across space and time, and therefore they are the strongest forces in the universe. We can put them into everything we do, and it will make our world better for everyone. Embracing love and kindness will free us to live our best lives.

THE DELICIOUSLY CHEESY HAPPINESS EQUATION

FOR THE COMING AGE OF FREEDOM

> *"Teach this triple truth to all: A generous heart, kind speech, and a life of service and compassion to others, this is what renews humanity."*
> — BUDDHA

Biologists Robert Sapolsky and Lisa Share followed and studied a group of baboons in Kenya for over twenty years. Baboons are typically very aggressive primates, especially the large alpha males, because they will belittle and torment the other males in the group. Baboons are also sometimes scavengers.

A group of baboons was living off a garbage dumpster in Kenya. An incident occurred after tainted meat, accidentally thrown into the dumpster, was consumed by the troop. The large alpha males ate most of the tainted meat, became sick, and died off. After this, the entire group became more emotionally mellowed and less aggressive toward each other. The emotional energy of the entire group changed to become more friendly and tolerant of each other. When a straggler from the outside would join this troop, the group would not tolerate the new member's aggressive behavior. Eventually, the straggler mellowed to the troop's new emotional and behavioral standard. The accidental baboon social experiment showed that we can change our social-emotional energy and that our nature is to show love and kindness to each other.[8]

The pattern in our human journey is the same. We are gaining more and more of our freedom from those that would once dominate us. We have grown to become more loving and kind toward each other, and we are more accepting and understanding of each other's differences. With each passing year and decade, our world is growing to accommodate new thoughts and accept new ideas of love and kindness that we didn't accept before. Our growing awareness and compassion will create more understanding and greater freedom. That trend will continue to grow. For higher thinking beings, love and kindness guide our actions, a newer pattern to nature's survival of the fittest. Once our hearts and minds become free of the dominance of others, we will never go back to what it was before. With our growing freedom, we can learn and grow to become better than our past.

Even baboons understand the need for love and kindness in social systems. They understand this law of nature. The accidental baboon social experiment shows that we are conductors of information and energy and that our fundamental nature is love and kindness. Once we are set free to love, we will not allow our past aggressive behavioral patterns to come into our social circles again. Once we rid ourselves of aggressive energy, we will conduct better emotional energy.

> *"If virtue promises happiness, prosperity, and peace, then progress in virtue is progress in each of these for to whatever point the perfection of anything brings us, progress is always an approach toward it."*
> — EPICTETUS

The world is becoming more open-minded and free as we become more connected to each other. The conduction of information and energy is becoming more open, clear, kind, and compassionate. We experience setbacks now and then, but the larger pattern going forward is a growing understanding, love, and kindness toward each other. Our cultures, social systems, and traditions need to adjust to the new information and energy. Traditions' role is to strengthen the hearts of those it serves. However, our traditions have to evolve with our changing and growing understanding. Our freedom will continue to grow. Our kindness and compassion will continue to grow. The coming age of freedom will free us to clear information and strong energy for a better life journey.

THE DELICIOUSLY CHEESY HAPPINESS EQUATION

Our growth and development in the universe

If our lives are fractal patterns of nature, we are like symmetrical quantum particles and their antiparticles. Our lives are very short in the eternity of time, and our creation has the symmetry of positive and negative energy inside. Suppose we allow the negative energy inside to fall into oblivion, like antiparticles falling into a black hole. In that case, our positive energy will escape into the world and live on like Hawking radiations adding matter to the visible universe. The darkness of the black hole inside our hearts will get smaller and smaller through time. Our positive energy lives on to beautify our world.

Our darkness will fall away and evaporate through each century and millennium, and our universe will become more self-aware and beautiful. We will continue to grow in ways that we cannot imagine because we have not opened up to its possibilities yet. We cannot understand what we cannot see or have yet to accept within our hearts. There will come new basic understandings and new ways of seeing our universe. New revelations of the laws of the heart will result in new ways and traditions that adapt to our growing understanding. There will be new information to guide and new energy to empower our hearts. Each growth stage requires failure and the pain of suffering to push it to the next level.

Imagine a very advanced human being a million years in the future. He will be all that we are and more, except in another few million years, another more advanced being will come, and so on and on. Each change, growth, and revelation will not occur the same way as the last, but it will be better in many ways. Each new revelation is subject to that particular space-time's need, suffering, understanding, and clarity. With our growing clear understanding of the universe will come new revelations for our journey ahead.

In *Contact* (1997 movie), based on Carl Sagan's novel, humans come together and build an alien-designed spacecraft for a one-person journey to the Vega star system, 26 light-years away. During the interview process, a panel member asks Dr. Eleanor

THE STARS

Arroway, when she meets the Vegans, what is the one question she would ask them. She said she would ask them how they grew past their early technological stage without destroying themselves.[9] The question from the panel to Dr. Arroway is Carl Sagan's question to all of us. He wants us to become aware of his concern. He wants us to think about the solution ourselves to benefit our species. Carl Sagan is a philosopher-scientist, and he was thinking about our growth and concerned about our survival along the way. For this reason, he is bringing awareness to a potential issue that could derail us on our journey to becoming a mature species of the universe. In Dr. Arroway's answer to the panel, Carl Sagan asks us to contemplate how to streamline our internal energy to grow to become better for our species.

As we advance technologically, the internal energy in our hearts will also grow. We will advance in both dimensions of information and energy. We will gain more wisdom, overcome our desires to take it all for ourselves or fight for limited resources, and learn to manage, share, and use our resources better. Thus, our hearts will grow to have more compassion for all living beings. Our desires and our fears will fade away. Without our desires and fears to overwhelm and create confusion inside, we will no longer need to take from or destroy each other. Our love and kindness are stronger than evil and hatred. The strength of our hearts will grow alongside our technological advances. Like the lotus flower, our species' heart strength will grow from the depths of confusion through the murky water into the light and bloom for others.

THE DELICIOUSLY CHEESY HAPPINESS EQUATION

The happiness of servicing life

> "Thousands of candles can be lighted from a single candle, and the life of the candle will not be shortened. Happiness never decreases by being shared."
> — BUDDHA

In every awakening of our consciousness, our objective is always the same. Whether we are on a starship headed for the stars, in the jungle living with primitive tools, or working in a business environment, we will service life's beauty. We will seek clear information and strong energy for our happiness and strength, and we will service life to the best of our ability in every space, time, purpose, or being. Using the Happiness Equation of giving, we will contribute a positive H to the world for others' benefit. A worthy and intelligent life is a life of service to others.

- We will service life's beauty with our first breath to bring happiness and hope to others' futures. They are ever looking for "The One" to bring balance.
- We will service life's beauty in our current environment.
- We will service life's beauty in the jungle.
- We will service life's beauty in a small village.
- We will service life's beauty in a large city.
- We will service life's beauty on the surface of Mars.
- We will service life's beauty in the stars.
- We will service life's beauty a thousand years in the future.
- We will service life's beauty a billion years in the future.
- We will service life's beauty in all the universe's changes.
- We will service life's beauty with our last dying breath to wish for happiness and a better future for others who remain in the world.

As each moment moves on to the next, the places and times of our lives become forever gone. One day our consciousness will

THE STARS

awaken in an alien world or civilization and, like the squirrel, call it our world. We will come in and out of existence in the googol years, like symmetrical quantum particles and their antiparticles. The length of our lives measured against near infinity will be similar to quantum particles measured against the length of our human lives. The particles blink in and out of existence when they form and then annihilate each other. When compared to the universe's timeframe, our lives blink in and out of existence. Thus, our lives meaning is not about us but about others. They are the continuation of the chain of life. The process of life in the cosmos is eternal and is not empty.

Our greatest purpose for our awakening is to bring joy and happiness to our world. Imagine what kind of world we would create or what kind of life we would have when we spend our days and nights dreaming about making it better for others. That would be a fantastic and amazing life of incredible happiness and success.

Our time here for indulgence and self-importance is meaningless because sensory stimulation is for the senses only, and it lasts only as long as the stimulant is present. Our happiness is in our hearts. Our energy of happiness lives on in the conduction of information and energy to others. We will find physical, emotional, and spiritual deterioration if we look to indulge in pleasure, comfort, and relaxation. Where we find our willingness to serve, we will find happiness, strength, and spiritual bliss. In the endless cycles of rest and growth, we are born and will die. That is our human perception of the process of nature, and our time here will pass in the blink of an eye. How we capture the importance of each moment is to give our information and energies to others. We must face our fears and understand our desires, thus, conquering ourselves from within, and we will have happiness for the strength to give our best. Our service to others is our best and happy life.

THE DELICIOUSLY CHEESY HAPPINESS EQUATION

> "Keep a clear eye toward life's end. Do not forget your purpose and destiny as God's creature. What you are in his sight is what you are and nothing more. Remember that when you leave this earth, you can take nothing that you have received ... but only what you have given; a full heart enriched by honest service, love, sacrifice, and courage."
>
> — SAINT FRANCIS OF ASSISI

We do not get to take anything with us, but we leave behind information and energy for others. If we leave behind clear information and strong energy, we will leave something wonderful behind to help light and strengthen others' journeys. By our commitment to service life, we will also be free of the suffering of desire. We will be free from the suffering of a large expectation $E(R)$; thus, we will have happiness and objectivity. In our commitment to serving life's beautiful balances, we are free to give the best of ourselves. When we commit to serve, our Happiness Equations become:

Happiness Equation of giving
We will raise our giving R
$$H = R - E(R) = 0$$
Raised R = +H
+H into the world

Happiness Equation of receiving
We will minimize our expectations $E(R)$
$$H = R - E(R) = 0$$
Lower $E(R)$ = +H
Our Happiness Equation = +H

The most successful and happy people in the world give their best to others every day, and they ask how they can do it better next time. The world will be more beautiful through our servicing and giving to life, and we will be happy due to our inner strength. Thus, how clear is our understanding of ourselves and our world? How deep is our love? How much do we want to give of ourselves to our world's processes and systems? If we are in love with the beauty of our world, the answer is we want to give *"everything."*

What's in it for me?

> *"The greatest happiness in the world is to make others happy."*
> — LUTHER BURBANK

But then there's a child inside who asks, *"What's in it for me?"* Due to unforeseen random events, we may suddenly depart tomorrow. In one hundred fifty years, everyone who is now alive will be gone, and in their place will be others. Our human journey will end, and the personal memories, names, and lives of those who came and went will become meaningless. Only the conduction of our information and energy will remain to light the way for others. Our attempts to preserve our memories through photographs become ghostly whispers to others of *"You can do it better than me."*

Life has existed on earth for a billion years before us, and it will continue to exist for billions more after we are gone. There will be new beings to replace us, and, in time, there will come a new species to replace humans as we know. In a million years, the next Homo evolutionary species will return from the stars to dig up our Homo Sapiens fossilized remains, and they will wonder how we lived and why we got off the third planet of this solar system.

Time goes on, and our journey is hardly about us or *"What's in it for me?"* Our importance is in our contributions during our brief time here. Our happiness is a balance of giving and receiving during our life's journey. A life focused on giving to others strengthens us and brings out our best to share. When we give ourselves for others' happiness, we will have inner strength, peace, purpose, and sometimes destiny. We will have freedom

THE DELICIOUSLY CHEESY HAPPINESS EQUATION

from suffering for our life's challenges during our journey. Thus, *"What's in it for us?"* are clear information and strong energy to balance our Happiness Equation, so H = R − E(R) = 0.

SUMMATION OF THE STARS

Our happiness

Ryonen's Clear Realization

> When Ryonen was about to pass from this world, she wrote another poem:
>
> Sixty− six times have these eyes beheld the changing scene of autumn.
>
> I have said enough about moonlight, ask no more. Only listen to the voice of pines and cedars when no wind stirs.

Ryonen's happiness requires almost nothing but a clear understanding, acceptance, and appreciation of how things are. When we all get to sixty-six years old, can we find peace listening to the voices of pines and cedars when no wind stirs? Will we achieve clarity of thoughts to give us such peace? When no wind stirs, we can't hear the movements of the pines and cedars. We cannot hear the rustling of leaves and pine needles in the wind. But, we can hear and feel the universe's vibration through the trees' peaceful and purposeful existence. And, we would hear their stories from their youth when they lived in the shadow of a great tree. We would hear of the trees' sad times, happy times, good ole days, and fear of death and the unknown. We would hear of the carefree days of their youth when they dwelled in the excitement of tomorrow while living under other great trees. We would hear how they serviced life when providing food and shelter for other living beings.

Their stories of struggles and happiness are our stories, as we all are part of the cosmos. We will understand their lives' balances and purpose upon listening to their stories. Our human journey's desires and fears will fade away, and we will have peace, knowing that we are one with the cosmos. Like all beings, we live in balance with the cycles of nature. If we have clarity in our thinking and understanding of the processes and systems, like Ryonen, we will find peaceful happiness basking in the universe's vibrations. Life is beautiful and filled with joy simply because we get to connect with the universe.

Evolutionary change will always be a part of nature and our universe, but our goal in every awakening is the same. We are to reach clarity in thinking, raise our heart's strength, and serve life during our time, and we will find peace and happiness in our hearts. Our purpose is very simple, bring joy and happiness to others and make the next generations stronger by being a conductor of clear information and strong energy.

The easiest and happiest way to live

Life is neither easy nor hard, filled with constant sadness or endless joy, but our perceptions and energy create those states in our minds and hearts. Thus, we cannot simply use the information and energy given to us by our environment. The deceptions of others' desires, pain, and suffering fill our environmental information and energy. We must absorb better information and energy from other space-times to raise the inside. Therefore, a better journey requires better information and energy. When we raise the inside, we raise many strength factors such as happiness, kindness, clarity, and endurance. When we raise our inner strength, our challenging tasks become easier to complete. We can make difficult decisions in favor of others. Our real strength is on the inside. We will be like the beast that became beautiful inside and, thus, changed the outside.

> *"Life is really simple, but we insist on making it complicated."*
> — CONFUCIUS

THE DELICIOUSLY CHEESY HAPPINESS EQUATION

There's only one way to end our suffering and live in happiness. When we hold back our inner growth, our lives become hard to do. The strength of our inside is less than the difficulty level of the outside. We struggle to accomplish our tasks, or we sometimes do things that we should not do. When we raise our inner strength to a 9, we can handle all the outside challenges. Our raised internal energy makes difficult tasks feel easy to do, and it gives us the strength to choose tasks that make sense. Therefore, the easiest way to live is to raise the inside to balance with the outside. So, we can easily complete most tasks.

The Easiest Way to Live

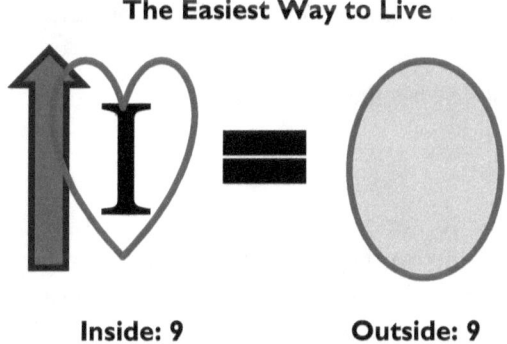

Inside: 9   **Outside: 9**

Match our inner strength to the outside tasks.

When we do less, it leads to our getting less. Our getting less leads to unhappiness. Once we have inner strength, we can do everything that makes sense. We lose nothing, and we will continue to become stronger because we get to do and grow stronger from our doing. We will also become happier because we have removed our expectation E(R). When we do more for others, we will bring joy and happiness wherever and whenever we go. We will live a purposeful life for our journey. If we want all the happiness in the world, then give all we have into the world. Like *The Rainbow Fish (1992)* by author Marcus Pfister, giving our best to others becomes our beauty and happiness. The happiest way to live is to give our inner beauty away for others' happiness.

THE STARS

The Happiest Way to Live

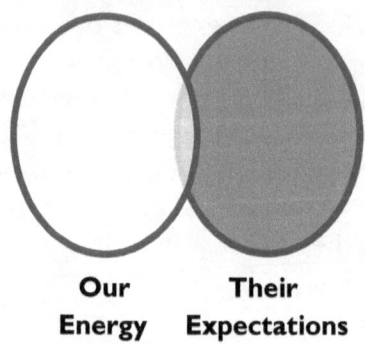

Our Energy   Their Expectations

Match our energy to their expectations.

> "You are the music while the music lasts."
> — T.S. ELIOT

If we commit to servicing life's beauty, it will mean doing, thinking, and giving our best for others. When we carry everyone else's burden, we will carry their weights and worries, growing to become stronger. We will be free of the suffering of our confusion that endlessly desires for ourselves. The easiest way to live is to raise our inner strength. The happiest way to live is to live our lives to meet and exceed others' expectations. Our best life is for others. By sharing our time and energy for everyone's happiness, we get to service life and be like water.

Be like water

> "Enlightenment for a wave is the moment the wave realizes it is water. At that moment, all fear of death disappears."
> — THICKE NHAT HANH

We didn't get a say in coming into this world, we simply awoke from the void into this world, but we do get a say in how we live in this world during our journey. We get to live in

THE DELICIOUSLY CHEESY HAPPINESS EQUATION

happiness while we are here, and then we leave. According to the late Louise Hay (October 8, 1926 - August 30, 2017), make sure to leave love behind for the next occupants when we move on. With our love that creates a positive H, we will leave love behind for those to come into our world. We get to become like water:

- According to Bruce Lee, be flexible, formless, and shapeless.
- According to Lao Tzu, be soft, yielding, ever obeying the laws of nature, yet unbeatable, and always completing our tasks.
- Be clear, transparent, and nurturing of life.
- Let principles guide our internal strength and beauty. Thus, we are constant, like the water temperature in a lake.
- Like a drop of water, do not waste an ounce of time and energy in the service of life's beauty.
- Because water services life and the cosmos. We are part of the cosmos.

> *"Go confidently in the direction of your dreams."*
> — HENRY DAVID THOREAU

There is only one journey through all our different exciting adventures. That is a journey of happiness. When we apply the Happiness Equation to our life's events, it is for our inner peace and happiness. When we have a clear view, we can see and understand our lives and match our expectations $E(R)$ to our reality R. Our clear understanding brings happiness to our hearts. Therefore, our happiness is ours to discover when we can balance our Happiness Equation, $H = R - E(R)$, from inside.

Our happiness is everything. Our level of happiness drives everything we do and don't do. The happier we are, the more we do. The happier we are, the more we give. To live is to give, and to show kindness to others is to grow in strength. Our happiness is in the strength of our information and energy. When we raise

THE STARS

the inside, our inner clarity and strength become our journey in the world. Like the prince in *Beauty and the Beast*, our world becomes more beautiful when we first put beauty inside and allow it to radiate outward into the world.

With clear information, we understand happiness; with our hearts' strength, we apply happiness; with wisdom, we live in happiness; and we share happiness with others on our journey. Our lives are exciting and amazing because we get to connect to the universe and give our best to others each day. We live, we are happy, and we give. The vibrations of our clear information and positive energy will ripple across space and time for others' happiness.

> *"An Old Pond"*
>
> *A timeless universe*
> *Our amazing journey to the stars begins*
> *Our contributions ripple across space and time*
>
> — TRANSLATED BY DUKE THAO

Thank you for coming along on this journey of our clear self-discovery for inner strength and happiness. The beautiful colors of our hearts paint themselves onto the world. The full potential of you is one of the most beautiful beings that ever lived on a special journey for this world's beauty, peace, and happiness. On your exciting and amazing journey to the stars, you will discover your inner beauty and free it into the world. May you rise to meet your best self to embark on your awaiting journey to let your clear information and strong energy vibrate across space and time for others. May you live in strength, confidence, and happiness all your life. May you touch the sky.

ACKNOWLEDGMENT

Thank you for all the powerful ideas of others that came before that are in this book. Our lives are conductions of information and energy. Thus, I am grateful for all the quotes, poems, songs, fables, or moral stories of others in the book: the clear information and strong energy of those who came before helped empower the book's purpose.

Thank you to Jason for being my first reader. Your kind words and clear analysis helped further encouraged me to keep moving forward. In addition, you enthusiastically wanted to share the manuscript with some of your peers to show that you truly believe in the book's ideas. I am deeply grateful for your kindness and positivity.

Thank you to Ashida Kim for allowing me to use Zen koans from his website https://ashidakim.com/zenkoans in the book. Fables demonstrate conditioned behaviors and show our human nature. Zen Stories are like fables but require thinking to arrive at a clear realization of our happiness. The following Zen stories are from Ashida Kim's website:

- A Cup of Tea
- Great Waves
- If You Love, Love Openly
- Is That So?
- Joshu's Zen
- No Loving Kindness
- Ryonen's Clear Realization
- The Giver Should Be Thankful
- The Moon Cannot be Stolen
- Zen in a Beggar's Life

ACKNOWLEDGEMENTS

Thank you to Krysti for being the greatest supporter of this project. Your enthusiasm helped move the project along at times. I greatly appreciated your exceptional energy and support for the book.

Thank you to Linda for your in-depth and caring critique during your reading. I appreciated all your insights and recommendations to make the book better. Your feedback was vital. You helped me realize that there is room for improvement.

Thank you to May for your detailed and thorough reading to assist with grammar and ideas to make it read better. You brought your expertise as a lifelong English teacher and helped uncover situations that I would have easily missed.

REFERENCES

Chapter One: The Happiness Equation

1. Lee, Bruce, Tao of Jeet Kune Do. Valencia, CA: Black Belt Books, 1991, Page 208.
2. Author N/A. "Fables" *Stories from around the world*, 16 June 2016, http://fablesss.blogspot.com/2016/03/farmer-and-wise-man-inspirational-story.html

Chapter Two: Clarity

1. Grubin, D. (Producer), & Grubin, D (Director). (2010). The Buddha – PBS Documentary (Narrated by Richard Gere) [Documentary Film].
2. Savant, Marilyn vos, Fleishcher, Leonore. Brain Building in Just 12 Weeks. New York, NY: Bantam Books, 1991, Page 215, 241-243.
3. Radhakrishnan, Reeja. "Siddhartha and the Wounded Swan" *The Indian Express*, 13 June 2014, https://www.newindianexpress.com/cities/bengaluru/2014/jun/13/Siddhartha-and-the-Wounded-Swan-624380.html
4. Noyce, P. (Director). (1997). The Saint [Film]. Mace Neufeld Productions and Rysher Entertainment.
5. Baldwin, James (1997). "The Sword of Damocles." The Book of Virtues: For Young People, edited by William J. Bennett, Simon & Schuster Books for Young Readers. Page 104-106.

REFERENCES

6. Collector (Taneleer Tivan). (2015, March Day N/A). In *Wikipedia*.
   https://en.wikipedia.org/wiki/Collector_(character)
7. The Wachowskis (Director). (1999). The Matrix [Film]. Warner Bros, Village Roadshow Pictures, Groucho II Film Partnership, and Silver Pictures.
8. Beman, Jennifer and Townshley, Graham (Writer), & Townsley, Graham (Director). (2009, November 3), Becoming Human: First Steps (Season 36, Episode 13) [Television series episode]. In P. S. Apsell (Executive Producer), *NOVA*. Shining Red Productions for NOVA.
9. Fleming, V (Director). (1939). Gone with the Wind [Film]. Selznick International Pictures.
10. Soul Asylum. "Runaway Train." *Youtube*, uploaded by Soul Asylum, 26 February 2010,
    https://www.youtube.com/watch?v=NRtvqT_wMeY
11. Mandino, Og. The Greatest Salesman in the world. New York, NY: Bantam Books, 1968.
12. Reiner, R (Director). (1987). The Princess Bride [Film]. Act III Communications and Buttercup Films The Princess Bride Ltd.
13. Hasher, Tom. "How Thomas Edison's Mother Was The Making of Him…" *Legends Report,* 24 May 2020,
    https://www.legends.report/how-thomas-edisons-mother-was-the-making-of-him/
14. Gunn, Alastair. "What is the largest object in the Universe? *Science Focus: The Home of BBC Science Focus Magazine*, date N/A,
    https://www.sciencefocus.com/space/what-is-the-largest-object-in-the-universe/
15. Zemach, Margot. It Could Always be Worse, A Sunburst Book: Farrar, Straus and Giroux, 1976.

THE DELICIOUSLY CHEESY HAPPINESS EQUATION

Chapter Three: The Heart

1. Donnor, R (Director). (1978). Superman [Film]. Dovemead Ltd. and International Film Production.
2. Oliva, J (Director). (2013). Justice League: The Flashpoint Paradox [Film]. Warner Premiere, DC Entertainment, Warner Bros. Animation Studio 4°C.
3. Bazalgette, E (Director). (2005). Genghis Khan [Film]. BBC and Discovery Channel Co.
4. Jurgens, Dan (p)Breeding, Brett (i)'Superman/Doomsday: Hunter/Prey 2: 14-31 (1994), DC Comics.
5. Starlin, Jim. *The Infinity Gauntlet,* No. 1 - 6, Marvel Comics, 1991.
6. Shooter, Jim. Marvel Superheroes Secret Wars. No. 1-12, Marvel Comics, 1984-1985.
7. Shooter, Jim. Secret Wars II. No. 1-9, Marvel Comics, 1985-1986.
8. Archibald, P, Oliva, J, and Sebast, R (Directors). (2007). Doctor Strange: The Sorcerer Supreme [Film]. Lionsgate Home Entertainment.

Chapter Four: Wisdom

1. McCoy, Daniel. "Why Odin is One-Eyed" *Norse Mythology for Smart People,* 2012-2019, https://norse-mythology.org/tales/why-odin-is-one-eyed/
2. Lee, A (Director). (2012). Life of Pi [Film]. Fox 2000 Pictures.
3. Prager, Dennis. "Fireside Chat Ep. 203 – Escaping Oppression: North Korean Defector Yeonmi Park." *YouTube,* uploaded by PragerU, 09 Sept. 2021, https://www.youtube.com/watch?v=ewGM1GZ8uqg
4. Ansari, Shaikh Mohammad Razaullah. "Ibn al-Haythan's Scientific Method" *The Unesco Courier*, 14 September

REFERENCES

2015, https://en.unesco.org/courier/news-views-online/ibn-al-haytham-s-scientific-method
5. *MythBusters*. Created by Peter Rees, Discovery, Inc. and Beyond Distribution, Discovery Channel 2003-2016, Science Channel 2017-2018
6. Frakes, Jonathan. (1996). Star Trek: First Contact [Film]. Paramount Pictures.

Chapter Five: The Stars

1. "Jack and the Traveling Creatures." *Samurai Jack*, created by Tartakovsky, Genndy, Season 3, Episode 6, Cartoon Network Studios, 2003.
2. Pinsker, Joe. "People Who Use Firefox or Chrome Are Better Employees" *The Atlantic*, 2015, https://www.theatlantic.com/business/archive/2015/03/people-who-use-firefox-or-chrome-are-better-employees/387781/
3. Tamahori, L (Director). (1996). The Edge [Film]. Art Linson Productions.
4. *Samurai Jack*. Created by Tartakovsky, Genndy, Season 5, Episodes 1-10 Cartoon Network Studios, 2017.
5. Weir, P (Director). (1989). Dead Poets Society [Film]. Touchstone Pictures and Silver Screen Partners IV.
6. Chow, S (Director). (2004). Kung Fu Hustle [Film]. Columbia Pictures Film, Production Asia, Star Overseas, Beijing Film Investment, Taihe Film Investment, China Film Group, and Huayi Brothers.
7. Schwager, Jack. Market Wizards. New York, NY: Harper Collins, 1989.
8. Sapolsky, Robert M and Share, Lisa J. "A Pacific Culture among Wild Baboons: Its Emergence and Transmission" *Plos Biology*, 13 April 2004.

THE DELICIOUSLY CHEESY HAPPINESS EQUATION

https://journals.plos.org/plosbiology/article?id=10.1371/journal.pbio.0020106

9. Zemeckis, R (Director). (1997). Contact [Film]. Southside Amusement Company.

INDEX

Aeschylus, 105
Aesop, 31, 60
African Proverb, 143
Alcott, Louisa May, 210
Alexander the Great, 202
Ali, Muhammad, 307
Angelou, Maya, 27, 153
Anonymous, 208, 230
Aristotle, 113, 165, 189, 198
Aurelius, Marcus, 20, 228
Barnum, P.T., 186
Basho, Matsuo, 256
Beatles, 22
Beckwith, Rev. Doctor Michael, 308
Bhagavad Gita, 219, 237
Book of Ruth, 158
Brooks, David, 300
Buddha, 4, 7, 40, 44, 64, 74, 86, 129, 137, 164, 166 180, 236, 274, 319, 323
Burbank, Luther, 326
Burke, Edmund, 297
Camus, Albert, 78
Castaneda, Carlos, 200, 306
Chinese Proverb, 235
Churchill, Winston, 292

Confucius, 63, 328
Count of Monte Cristo (2002 Movie), 73
Cousins, Norman, 123
Covey, Dr. Stephen, 90
Davis, Miles, 115
de Saint-Exupéry, Antoine, 176
DeSouza, Clyde, 217
Dior, Christian, 257
Dyer, Wayne, 55
Dyson, Freeman, 196
Einstein, Albert, 75, 95, 121, 183
Eliot, T.S., 204, 261, 330
Emerson, Ralph Waldo, 75, 200
En Vogue, 281
Epictetus, 34, 65, 179, 237, 275, 320, 323
Feynman, Richard, 114
Fleischer, Leonore, 94
Frankl, Viktor, 13, 17, 25, 101, 131, 262, 264
Galatians 6:7, 60
Garfunkel, Art, 144
Genesis 6:14-16, 239

INDEX

Genesis 27:5-7, 153
Gandhi, Mahatma, 177
Greene, Brian, 125, 196
Guest, Edgar Albert, 288
Hafiz, 147
Hanh, Thich Nhat, 224, 228, 330
Hawking, Doctor Stephen, 260
Henley, William Ernest, 191
Hillary, Edmund, 127
Ingersoll, Robert Green, 82
Jobs, Steve, 62, 84
John 9:7, 84
Joseph, Dr. Ivan, 307
Jung, Carl, 106, 158, 191
Keller, Helen, 271, 295
Khayyam, Omar, 36
King, Jr., Martin Luther, 273, 316
Lincoln, Abraham, 156
Livgren, Kerry A, 193
Lombardi, Vince, 59
Longfellow, Henry Wadsworth, 296
Luke 12:46, 100
Macaulay, Thomas Babington, 289
Mahes, Prasad, 273
Maillart, Ella 107
Maimonides, 249
Manchester, Melissa, 155
Mandela, Nelson, 241
Maraboli, Steve, 299
Mark 2:1-12, 174
Maslow's Hierarchy of Needs, 49, 99
McGonigal, Karen, 125
McGregor, Conor, 62
Meir, Golda, 211
Melua, Katie, 219
Mike and the Mechanics, 283
Musk, Elon, 239, 285, 290
Nietzsche, Frederick, 39, 130
Noble EightFold Path, 70
Oberlander, Henry, 54
Ockham, William, 63
Paolini, Christopher, 201
Pirsig, Robert M., 306
Poetry, Perry, 277
Peterson, Wilferd, 315
Pfister, Marcus, 330
Plato, 171, 269
Rocketman (2019 Movie), 284
Roosevelt, Theodore, 33
Rumi, 67, 91, 104, 106, 148, 149, 191, 244, 253, 255, 278, 279, 285, 288, 293, 314, 315
Sagan, Carl, 322
Saint Francis of Assisi, 325
Savant, Marilyn vos, 94
Schwager, Jack, 305
Scientific Method, 221
Scorpion and the Frog, 43

Seuss, Dr., 258
Shakespeare, William, 47, 175
Shapiro, Shauna Professor, 229
Shelley, Percy, 206
Spence, Herbert, 150
Suzuki, D.T., 256
Steve Jobs Movie, 84
Stoic Philosophy, 12
Strictly Ballroom Movie (1992), 203
Superman, 166
Tagore, Rabindranath, 128, 207, 213, 243, 302, 316
The 47 Ronin (2013 Movie), 79
The Matrix (film 1999), 291
Thoreau, Henry David, 83, 331
Tolstoy, Leo, 10, 318
Tortoise and the Hare, 60, 153
Twain, Mark, 256
Tzu, Lao, 13, 66, 95, 116, 122, 136, 191, 252, 269
Von Goethe, Johann Wolfgang, 134, 146, 303
Ware, Nat, 11
Wilde, Oscar, 5
Williamson, Marianne, 28
Wooden, John, 220, 308
Zengetsu 10, 120